Cultural Studies and Discourse Analysis

04

Cultural Studies and Discourse Analysis

A Dialogue on Language and Identity

Chris Barker and Dariusz Galasiński

SAGE Publications

London • Thousand Oaks • New Delhi

First published 2001

 SAGE Publications Ltd
6 Bonhill Street
London EC2A 4PU

SAGE Publications Inc.
2455 Teller Road
Thousand Oaks, California 91320

SAGE Publications India Pvt Ltd
32, M-Block Market
Greater Kailash – I
New Delhi 110 048

British Library Cataloguing in Publication data

A catalogue record for this book is available
from the British Library

ISBN 0 7619 6383 9
ISBN 0 7619 6384 7 (pbk)

Library of Congress Control Number available

Typeset by Mayhew Typesetting, Rhayader, Powys
Printed in Great Britain by Biddles Ltd, Guildford, Surrey

With love for Julie and our far flung families – Chris Barker

Michałowi i Ani. Tata.

Contents

Acknowledgements

Our thanks go to all those who agreed to be interviewed for this book. CB and DG

I would also like to thank Elżbieta Chrobak who persuaded some of my interviewees to talk to me. DG

1

Language, Culture, Discourse

Cultural studies has for sometime been a constituent part of the 'lin-guistic turn' in the humanities and social sciences with writers arguing that language is the central means and medium by which we understand the world and construct culture. Indeed, the contemporary emphasis given to language within cultural studies is itself a part of a wider 'cultural turn' that is constituted in two ways. First, culture is explored through its own specific mechanisms and logic without reduction to any other phenomenon (e.g. the mode of production). Second, facets of a social formation that had previously been considered to be quite separate from culture can themselves be understood as cultural. For example, 'economic forces' are cultural because they involve a set of meaningful practices, including the social relations of production and consumption, along with questions of design and marketing. Thus, to put meaning at the heart of human activity is also to place the examination of culture at the top of the agenda of the humanities and social sciences. As Du Gay et al. argue, 'rather than being seen as merely reflective of other processes – economic or political – culture is now regarded as being as constitutive of the social world as economic or political processes' (du Gay et al., 1997: 4).

It is a core case of cultural studies that language does not mirror an independent object world but constructs and constitutes it. Culture is said to 'work like a language' and identities, which were the central category of cultural studies in the 1990s, are held to be social and dis-cursive constructions (see Barker, 2000). Though cultural studies has convincingly argued the philosophic case for the significance of language and has produced a large body of textual analysis, it is rarely able to show how, in a small-scale technical sense, the discursive construction of cultural forms is actually achieved. Here, we will argue, critical discourse analysis (CDA) is able to provide the understanding, skills and tools by which we can demonstrate the place of language in the construction, constitution and regulation of the social world. That is, CDA is a methodological approach that can add to and enrich cultural studies. Consequently, we hope to forge a useful interdisciplinary dialogue between two fields of inquiry that have for sometime been interested in similar areas of study.

About this book

This book is constructed as a productive dialogue between cultural studies and CDA, bringing together the insights and analytical capabilities of these two domains. In doing so, we hold that an analytical strength of our book derives from the analysis of the utterances of speaking subjects.

In this chapter we set out the philosophy of language which has informed cultural studies before suggesting that critical discourse analysis is a necessary addition to it. Chapter 2 investigates the implications of the 'linguistic turn' for the self and cultural politics while Chapter 3 explores the tools which CDA brings to the investigation of culture and cultural politics. Having established the theoretical and practical advantages of a dialogue between cultural studies and CDA, Chapters 4 and 5 offer case studies, of gender and ethnicity respectively, to illustrate the gains that the alliance we propose can bring. In the final chapter (6) we explore the intersections in the production of masculinity and ethnicity through a fusion of cultural studies and CDA.

This opening chapter serves a dual purpose. It acts as an introduction to theories of language for the 'new' reader and as a 'position' chapter for an audience familiar with the philosophy of language. The chapter will review the core arguments that cultural studies has taken up from Saussure, Barthes, Derrida and Foucault and in doing so state our own position.

First, we will outline the central argument of cultural studies: that language is relational in character; that signs have no direct referents in an independent object world but generate meaning through their relationships to other signs organized into syntagmatically and paradigmatically structured codes. From this, it is argued that all cultural forms can be analysed 'like a language' (Barthes, 1967, 1972).

Second, we forward the argument adopted by a good many cultural studies writers (following Derrida, 1976) that the binary relations between signs proposed by structural linguistics are not stable, rather, meaning is unstable and slides down the infinite play of signifiers. That is, *differance* – difference and deferral. Nevertheless, we argue, though meaning is formally undecided, in social practice it is regulated and temporarily stabilized into pragmatic narratives or discourses. Discourses, which after Foucault (1972, 1977, 1980) refer to language and practice, are regulated ways of speaking about a topic which delimit the sayable and unsayable.

Third, we take Wittgenstein (1953) as a mediating figure between the Derridean notion of differance and the Foucauldian concept of discourse. Like Derrida, Wittgenstein argues that meaning is relational, formed within language games. However, he also suggests that meaning is stabilized and regulated in use, embedded as it is in pragmatic narratives. Using the metaphor of the 'tool', we are directed to the diverse functions words play in human life. To see language as a tool is to suggest that we do things with language so that, in the context of social usage, meanings can be temporarily stabilized for practical purposes. As Rorty (1991a) argues, we have a variety of languages because we have a variety of purposes. Indeed, we suggest that Rorty's blending of Wittgenstein and Davidson is useful to cultural studies in helping us to regard language as a series of marks and noises used by human animals to achieve their goals. Knowledge is not a matter of getting an accurate picture of reality, but of learning how to contend with the world in the pursuit of our various purposes.

Wittgenstein was, of course, a key influence on the formation of discourse analysis and it is CDA, we suggest, that can show us the detail of how the social world is constructed and regulated. CDA augments cultural studies by showing us the technical linguistic building bricks of social construction.

Culture and language

As Raymond Williams (1983) observed, the concept of culture is 'one of the two or three most complicated words in the English language'. Indeed, it is best not to pursue the question 'what is culture?' but rather to ask about how we talk about culture and for what purposes. Culture has been variously described as 'cultivation', as 'a whole way of life', as 'like a language', as 'power' and as a 'tool' etc. That is, the abstraction 'culture' covers a variety of ways of looking at human conduct and can be used for a range of purposes.

Williams understood culture as constituted by the meanings and practices of ordinary men and women. For him, culture is lived experience; the texts, practices and meanings of all people as they conduct their lives within the totality of 'a whole way of life'. Williams insisted that culture be understood through 'the analysis of all forms of signification . . . within the actual means and conditions of their production' (Williams, 1981: 64–65). In so far as contemporary cultural studies has a distinguishing 'take' on 'culture' it is one which stresses the intersection of language, meaning and power. Culture is said to be centrally concerned with questions of shared meanings so that

> To say that two people belong to the same culture is to say that they interpret the world in roughly the same ways and can express themselves, their thoughts and feelings about the world, in ways which will be understood by each other. Thus culture depends on its participants interpreting meaningfully what is happening around them, and 'making sense' of the world, in broadly similar ways. (Hall, 1997: 2)

The shared meanings of culture are not 'out there' waiting for us to grasp them. Rather, they are the product of signifying practices, most notably those of language. Language constitutes material objects and social practices as meaningful and intelligible, it structures which meanings can or cannot be deployed under determinate circumstances by speaking subjects. To understand culture is to explore how meaning is produced symbolically through the signifying practices of language within material and institutional contexts. Indeed, the currently ascendant strand of cultural studies holds the field to be centrally concerned with culture as the signifying practices of representation (see Hall, 1997).

Signs, texts and codes: structuralism in cultural studies

The breach between Williams' concern with meaning produced by active human agents and an understanding of culture centred on signifying systems, cultural texts and the 'systems of relations' of language marks the shift in cultural studies from 'culturalism' to 'structuralism' (Hall, 1992a). Structuralism is anti-humanist in its de-centring of human agents from the heart of inquiry. For structuralism, signifying practices generate meaning as an outcome of structures or predictable regularities that lie outside of any given person. Structuralism is largely synchronic in approach analysing the structures of relations in a snap shot of a particular moment. In this, structuralism is also asserting the specificity of culture, and its irreducibility to any other phenomenon, taking culture to be analogous to, or structured like, a language.

It is noteworthy that structuralism is more concerned with the structures of language which allow linguistic performance to be possible than actual performance in its infinite variations. Crucially, in Saussure (1960) and Levi-Strauss (see Leach, 1974) – both critical figures in the development of structuralism – meaning is generated through the rules and conventions which organize language (langue) rather than the specific uses and utterances which individuals deploy in everyday life (parole).

For Saussure, signs, which are constituted by signifiers (medium) and signifieds (meaning), do not generate sense by virtue of reference to entities in an independent object world, rather, they create significance through reference to each other. Meaning is a social convention generated by signifying practices that organize the relations between signs. This involves a process of selection and combination of signs along the syntagmatic (linear – e.g. a sentence) and paradigmatic (a field of signs – e.g. synonyms) axes.

The relationship between signifiers and signified is said by structuralism not to be held in any fixed eternal relationship. Rather, their arrangement is arbitrary, suggesting that meaning is culturally and historically specific. The relations between signifiers and signifieds are organized (and maintained) through social conventions into cultural codes. Signs become naturalized codes and the transparency of meaning we give to words and sequences of signs are an outcome of a cultural habituation that conceals from us the practices of cultural coding. Thus, the cultural code of traffic systems temporally fixes the relationship between colours and meanings into a code so that 'red' signifies 'stop' and 'green' signifies 'go'.

Signs of popular culture

Structuralism extends its reach from 'words' to the language of cultural signs in general. Barthes in particular became an influential figure within cultural studies through his expansion of the structuralist account of language to include the practices of popular culture which, read as texts, are not to be grasped in terms of the utterances or interpretations of specific human beings but as a set of signifying practices. It is in this sense that all cultural practices become open to semiotic analysis. While everyday usage of the word 'text' refers to writing, it has become an axiom of cultural studies that a text is any phenomenon that generates meaning through signifying practices. Hence, dress, television pro-grammes, advertising images, sporting events, pop stars, etc. can all be read as texts.

In his early work, Barthes (1967, 1972) spoke of two systems of signification; denotation and connotation. Denotation was said to be the descriptive and literal level of meaning generated by signs and shared by virtually all members of a culture. Thus, 'man' denotes the concept of a male member of the human species. At the level of connotation, meanings are generated by connecting signifiers to wider cultural codes of meaning. Thus, 'man' may connote toughness, hardness and ration-ality, or violence and injustice according to the sub-codes or lexicans at work. Further, the sign 'member' may now multiply up to carry the expressive value of the penis being the central symbol of masculinity coded as sexual performance.

Connotations which have become naturalized as hegemonic, that is, accepted as 'normal' and 'natural' are described by Barthes as myths. These act as conceptual maps of meaning through which to make sense of the world and turn cultural constructions into pre-given universal truths. For example, just as red signifies 'stop' within one cultural code, so 'biceps' signifies a male with connotations of strength within a popular code of masculinity. The myth of masculinity suggests that men are strong physically and mentally with the latter marked by emotional stoicism. Myths work by naturalizing culturally contingent codes into unchallengeable commonsense. 'Myth has the task of giving an histori-cal intention a natural justification, and making contingency appear eternal' (Barthes, 1972: 155).

Reading signs

What Hall (1992a) calls the 'moment of structuralism' in cultural studies was important because, in giving us the language of signs and codes, it laid the foundations for a stream of analyses of popular cultural documents, artifacts and practices all treated as texts. That which Williams called 'lived experience' is now held to be textual. The consequences of this were that while Paul Willis (1977;1978), under the influence of Williams, was exploring the lives of young men ethnographically, Hebdige (1979) turned to semiotics to explore the meaning of youth cultures, and Punk in particular, through the textual category of style.

Punk semiotics

For Hebdige, style is a signifying practice achieved through the transformation of the signs of commodities through the process of bricolage. Bricolage involves the rearrangement and juxtaposition of previously unconnected signifying objects to produce new meanings in fresh contexts. It is a process of re-signification by which cultural signs with established meanings are reorganized into new codes of meaning.

Punk, Hebdige said, was a dramatization of British economic and social decline and an expression of anger and frustration. Punk style was an especially dislocated, self-aware and ironic mode of signification. As bricolage signifying noise and chaos at every level, Punk style was held to be ordered and meaningful, a 'revolting style' which created an ensemble of the perverse and abnormal; safety pins, bin liners, dyed hair, painted faces, graffitied shirts and the iconography of sexual fetishism (leather bondage gear, fishnet stockings etc.). Through disordered dancing, cacophonous sound, desecrating lyrics, offensive language and anarchic graphics punk 'did more than upset the wardrobe. It undermined every relevant discourse' (Hebdige, 1979: 108).

The influence of structuralism also lay behind a number of investigations of popular cultural texts including news (Brunsdon and Morley, 1978; Hartley, 1982) and Soap opera Dyer et al. (1981). Noteworthy was Williamson's (1978) pioneering exploration of advertising in which semiotics is deployed to address their formal qualities. She pointed to the way in which objects in advertisements are signifiers of meaning that we decode in the context of known cultural systems, associating products in adverts with other cultural 'goods'. While an image of a particular product may denote only beer or perfume it is made to connote 'male fun' or 'female sexuality' so that advertising creates a world of differences between products and lifestyles which we 'buy into'. For Williamson, such advertising is ideological in that its images of consumption obscure economic inequality that is generated at the level of production.

Talking to people

In response to Hebdige's work on youth culture, Cohen (1980) expressed the core concern 'that these lives, selves and identities do not always coincide with what they are supposed to stand for' (Cohen, 1980: xviii). The problem is one of relating an analyst's structural interpretations to the meanings held by knowing subjects. Cohen suggests that not only are the semiotic inspired interpretations of youth culture offered by Hebdige and others disputable, but that young people are made to 'carry too much'. At heart is the criticism that such analysis fails to engage with members' accounts of subcultural involvement (Widdicombe and Wooffitt, 1995). This point is of course core to Paul Willis's long-standing commitment to ethnography as the means to 'represent the subjective meanings, feelings and cultures of others' (Willis, 1980: 91).

The active audience

Structuralist-inspired textual analysis assumed that meaning lay in the text. Critics challenged this view on grounds that texts are unable to police the meanings created by readers/audiences. Texts are said to be polysemic, that is, they embody the potential for a number of different meanings to be constructed from them. Cultural understanding of texts cannot remain with the text but must concern itself with the processes involved in the realization of meaning by readers (Gadamer, 1976; Hall, 1981; Iser, 1978). Consequently, cultural studies spawned a range of audience and consumption studies that repeatedly held audiences and consumers to be active creators of meaning and not the cultural dopes of textual positioning.

Morley (1980) led the way with his study of the audience for the news magazine *Nationwide*, where he argued that class provided the basis for resistant and oppositional readings of a textually embedded ideology. He was closely followed by Hobson (1982) and Ang's (1985) examinations of the female audiences for the soap operas *Crossroads* and *Dallas* respectively. These women were held to be active viewers with a range of genre competencies capable of generating meaning in the interaction between texts and audience talk. Subsequently, numerous studies of television audiences have reiterated these fundamental points (Barker, 1998; Gillespie, 1995; Miller, 1995; Seiter, 1989).

During the 1980s and 1990s a critical mass of consumption studies built up, extending beyond television to a concern with commodities in general. Here, consumers were held to be active creators of meaning bringing previously acquired cultural competencies to bear on texts. Fiske (1987) in particular argued that popular culture is constituted not by texts but by the meanings that people produce through them. Similarly, Willis argued (1990) that young people have an active, creative and symbolically productive relation to the commodities that are constitutive of youth culture. Meaning, he suggests, is not inherent in the commodity but is produced through actual usage.

The turn to audiences and consumers was a welcome break from the study of signs without reference to the voices of living and breathing people. However, this is not to dismiss the innovative work done under the banner of semiotics; Hebdige's work cited above is ground-breaking, provocative, readable and pioneering. Further, the study of texts remains an important activity of cultural studies. For example, the texts displayed on television allow us all to be armchair travellers and experience something of the lives and cultural identities of others even as we stay at home. Consequently, television, as it spreads across the globe, is a major and proliferating resource for the construction of cultural identities. The concept of 'resource' is significant here since television is actively appropriated and deployed by audiences in making sense of their lives. In other words, the meanings that people produce interactively with television texts are woven into their identity projects (Barker, 1997a, 1999).

The specificity of speech

Television does not construct identities in the manner of a hypodermic needle but provides materials to be worked on. As Tomlinson (1991) has argued, the media is the dominant representational aspect of modern culture but its meanings are mediated by the 'lived experience' of everyday culture. The relationship between media and culture is therefore one of the subtle interplay of mediations. This suggests that textual analysis alone is insufficient for a domain of study that calls itself cultural studies. The study of texts and the study of audiences can felicitously be done together. Indeed, the talk produced by audiences in relation to texts is another form of text so that the study of culture involves the relationship between different *types* of text. Nevertheless, we will need to bear in mind the *specific qualities* of speech texts produced by active persons.

While the exploration of audiences and consumers has commonly involved talking to people and reporting on their attitudes, none of the key audience studies cited above brings to bear anything close to detailed language analysis. Semiotics taught us that texts were not to be taken at face value but were to be approached as constructions of signs which could be analysed to illustrate how meaning was generated. The same lesson was not applied to talk as a text. Not only does textual analysis not have to be in opposition to ethnography and consumption studies, but the methods and tools of text analysis can be brought to bear on talk (this is not to say that semiotics *per se* provides the best tools for this purpose).

Poststructuralism and the crisis of representation

While the pendulum of cultural studies swung from the structuralist study of texts to the interpretative exploration of audiences, the idea that it is possible to represent in a naturalistic way the 'real' experience of people, as ethnography and reception studies claimed to do, became the subject of considerable criticism. The most telling of these was the post-structuralist inspired critique of realist epistemology and the argument that ethnography is a genre of writing which deploys rhetorical devices, often obscured, to maintain its realist claims (Clifford and Marcus, 1986). In other words, the products of ethnography are always texts. This assertion leads to the examination of ethnographic texts for their rhetorical devices, along with a more dialogical approach to research so that ethnography becomes less an expedition in search of 'the facts' and more a conversation between participants in an investigative process.

However, it would not do to bring the tools of structuralist semiotics to bear on ethnographic texts, for the very principles on which it was founded were under suspicion. Notably, the stability of the binaries of structuralism (e.g. denotation–connotation, signifier–signified) and its claims to surety of knowledge were the subject of attack by Derrida and poststructuralism. That is, Derrida deconstructs the very notion of the stable structures of language.

The instability of language

Cultural studies has taken from Derrida the key notions of intertextuality, undecidability, deconstruction, differance, trace and supplement all of which stress the instability of meaning, its deferral through the interplay of texts, writing and traces. Here, words have no universal meanings and do not refer to objects that possess essential qualities.

Derrida's critiques of 'logocentrism' and 'phonocentrism' seek to undermine any reliance on fixed *a priori* transcendental meanings, in other words, universal meanings, concepts and forms of logic that exist within human reason before any other kinds of thinking occur. Derrida attacks the idea that speech, by virtue of being apparently prior to writing, represents a universal transcendental truth through which subjects ground themselves as their own pure and spontaneous source. Derrida contends that the privileging of speech relies on the untenable idea that there is direct access to truth and stable meaning. This idea is fallacious because, in representing a truth that is argued to exist outside of representation, one must be re-representing it. That is, there can be no truth or meaning outside of representation. 'From the moment that there is meaning there are nothing but signs. We think only in signs' (Derrida, 1976: 50). There is no original meaning outside of signs, which are a form of graphic 'representation', so that writing is in at the origin of meaning. We cannot think about knowledge, truth and culture without signs, that is, writing. Writing is always already part of the outside of texts and texts are constitutive of their outsides. This is what Derrida calls 'arche-writing'.

Derrida argues that since meaning is generated through the play of signifiers and not by reference to an independent object world it can never be 'fixed'. Words carry multiple meanings, including the echoes or traces of other meanings from related words in other contexts. Language is non-representational and meaning is inherently unstable so that it constantly slides away. Thus, by *differance*, a sense of 'difference and deferral' is suggested. The production of meaning in the process of signification is continually deferred and supplemented in the play of more-than-one. The continual supplementarity of meaning, the continual substitution and adding of meanings through the play of signifiers, challenges the identity of noises and marks with fixed meaning. The meaning of signifiers can never be identical with a fixed entity to which a word refers because a supplement adds to and substitutes meanings.

Derrida is widely associated with the practice of deconstruction. To deconstruct is to take apart, to undo, in order to seek out and display the assumptions of a text. It involves the dismantling of hierarchical binary oppositions such as speech/writing, reality/appearance, nature/culture, reason/madness etc. that are said to guarantee truth through excluding and devaluing the 'inferior' part of the binary. In deconstructing the binaries of western philosophy and attacking the 'metaphysic of presence' (i.e. the idea of a fixed self-present meaning) Derrida must use the very conceptual language of the western philosophy he seeks to undo. To mark this tension, which can be exposed by a strategy of reversal (i.e. putting writing before speech, appearance before reality) but not overcome or replaced, Derrida places his concepts 'under erasure'. To place a word under erasure is to first write the word and then cross it out, leaving both the word and its crossed out version. The use of accustomed and known concepts 'under erasure' is intended to destabilize the familiar as at one and the same time useful, necessary, inaccurate and mistaken. Thus does Derrida seek to expose the undecidability of metaphysical oppositions, and of meaning as such.

Derrida and cultural studies

The authority and sway of Derrida in cultural studies has been considerable, underpinning the widespread adoption of anti-representationalism, social constructionism, anti-essentialism and textual deconstruction. It can be seen at its most useful in Hall's (1992b, 1996a) theorization of identity as an unstable description in language; a becoming rather than an entity (Chapter 2). It is also a presence in that feminism (Nicholson,

1990; Weedon, 1997) which holds sex and gender to be wholly social and cultural constructions that are not reducible to biology. This anti-essentialist stance argues that femininity and masculinity are not essential universal and eternal categories but plastic, malleable, cultural constructions. This enables the production of a range of possible masculinities and femininities.

Through the work of Spivak and Bhabha, Derrida has also been a significant presence in postcolonial theory prompting deconstruction of colonial categories and a realization of the indivisibilty of the colonial 'master' and the colonized 'native'. Neither the colonial nor colonized cultures and languages can be presented in 'pure' form, nor separated from each other (Bhabha, 1994). This gives rise to a hybridity which challenges not only the centrality of colonial culture and the marginalization of the colonized, but the very idea of centre and margin as being anything other than 'representational effects'. This body of work explores postcolonial discourses and their subject positions in relation to the themes of race, nation, subjectivity, power, subalterns, hybridity and creolization. Further, the instability of meaning in language leads us to think of culture, identities and identifications as always a place of borders and hybridity rather than fixed, stable entities (Bhabha, 1994). All cultures are zones of shifting boundaries and hybridization.

Laclau and Mouffe's (1985) critique of the essentialism, foundationalism and reductionism of Marxism is also indebted to Derrida. Laclau and Mouffe argue that the 'social' is not to be thought of as a totality but as a set of contingently related aggregates of difference articulated or 'sutured' together. For Laclau and Mouffe the 'social' involves multiple points of power and antagonism rather than cohering around class conflict as in classical Marxism. The complex field of multiple forms of power, subordination and antagonisms are not reducible to any single site or contradiction. Consequently, any radical politics cannot be premised on the domination of any particular political project (e.g. the proletariat of Marxism) but must be constructed in terms of the recognition of difference and the identification and development of points of common interest. Thus are we led to the politics of coalition and alliance in the pursuit of radical democracy.

Problems with decontructionism

The influence of Derrida within cultural studies has not been wholly benign. Analytically, deconstruction in cultural studies remains bound into a high textualism that rejects any kind of ethnographic or empirical work. It has become a kind of formalism. Politically, the unbounded deconstruction of foundational categories, the endless unfolding of meaning, the undecidability of concepts like justice or identity has limited practical use. Indeed, deconstruction may be a barrier to action founded on the arbitrary but necessary closure of meaning. Great claims are made for the political importance of deconstruction yet much of this campus-based work is unintelligible to other than highly trained philosophers and literary critics. Ironically, deconstruction is a new language all of its very own and one confined to an elite intelligentsia.

Later in the chapter we will suggest that despite the poststructuralist critique of representational realism, ethnography, discourse analysis of everyday talk and other forms of empirical work continue to have analytical and political value. For the time being we want to examine the idea that while meaning may formally proliferate endlessly in the rarified world of texts, this is not so in social practice where meaning is regulated and stabilized for pragmatic purposes. This will be demonstrated through the work of Foucault and Wittgenstein.

The regulation of language

Foucault, discourse and subject positions

Foucault (1972), in common with Derrida, argues against structuralist theories of language that conceive of it as an autonomous rule governed system. Rather, he is more concerned with the description and analysis of the surfaces of discourse and their effects under determinate material and historical conditions. From Foucault, cultural studies has derived the idea of discourse as a regulated way of speaking that defines and produces objects of knowledge, thereby governing the way topics are talked about and practices conducted. For Foucault, discourse constructs, defines and produces objects of knowledge in an intelligible way while at the same time excluding other ways of reasoning as unintelligible. He explores the circumstances and rules under which statements are combined and regulated to form and define a distinct field of knowledge/objects requiring a particular set of concepts and delimiting a specific 'regime of truth' (i.e. what counts as truth).

In this argument, meaning does not proliferate in an endless deferral but is regulated by power which governs not only what can be said under determinate social and cultural conditions but who can speak, when and where. Much of Foucault's work is concerned with the historical investigation of discipline and the production of subjects through that power. For example, he analyses statements about madness which give us knowledge about it, the rules which prescribe what is 'sayable' or 'thinkable' about madness, subjects who personify madness and the practices within institutions which deal with madness (Foucault, 1973). He shows us how classificatory systems are essential to the process of 'normalization' (the distribution of categories around a central norm) and thus to the production of a range of subjects.

For Foucault, the subject is not a stable universal entity but an effect of discourse that constructs an 'I' in grammar. Subjectivity is held to be a discursive production and the speaking subject is dependent on the prior existence of discursive subject positions, that is, empty spaces or functions in discourse from which to comprehend the world. Living persons are required to 'take up' subject positions in discourse in order to make sense of the world and appear coherent to others. A subject position is that perspective or set of regulated discursive meanings from which discourse makes sense. To speak is to take up a subject position and to be subjected to the regulatory power of that discourse.

Use and abuses

Foucault is useful to us when we want to understand the way the social order is constituted by discourses of power that produce subjects who fit into, constitute and reproduce that order. He turns our attention to questions of power and its dispersal through the social world. Foucault is at his most valuable when exploring the concept of governmentality (Foucault, 1991), understood as the regulation or 'policing' of societies by which a population becomes subject to bureaucratic regimes and modes of discipline. This includes modes of regulation that operate through medicine, education, social reform, demography and criminology by which a population can be categorized and ordered into manageable groups.

The concept of governmentality emphasizes that processes of social regulation do not so much stand over and against the individual but are constitutive of self-reflective modes of conduct, ethical competencies and social movements. Culture in this reading is understandable in terms of governmentality since

> the relations of culture and power which most typically characterize modern societies are best understood in the light of the respects in which the field of culture is now increasingly governmentally organized and constructed. (Bennett, 1998: 61)

For Bennett, culture is caught up in, and functions as a part of, cultural technologies that organize and shape social life and human conduct. A cultural technology is part of the 'machinery' of institutional and organizational structures that produce particular configurations of power and knowledge. Culture is not just a matter of representations and consciousness but of institutional practices, administrative routines and spatial arrangements. In Bennett's reading, Foucault demands a 'politics of detail' in order to be effective in relation to the specificities of cultural institutions, governmental technologies, cultural technologies and cultural policy.

Conversely, Foucault is at his least useful in relation to the utterances and actions of speaking subjects. In his hands, the authority of discourse can appear to be external to persons and disconnected from utterances as if it were an anonymous power lurking behind us with its fingers wrapped around the puppet's strings. A form of functionalism dressed up in attractive packaging. The notion of subject position and the description of subjects as 'docile bodies' threatens to deprive the self of the agency required for political (or any other) action.

It is arguable that Foucault's later work centred on 'techniques of the self', including how the subject is 'led to focus attention on themselves, to decipher, recognize and acknowledge themselves as subjects of desire' (Foucault, 1987: 5), does reintroduce agency and the possibility of resistance and change. This concern with self-production as a discursive practice is centred on the question of ethics as a mode of 'care of the self'. For Foucault, ethics is concerned with practical advice as to how one should concern oneself with oneself in everyday life. That is, ethics centre on the 'government of others and the government of oneself' and form part of our strategies for 'conduct about conduct' and the 'calcu-lated management of affairs' (Foucault, 1979, 1984a, 1984b).

McNay (1992) asserts that this more dynamic conception of the self enables the exploration of a variety of sexualities and suggests a route for feminist political activity. She argues that 'Foucault's idea of prac-tices of the self parallels developments in feminist analysis of women's oppression that seek to avoid positing women as powerless victims of patriarchal structures of domination' (McNay, 1992: 66). Nevertheless, to date, Foucault's work has inspired more studies of power as constraint and discipline than the enabling 'power to'. In order to make Foucault's conception of ethics more workable we would need to understand how subjects construct the language of ethics and agency and how this empowers them to reflect upon their own actions even as that very language constitutes them as social subjects. This is a project in which CDA can be of use to us. However, we first need to establish how it is that human beings use language in, or as, action.

Wittgenstein and the uses of language

Writers as diverse as Saussure, Barthes, Foucault and Derrida all have a tendency to reify language or discourse into a 'thing'. However, if we give up the idea that the job of the marks and noises we call language is to generate such an entity called 'representational meaning' then there is no problem of instability. Nor would we treat discourse as a hidden presence but would take it as a metaphor suggesting the regulation and patterning of human marks and noises. If we consider language to be a tool (but not one wedded to intentionality) for achieving our purposes then the meaning of words lies in their use and 'nothing is hidden'. We know what words 'mean' when we are able to use them so that the apparent undecidability of meaning is stabilized in pragmatic narratives and social practice.

While there are similarities between the writings of Derrida and Wittgenstein (Staten, 1984), for instance, the non-representational character of language and the contextual nature of 'truth', Wittgenstein more than Derrida underlines the pragmatic and social character of language. For Wittgenstein, while the meanings of language do derive from relations of difference, they are given a degree of stability by social convention and practice. Language is not a metaphysical presence but a tool used by human animals to do things in the context of social relationships. The endless play of signification that Derrida explores is regulated and partially stabilized through pragmatic narratives.

Wittgenstein suggests that looking for universal theoretical explanations for language is not the most profitable way to proceed. 'The meaning of a word is its use in the language' (Wittgenstein, 1953 #43: 20). What is important is that we ask 'in what special circumstances this sentence is actually used. There does it make sense' (Wittgenstein, 1953 #117: 48). In his discussion of the word 'game' Wittgenstein suggests that:

> you will not see something that is common to all, but similarities, relationships, and a whole series of them at that . . . Look for example at board-games, with their multifarious relationships. Now pass to card-games; here you find many correspondences with the first group but many common features drop out, and others appear. When we pass next to ball-games, much that is common is retained, but much is lost . . . And the result of this examination is: we see a complicated network of similarities overlapping and criss-crossing: sometimes overall similarities, sometimes similarities of detail. (Wittgenstein, 1953: 31–32)

Language as practice

The meaning of the word 'game' derives not from some special or essential characteristic of such an activity, but through a complex network of relationships and characteristics, only some of which are ever present in a specific game. Thus, games are constituted by a set of 'family resemblances'. Members of a family may share characteristics with one another without necessarily sharing any specific feature in common. In this sense the word 'game' is relational; the meaning of 'card-game' depends on its relations to board-games and ball-games. Nevertheless, when it comes to explaining the word game to others we are likely to show them different games and to say 'this is what games are'. In doing so, we draw boundaries for pragmatic purposes and give examples, not as 'meanings' generated by an abstract and reified 'language', but as practical explanation for specific purposes. In a sense, to know what games are is to be able to play games. While language games are rule bound activities, those rules are not abstract components of language (as in structuralism) but constitutive rules, rules that are such by dint of their enactment in social practice. The rules of language constitute our pragmatic understandings of 'how to go on' in society.

For Wittgenstein, a meaningful expression is one that can be given a use by living human beings. That is, language is directly implicated in human 'forms of life'. Thus, in so far as the meaning of the word 'love' is generated through the relationship of signifiers – love, affection, adoration, devotion etc. – it is unstable. Nevertheless, it is stabilized by social knowledge of the word 'love', of what it is used for, when, under what circumstances and so forth. In other words, the meaning of the word 'love' is stabilized by its uses in the pragmatic narratives or language games in which it appears. When we are trained into the language-game of love within our form of life so we come to behave in specific ways which constitute our love relations and actions. This is what love 'is' . . .

Rorty and the revival of pragmatism

In recent years some of the most interesting and useful writings to have deployed or critiqued the work of Derrida, Foucault and Wittgenstein come from the pen of Richard Rorty (1980, 1989, 1991a, 1991b, 1998) who puts them into productive dialogue with the pragmatist tradition of James and Dewey. West (1993) offers the following as a good definition of pragmatism:

> Pragmatism could be characterized as the doctrine that all problems are at bottom problems of conduct, that all judgements are, implicitly judgements of value, and that, as there can be ultimately no valid distinction of theoretical and practical, so there can be no final separation of questions of truth of any kind from questions of the justifiable ends of action. (C.I. Lewis cited in West, 1993: 109)

Pragmatism shares with the poststructuralist strand of cultural studies an anti-foundationalist, anti-representationalist, anti-realist view of truth. However, this is combined with a commitment to pragmatic social reform. Pragmatism suggests that the struggle for social change is a question of language/text and of material practice/policy action. Like cultural studies, pragmatism attempts to render contingent that which appears natural in pursuit of a better world. However, unlike the revolutionary rhetoric of many followers of poststructuralism, pragmatism weds itself to the need for piecemeal practical political change. Unlike much of the cultural left, but in common with cultural policy arguments, pragmatism regards liberal democracies as the best kind of system the world has yet come up with, requiring us to work within them even as they are urged to do better. In this sense, pragmatism has a 'tragic' view of life for it does not share the utopian push of, for instance, Marxism. In contrast, it favours a trial and error experimentalism that seeks new ways of doing things which can we describe as 'better' measured against our values.

Like postmodern cultural studies, pragmatism is against 'grand theory', agreeing with Lyotard's (1984) 'incredulity towards metanarratives'. Pragmatists have a radically contingent view of the world where truth ends with social practice. However, this does not mean that all theory is to be jettisoned. Rather, local theory becomes a way of re-describing the world in normative ways. That is, theory may enable us to envisage possible new and better ways of doing things. Theory does not picture the world more or less accurately, rather, it is a tool, instrument or logic for intervening in the world through the mechanisms of description, definition, prediction and control.

Since pragmatism holds the universe to be always 'in the making' so the future has ethical significance. We can, it is argued, make a difference and create new 'better' futures. In this sense, pragmatism insists on the irreducibility of human agency even as it recognizes the causal stories of the past. Agency is to be understood as the socially constructed capacity to act and is not to be confused with a self-originating transcendental subject. We are not made up of an inner core self which possesses attitudes, beliefs, and the capacity to act. We are a network of attitudes, beliefs etc. which does act. Pragmatism shares with post-structuralist post-marxist cultural studies the idea that social and cultural change is a matter of 'politics without guarantees'. Without Marxism's 'laws of history' politics is centred on small-scale experimentalism, value-commitment and practical action.

Anti-representationalism and the final vocabulary

Rorty draws on the insights of Wittgenstein and Davidson to show that human beings use the noises and marks of language to co-ordinate action and adapt to the environment. The relationship between language and the rest of the material universe is one of causality and not of adequacy of representation or expression. That is, we can usefully try to explain how human organisms come to act or speak in particular ways which have causal relationships, but we cannot usefully see language as representing the world in ways which more or less correspond to the material world. For Rorty, 'no linguistic items represent any non-linguistic items' (Rorty, 1991a: 2). That is, no chunks of language line up with or correspond to chunks of reality. 'There is no skyhook-something which might lift us out of our beliefs to a standpoint from which we glimpse the relations of those beliefs to reality' (Rorty, 1991a: 9).

While we can describe this or that discourse, or chunk of language, as being more or less useful and as having more or less desirable consequences, we cannot do so by reference to its correspondence with an independent reality. The discovery of truth as the correspondence between words and the world cannot be the aim of inquiry or the function of language. For Rorty, to say that most of our beliefs are true is to say that we use a coherent pattern of noises and actions which line up with those of others and which enable us to co-ordinate actions with others. That is, 'true' is not an epistemological term referring to the relationship between language and reality but a consensual term referring to degrees of agreement and co-ordination of habits of action. Truth is social commendation. To say that something is 'not true' is to suggest that there is a better way of describing things, where 'better' refers to a value judgement about the consequences of describing the world in this way (including its predictive power). Truth is the literalization (or temporary fixing through social convention) of metaphors within a language-game into what Rorty (1989) calls a contingent 'final vocabulary'.

Through Wittgenstein and Rorty we can view language as a series of marks and noises made by human animals by which they attempt to achieve their purposes. Knowledge is not a matter of getting a true or objective picture of reality, but of learning how best to cope with the world. We produce various descriptions of the world and use those that seem best suited to our purposes. We have a multiplicity of vocabularies because we have a multiplicity of objectives. This argument allows us to re-examine the merits of ethnography and other empirical work, not in terms of truth or representational value, but in relation to its purposes.

Ethnographic and qualitative empirical work

Ethnographic research within cultural studies has been concerned with the qualitative exploration of values and meanings in the context of a 'whole way of life', that is, with questions of cultures, life-worlds and identities. As Morley remarks, 'qualitative research strategies such as ethnography are principally designed to gain access to "naturalized domains" and their characteristic activities' (Morley, 1992: 186). Notwithstanding qualifications about 'reflexivity', this has involved the wish to 'represent the subjective meanings, feelings and cultures of others' (Willis, 1980: 91).

However, if we think that the purpose of ethnography and other forms of qualitative empirical work lies in the discovery or accurate representation of an objective reality then the poststructuralist inspired critique of its realist pretensions is devastating (Clifford and Marcus, 1986). Wittgenstein, Rorty and Derrida among others have taught us that that the 'real' is always already a representation. We need to be less concerned with questions of representational adequacy and more with a 'politics of representation' in which marginality or subordination can be understood as a constitutive effect of representation realized or resisted by living persons. We have to be concerned with how representations signify in the context of social power and with what consequences.

The critique of the epistemological claims of ethnography does not leave this practice without worth or significance for its purposes do not lie in the production of a 'true' picture of the world. There is no funda-mental epistemological distinction between ethnography, physical science and a multi-layered novel; they all involve socially agreed pro-cedures which produce texts of more or less use to us in guiding our conduct. The differences are not degrees of correspondence with reality but matters of purpose and genre. Science has proved itself to be good at prediction and control of the natural environment while ethnographies and novels have among their achievements the production of empathy and the widening of the circle of human solidarity (Rorty, 1989).

Methods and purposes

Ethnography has personal, poetic and political, rather than epistemo-logical, justifications. This does not mean that we can abandon all methodical rigour. First, evidence and poetic style are pragmatically useful warrants for truth and action being epistemologically equivalent to the procedural agreements of the physical sciences. That is, scientific 'objectivity' is to be read as social solidarity and truth signals maximum social agreement (Rorty, 1991a). Second, the languages of observation and evidence are among the conventions that divide the genre of ethnography from the novel. Third, the rejection of a universal objective truth is based on the impossibility of word–world correspondence and therefore of accurate or adequate representation. This does not mean that we have to abandon word–word translation. We can achieve 'good enough' reporting of the speech or action of others without making claims to universal truth. It is better to use a tape recorder to document the utterances of research subjects rather than invent their speech because (a) we will be better able to translate and understand the words of others for practical purposes and (b) we will be better able to predict the actions of others.

The problems of ethnography are problems of translation and justi-fication, not of universal or objective truth. Since all languages are culture-bound and knowledge is positional, then languages, along with cultural and political discourses, can be incommensurable for there is no meta-language of translation. There would appear to be no shared rules or point of potential arbitration for coming to agreement as to what would constitute the meaning of words so that ethnography could not bridge cultures. However, we can recognize others as language users. If we then consider languages (and thus culture and knowledge) as constituted not by untranslatable and incompatible rules but as learnable *skills* then incommensurable languages could only be unlearnable languages (Rorty, 1991a).

According to Davidson (1984), there can be no such thing as an untranslatable language, for under such circumstances we would be unable to recognize others as language users in the first place. Thought of as the learning of language skills, ethnography would encourage dialogue and the attempt to reach pragmatic agreements. There is no *a priori* reason why this should succeed, agreement may never be reached, but there is no *a priori* reason why it should fail either. If it should succeed then those to whom we can speak are held to be 'like us' and are treated as part of the 'we' of human solidarity.

Combatting ethnocentrism

Truth, knowledge and understanding can only be from within particular language-games and thus truth is the consequence of particular kinds of acculturalization. Ethnography as a part of the continued re-description of the world can help to supply those 'toe holds for new initiatives' which combat ethnocentrism and help enrich our own culture with new ideas:

> no description of how things are from a God's-eye-view, no skyhook provided by some contemporary or yet-to-be developed science, is going to free us from the contingency of having been acculturated as we were. Our acculturation is what makes certain options live, or momentous, or forced, while leaving others dead, or trivial, or optional. We can only hope to transcend our acculturation if our culture contains (or, thanks to disruptions from outside or internal revolt, comes to contain) splits which supply toe holds for new initiatives . . . So our best chance for transcending our acculturation is to be brought up in a culture which prides itself on not being monolithic – on its tolerance for a plurality of subcultures and its willingness to listen to neighbouring cultures. (Rorty, 1991a: 13–14)

Ethnographic data can be seen as giving poetic expression to voices from other cultures or from the 'margins' of our own culture. Writing about such voices is no longer to be regarded as a 'scientific' report, but a poetic exposition and narration that brings new voices into what Rorty (1980) calls the 'cosmopolitan conversation of humankind'. Thus, ethnographic data can be the route by which our own culture is made strange to us, allowing new descriptions of the world to be generated. The continued re-description of our world which ethnographic research can achieve is a desirable thing to do because it offers the possibility of an improvement of the human condition. Different practices and descriptions of the world can be played off against each other, compared and juxtaposed, in order to generate yet more new descriptions in the ongoing conversation of humanity and its search for betterment.

The story so far . . .

We may summarize the argument at this point by stating that we agree with the mainstream of cultural studies that meaning in language is generated through the relations of difference between signs and that, as a consequence, language cannot produce truth as a correspondence of the word–world relationship. We have argued that [to date cultural studies has centred on the politics of signification in the context of textual analysis.] Here, the structuralist language of signs and codes, together with the poststructuralist tropes of discourses and texts, has proved to be good at telling the story of how power is implicated in all forms of cultural representation. However, cultural studies has been lopsided in its concentration on 'dead' texts and its general failure to analyse the utterances of living speaking subjects. Even where, as in ethnographic, reception and consumption studies, cultural studies has explored the speech of living persons it has rarely brought the tools of linguistic analysis to bear.

One of the reasons for this imbalance within cultural studies is the pervading influence of structuralist and poststructuralist theories of language that concentrate on the grammar of language (to the detriment of utterances) and efface the speaking subject as the product or effect of discourse. By contrast, we argued that language is a tool used to achieve our aims and cope with the world – we have many languages because we have many purposes. The instability of signs is temporarily halted in the context of pragmatic narratives since we comprehend the meaning of words when we are able to use them. This points to the need for a language of agency and utterances to explore persons as social actors in contexts that would sit alongside and interact with the languages of structure and determination. The qualitative empirical research that stems from this argument is not premised on a search for truth as correspondence but upon the possibility of better understanding and predicting the behaviour of others while widening the circle of human solidarity.

In the context of cultural studies CDA can enrich the study of human beings talking. If language is a tool, CDA may help us wield it in ways better suited to our purposes. For analytic purposes the detailed analysis of language-in-use can show us how social constructions are built. We can see not just the building but the design and deployment of individual bricks. Allied to a discursive psychology, discourse analysis can explore how consciousness is constituted through language and the manner in which psychological states are assembled within language, rather than being entities that lurk behind it. Through the study of language usage we can explore how people make emotional and identity-related claims about themselves and what they are achieving as they do so (Billig, 1997).

From a political perspective, CDA can reveal our participation in patterns of the linguistic dance of which we are not conscious and that have consequences which we find undesirable. In particular, critical discourse analysis can help us be more reflexive about power relations between speakers within and between language communities. Armed with an improved grasp of the way we are constructed/construct ourselves as men or women, Poles or Ukrainians, we may be better positioned to change ourselves, talk to each other and construct workable political and policy initiatives.

Critical discourse analysis (CDA)

CDA, a particular version of which we describe in Chapter 3, represents an aid in the analysis of language-based data. In addition, this approach offers a repeatable method capable of tackling the data regardless of the who, where and when involved. As such, we position CDA as a means of coping with two potential problems for the analysis of talk within cultural studies. The first is the problem of the positionality. That is, 'knowledge' is never a neutral or objective phenomenon but a matter of the place from which one speaks, to whom, and for what purposes. The second is the question of evidence and in particular the issues of verifiability and repeatability.

The personal is cultural

It is often argued that ethnographic and/or empirical data can be the route by which our own culture is made strange to us (Hammersley and Atkinson, 1983) or surprises us (Willis, 1980). That is, ethnographic work allows new descriptions of the world to be generated as new forms of knowledge which are the product of the juxtaposition of perspectives; new methods or viewpoints applied in familiar contexts, and/or tried and trusted methods applied to new situations. In neither case does knowledge production involve claims to universal truth but the generation of a context-bound 'regime of truth', what counts as truth, given the specific acculturation of the persons involved.

This familiar intellectual argument was made more concrete and given an affective undercurrent for us by our own personal circumstances. One of us, Chris Barker, is English-born, now living in Australia and, despite a certain shared history and the apparent similarity of English and Australian culture, has experienced a degree of cultural dislocation. On one level this concerns the challenges to one's taken-for-granted stocks of day-to-day 'how to get along' knowledge. On another level it concerns the acquisition of a new Australian perspective on history and world events to set alongside an older acculturated outlook that effectively relativizes both.

The other author, Dariusz Galasiński, is Polish, born and educated up to doctorate level in Communist Poland. Going to school in the period of deep Communism, living through the time of *Solidarity*, or experiencing martial law in 1981 are all important parts of the background with which he as an analyst is burdened. So, incidentally, is the experience of living abroad as a 'legal alien' from a 'non-elite', non-EU country. This has involved enduring the same absurd questions at British airports from immigration officers positioned on a platform so as to tower over you or having to report your whereabouts to the police every six months.

These experiences are not merely part of a private person's make-up, rather, they are also cultural patterns that form a part of the analyst's approach to data that will manifest themselves to a greater or lesser extent depending on the kinds or origins of observations under review. This closeness to the data poses problems of reliability and verifiability where no 'controlling mechanisms' are offered, but also proves fruitful in providing insight and perspective on the problems at hand. (For an extended discussion of the problems of background in discourse analysis, see Galasiński, 1997b.)

One does not have to be a migrant or have been raised in a totalitarian country to be able to see that one's individual background can easily have an impact on, perhaps not the quality, but at least the scope and extent of one's analysis. For example, one of the criticisms that can be levied at the semiotic or iconological analyses conducted by Barthes (1972) and Panofsky (1955), or at the Derridean-inspired techniques of decontructionism (all of which have formed the mainstay of textual analysis with cultural studies) is that they rely too heavily on the erudition of writers that is not easily matched by others.

Objectivity as solidarity

There is, of course, nothing wrong with erudition itself. However, semiotic and deconstruction theories, despite their claims to scientific or philosophic sophistication respectively, remain highly individualistic and essentially literary approaches. For the kinds of analysis that we are proposing, what is required is an agreed method of analysis that will provide the investigator with a means of tackling the data in ways that address the data irrespective of the specificities of the analyst's cultural background. This does not involve making claims for universal objective truth. Rather it involves making claims for the context-bound veracity generating achievements of consensually validated sets of procedures.

Here, evidence is a pragmatically useful warrant for the integrity of truth and action being epistemologically equivalent to the procedural agreements of the physical sciences.

Scientific 'objectivity' is a matter of procedural solidarity and social commendation rather than universal accuracy. Thus, given a certain acceptance of the 'rules' and procedures of the English language that provide lexico-grammatical analysis with validation and quasi-objectivity within the cultural context of its use, CDA can offer a degree of repeatable and empirically verifiable analysis. Given the grammatical rules of English, CDA can offer forms of analysis that cannot be reasonably or intelligibly disputed. Further interpretation, however contentious and ideologically motivated, follows on from an empirically verifiable analysis of the text. As we shall make clear in Chapter 3, insights into the context of discourse are an indispensable part of discourse analysis. However, here we are not so much talking about the context, but rather about the entextualization (i.e. making textually relevant, see Blommaert, 1997) of traditions that may or may not have been part of the analysed discourses.

This argument has led us to the second problem frequently faced by cultural studies from its critics, namely the need (or failure) to base analysis on some sort of 'hard' evidence. That is, evidence that can be empirically accessed not only by the 'erudite's club', or by members of the same culture. The method that we are seeking is not one that will rely solely on one's fine-tuned command of the local language or culture. Incidentally, if this were the case, we as joint authors of this book would be very hard pushed to say anything about the other contributor's data in English and Polish. Furthermore, we do not want to convince our readers that we only have an instinctive feeling that a particular phrase means this or that. Rather, we want to say to readers that there are certain agreed features of the analysed talk upon which our subsequent interpretation is based.

CDA within cultural studies

Needless to say, we do not want to claim that all the analyses carried out within semiotics or cultural studies are useless because they have not espoused discourse analysis. Rather, what we are suggesting is that such analyses might be enriched through the benefits of detailed linguistic insights. Second, we do not want to claim that CDA is the only useful method available for the analysis of language data. What we are saying is that method and truth claims are always related to, and contingent upon, purposes. Given the aspiration to uncover certain discursive constructions of reality, as opposed for example to the description of the organizational patterns of social actors' interactions in talk, it is CDA that offers the most adequate tools.

The kind of critical discourse analysis with which we have sympathy aims to unravel the ideological framings of discursive practices and is firmly grounded in the analysis of the lexico-grammatical structures of language. In this context, the kind of CDA that we advocate points to what can be seen on the 'surface' of language and argues that such constructions have ideological potency. In other words, CDA focuses upon the social meanings of linguistic structures, whether lexical, syntactic or other. In such a way, what CDA offers is a checklist of a number of aspects of language that can be systematically investigated in the data (for one such checklist, see Fairclough, 1989, Chapter 5).

By ideology we mean something akin to Foucault's conception of power/knowledge (Foucault, 1980) even though we acknowledge his rejection of the concept of ideology *per se* (see Chapter 3). We hold ideology to be forms of power/knowledge used to justify the actions of persons or groups and which have specific consequences for relations of power. As such ideology is not to be counterpoised to truth. Ideologies are structures of signification that constitute social relations in and through power. Indeed, if there is one thing that most cultural studies writers and advocates of CDA could agree on it is the centrality of the concept of power. Power is not simply the glue that holds the social together, or the coercive force which subordinates one set of people to another, though it certainly is this, but the processes that generate and enable any form of social action. In this sense, power, while certainly constraining, is also enabling. Having said that, cultural studies and CDA have both shown a specific concern with subordinated groups.

Thus, Bennett's (1998) 'element of a definition' of cultural studies suggests that it is an interdisciplinary field in which perspectives from different disciplines can be selectively drawn on to examine the relations of culture and power. The forms of power that cultural studies explores are diverse and include: gender, race, class, colonialism etc. Cultural studies seeks to explore the connections between these forms of power and to develop ways of thinking about culture and power that can be utilized by agents in the pursuit of change. Hence, cultural studies is generated by thinkers who regard the production of theoretical knowledge to be a political practice where 'the theory to be constructed is not a system but an instrument, a logic of the specificity of power relations and the struggles around them' (Foucault cited in Best, 1997: 26). Further, one need not look beyond the titles of two of Fairclough's CDA texts, *Language and Power* (1989) and *Discourse and Social Change* (1992) to appreciate the overlapping concerns of cultural studies and CDA with regard to power and the politics of change.

In this context, CDA offers the potential for a systematic and repeatable insight into the linguistic form capable of unravelling social practice and, as we shall show in the data-analytic chapters, offering insights that are capable of sustaining and enhancing those offered by cultural studies. The difference that CDA analysis makes to cultural studies is precisely a more close and clear identification of the evidence upon which to base interpretation of data. For example, whether we sympathize with 'New Labour' in Britain or with Prime Minister Tony Blair, it will not be a matter of judgement or political sympathy to collate and analyse the use of pronouns in their documents. Thus, Fairclough (2000) suggests that the pronoun 'we' is one of New Labour's keywords, i.e. one that occurs within the analysed corpus most frequently. In this way, what we arrive at is a method of analysing texts which can be easily repeated by analysts of varied backgrounds – what can be made of it is, of course, another matter.

Moreover, this systematic focus on the linguistic data turns the issues of the analyst's background as well as the analysable context into potential advantages. CDA offers the possibility of dialogue between the non-linguistic and the linguistic precisely because the latter remains at the core of the analysis. The non-linguistic, however, can very fruitfully inform the findings of the language analysis and offer ways in which to interpret them. The Gadamerian constant rereading of the text can safely continue because linguistic analysis offers a methodologically sound anchor.

Some limitations of CDA

None of the arguments we have put forward means that CDA is without its own particular shortcomings. CDA is essentially a labour-intensive, micro-linguistic enterprise requiring a lot of time and, as such, it is very difficult to apply to large corpora of texts. There are at least two, mutually complementing solutions, both made easier by the increasingly user-friendly text-analysis software.

The first solution is the employment of a global and statistically viable content analysis (e.g. Bouma and Atkinson, 1995; Krippendorf, 1981; Weber, 1990) that can set up a conceptual framework within which CDA might operate. This quantitative content analysis can provide information as to the frequency with which, and the contexts in which, certain kinds of actors, topics, issues or events occur in the corpus (for an example of a successful combination of CDA and quantitatively oriented content analysis, see Galasiński and Marley, 1998). The second solution is to combine the advances in corpus linguistics (e.g. Fairclough, 2000), with the increased availability of qualitative text analysis software that enables a data-driven survey of the data with a view to the creation of a corpus manageable for the purposes of CDA.

Finally, it can be argued that CDA analysis does not achieve anything that any competent language user could not say. This argument has strength to the extent that everyday competent language users do have insights into their own uses of language. Many actors do have, on the level of pragmatic consciousness, a grip on the difference between addressing someone as 'she' or 'it' (see Chapter 5 on ethnicity). However, theory construction is a self-reflexive discursive endeavour that seeks to interpret and intervene in the world. Theory seeks to distinguish and account for the general features that describe, define and explain persistently perceived occurrences. If one does not have the necessary tools at hand, then there are limits to what can be achieved. The fact that any competent car driver knows roughly that s/he is in control of a vehicle powered by an internal combustion engine does not mean that they can repair it without the necessary conceptual and physical tools. Similarly, that ordinary language users possess linguistic insight does not enable them to carry out detailed language analysis of the kind CDA offers without the requisite tool-kit (Chapter 3).

Conclusions

In this chapter we have argued that cultural studies and CDA share a concern with the constitution of culture in the matrix of language and power. However, they approach these questions with different tools and purposes. The central aim of this book is to argue, and subsequently to demonstrate through analysis, that these two important perspectives can be put into a productive dialogue. In particular, we hold that the structuralist and poststructuralist legacy, though enormously productive in some respects, has produced crucial blind spots in cultural studies analyses.

Specifically, though cultural studies has produced a large body of textual analysis and made claims regarding the social construction of gender, ethnicity, class, age etc., it has only rarely attended to the day-to-day speech of acculturated persons. Consequently, cultural studies has been unable to show how precisely the discursive construction of cultural forms is achieved in everyday life. Here, it was argued, CDA is able to provide the methodological tools by which to demonstrate the place of language in the constitution and regulation of cultures and cultural identities. Further, CDA can provide cultural studies with sets of linguistic procedures validated by agreement regarding the rules of language. This enables cultural analysis to make claims to repeatability and verifiability which are so often the Achilles heel of cultural studies as far as its critics are concerned.

Consequently, studies of identities, which have comprised a major theme of contemporary cultural studies and which include Chapters 4–6 of this book, can become more grounded in 'real-life' language use. However, we first need to consider what cultural studies has had to say about the self, identity and cultural politics. This forms the substance of our next chapter.

2

Language, Identity and Cultural Politics

This chapter explores the character of subjectivity and identity as cultural constructions to which language is central. Identity is the focus of the chapter for two reasons. First, it is through the identity categories of gender and ethnicity that, in later chapters, we explore the potential of CDA to contribute to the project of cultural studies. Second, identity has been the primary domain with which cultural studies has been concerned during the 1990s. It will be argued that the plasticity of identity, manifested as the ability to talk about ourselves in a variety of ways, leads us to a form of cultural politics centred on the re-description of persons and social situations. This politics of re-signification is not opposed to, indeed is complementary with, a cultural politics of institutions and policy initiatives.

We will take the concept of subjectivity to be the tool by which to talk about the processes and condition of being a person. That is, how we are constituted as subjects through social processes that bring us into being as subjects for ourselves and others. Identity as a concept pertains to descriptions of persons with which we emotionally identify. Identities are discursive–performative (Butler, 1993, 1994) in the sense that they are best described as constructed through discursive practice which enacts or produces that which it names through citation and reiteration of norms or conventions.

The popular cultural repertoire of the western world holds that we have a true-self, an identity which we possess and which can become known to us. Identity is thought to be a universal and timeless core, an 'essence' of the self that is *expressed* as representations recognizable by ourselves and others. That is, identity is an essence signified through signs of taste, beliefs, attitudes and lifestyles.

Particular philosophers and cultural studies writers have questioned the assumption that identity is a fixed 'thing' that we possess. Identity, it is argued, is not best understood as an entity but as an emotionally charged description of ourselves. Rather than being a timeless essence, what it is to be a person is said to be plastic and changeable being specific to particular social and cultural conjunctures. In particular, subjectivity and identity mark the composition of persons in language and culture.

Language and the cultured self

The limits of language mark the edge of our cognitive understanding of the world, for our acculturalization in and through language is indicative of our values, meanings and knowledge. Indeed, the very notion of what it is to be a person is cultural and consequently variable. For example, the individualism and self-centredness of western societies is not shared by cultures for whom personhood is inseparable from a network of kinship relations and social obligations. Drawing on cross-cultural research, anthropologist Clifford Geertz suggests that;

> The Western conception of the person as a bounded, unique, more or less integrated motivational and cognitive universe, a dynamic center of awareness, emotion, judgement and action organized into a distinctive whole and set contrastively against a social and natural background is, however incorrigible it may seem to us, a rather peculiar idea within the context of the world's cultures. (Geertz, 1979: 229)

For Elias (1978, 1982), the Western 'I' as a self-aware object is a modern conception which emerged out of science and the 'Age of Reason'. It was at this point in time that the more obviously group- and moral-based identities of the middle ages began to be surpassed by considerations of the self as possessing reason, knowledge and an inner world. Increasingly the predominance of external, abstract regulatory rules of governance backed up by punishment gave way to a reliance on the 'internalization' of morality and the rules that regulate conduct.

Thus, historical and cross-cultural work suggests that the resources that form the material for personhood are the language and cultural practices of specific times and places. We are born into a world that pre-exists us and learn to use a language which was here long before we arrived. In short, we are formed as individuals in a social process using culturally shared materials. Without language, not only would we not be persons as we commonly understand that concept, but the very concept of personhood and identity would be unintelligible to us.

Identity as a becoming

The philosophical argument that identity is not a universal entity but a culturally specific discursive construction is grounded in the anti-representationalist understanding of language (see Chapter 1). That is, language does not act as a mirror able to reflect an independent object world, but is better understood as a tool that we use to achieve our purposes (Rorty, 1980). Language 'makes' rather than 'finds'; representation does not 'picture' the world but constitutes it. As such, language can be thought of as a resource which 'lends form' to ourselves and the world out of the contingent and disorderly flow of everyday talk and practice (Shotter, 1993).

If language does not reflect an independent object world then it cannot be said that language directly *represents* a pre-existent 'I'. Rather, language and thinking *constitute* the 'I', they bring it into being through the processes of signification. Subjectivity and identity are constituted through the regulatory power of discourse. Descartes' famous phrase 'I think therefore I am' now becomes deeply problematic. 'I think therefore I am' suggests that thinking is separate from and represents the pre-existent 'I'. However, since there is no 'I' outside of language, then thinking *is* being, 'I' is a position in language.

The contrast between an eternal metaphysical self and a contingent linguistic self has been explored through debates about essentialism and anti-essentialism (Hall, 1990, 1992b). The essentialist argument holds identity to be the name for a 'one true self'. The underlying assumptions of this view are that identity exists and that it is 'a whole' expressed through symbolic representation. By this token there would be an essence of, for example, masculine identity based on similarity of experience and expressed through representations of men in film, television and the print media. Men might be held to be tough, heterosexual, stoic, action-oriented and work-directed. However, men can also be verbally and emotionally expressive, inwardly reflective and homosexual with a balanced view of the relationship between paid work and personal recreation. Thus, the assumptions of an essentialist argument are immediately made problematic for men are not and cannot be one universal 'entity'.

The anti-essentialist position stresses that identity is a process of *becoming* built from points of similarity and difference. There is no essence of identity to be discovered, rather, cultural identity is continually being produced within the vectors of resemblance and distinction. Cultural identity is not an essence but a continually shifting description of ourselves. The meaning of identity categories – Britishness, Blackness, masculinity etc. – are held to be subject to continual deferral through the never-ending processes of supplementarity or differance (Derrida, 1976). Since meaning is never finished or completed, identity represents a 'cut' or a snap shot of unfolding meanings, a strategic positioning which makes meaning possible. This anti-essentialist position points to the political nature of identity as a 'production' and to the possibility of multiple, shifting and fragmented identities which can be articulated together in a variety of ways (Hall, 1990, 1992b).

Discourse and the regulation of identity

As Saussure, Derrida and Wittgenstein all argue, language generates meanings through a series of unstable and relational differences

(Chapter 1). However, it is also regulated within discourses which define, construct and produce their objects of knowledge. Consequently, what we can say about the identity characteristics of, for example, men, is socially circumscribed. Identities are both unstable *and* temporarily stabilized by social practice and regular, predictable behaviour.

The argument that subjectivity is a discursive construction owes much to Foucault's genealogy of the modern subject in which the self is radically historized, i.e. the subject is wholly and only the product of history. For Foucault (1972), discourse (as regulated ways of speaking/ practice) offers speaking persons subject positions from which to make sense of the world while 'subjecting' speakers to the regulatory power of those discourses. A subject position is that perspective or set of regulated discursive meanings from which discourse makes sense. To speak is to take up a pre-existent subject position and to be subjected to the regulatory power of that discourse.

Foucault (1977, 1979, 1980) describes a subject which is the product of power through the individualization of those subject to it. For Foucault, power is not simply a negative mechanism of control but is productive of the self. The disciplinary power of schools, work organizations, prisons, hospitals, asylums and the proliferating discourses of sexuality produce subjectivity by bringing individuals into view. The body is the site of disciplinary practices which bring subjects into being, these practices being the consequences of specific historical discourses of crime, punishment, medicine, science, sexuality and so forth.

Foucault provides us with useful tools for understanding the connections between subjectivity and the social order. However, he does not provide us with an understanding of how and why particular discourses are 'taken up' by some subjects and not by others or how a subject produced through disciplinary discursive practices can resist power (Hall, 1996a). He does not provide us with an understanding of the emotional investments by which subjects are attached to discourse nor with a theory of agency. Consequently, Hall (1996a) has looked to psychoanalysis to shed light on how identifications of the 'inside' link to the regulatory power of the discursive 'outside'. That is, the processes by which discursively constructed subject positions are taken up (or otherwise) by concrete persons, fantasy identifications and emotional 'investments' (Henriques et al., 1984).

The metaphorical interior

The interface between the discursive 'outside' as described by Foucault and the identifications of the 'inside' as illuminated by psychoanalysis is central to Hall's conceptualization of 'identity' as the point of suture, between on the one hand the discourses and practices which attempt to 'interpellate', speak to us or hail us into place as the social subjects of particular discourses, and on the other hand, the processes which produce subjectivities, which construct us as subjects which can be 'spoken'. Identities are thus the points of temporary attachment to the subject positions which discursive practices construct for us. (Hall, 1996a: 5–6)

Lacan and the symbolic order

Lacanian theory has proved to be the most influential form of psycho-analysis within cultural studies, in part because of the crucial role that language plays within it. According to Lacan (1977), language formation is motivated by the pleasure that comes through feelings of control. Language acquisition represents the wish to regulate desire through occupying the place of symbolic power. It is a manifestation of the *lack* which Lacan sees at the core of subjects. Specifically, this is the lack of the mother as a result of separation at the mirror phase and, more generally, the lack that human subjects experience by virtue of the prior existence of a symbolic order which they cannot control. Language is the symbolization of desire in a never-ending search for control.

For Lacan it is through entry into the symbolic order that subjects are formed. Outside of the symbolic order, i.e. the overarching structure of language and received social meanings, lies only psychosis. The symbolic is the domain of human law and culture whose composition is materialized in the very structure of language that forms the subject positions from which one may speak. Crucially, these are gendered subject positions as the Phallus serves to break up the mother–child dyad and stands for entry into the symbolic order. Indeed, it is the Phallus as 'transcendental signifier' which enables entry to language (for both sexes) and, by standing in for the fragmented subject, allows the construction of a narrative of wholeness. The symbolic Phallus is the privileged and universal signifier because it is the law of the Name-of-the-Father (resonant of God as the place of creation and power in Judaic-Christian culture) which organizes the symbolic order and the infant's entry into it (since it is the symbolic father that prohibits desire for the mother).

The unconscious as 'like a language'

The unconscious is the site for the generation of meaningful represen-tations that, in Lacanian terms, are structured 'like a language'. Not only is language the route to the unconscious, but the unconscious is a site of signification, i.e. the generation of meaningful activity. In particular, the mechanisms of condensation and displacement, which Freud saw as the most important of the 'primary processes', are held by Lacan to be analogous to the linguistic functions of metaphor and metonymy.

Condensation and metaphor are processes by which one idea comes to stand for a series of associated meanings along a chain of signifiers. While meaning is never fixed (or denotative) because generated through difference/differance, nevertheless, under the force of repression, a signifier comes to acquire the status of a signified. A conscious idea represents, as metaphor, a whole chain of unconscious meanings. Displacement involves the redirection of psychic energy due to one object or idea onto another. Metonymy, a process whereby a part stands for the whole, involves the displacement of energy and therefore meaning along a chain of signifiers. While meaning is differed, because generated by difference, displacement/metonymy is motivated by the desire for satisfaction that such a fixing could bring. It involves the attempt to control the symbolic and overcome lack. The continual sliding of meaning is prevented, or temporarily stabilized, by its metonymic organization around key cultural *nodal points* which structure (and gender) the unconscious.

Problems with Lacan

Although influential in cultural studies, the Lacanian reading of Freud poses a number of unanswered questions:

1. Is the unconscious 'like a language' or is it constituted by language?
2. Is structuring of the symbolic order by the Phallus and the regulation of our entry into it by the law of the father a universal human condition, or is it culturally and historically specific?
3. Is it possible to struggle against, and change, the language of patriarchy or are we forever formed in this way?

Cultural studies and feminism alike have been attracted and repelled by psychoanalysis (and Lacan specifically) because this body of work offers an account of the constitution of gendered subjects yet places the formation of subjectivity in a set of universal, ahistorical and patriarchal processes. This is the case for Lacanians (Mitchell, 1974; Rose, 1997) and object-relations theorists (Chodorow, 1978, 1989) alike. Whatever its strengths and weaknesses, psychoanalysis must be taken as an historically specific account of human sexuality and subjectivity. The particular kinds of psychic resolutions which psychoanalysis describes are not universals of the human condition but particular to specific times and places. Indeed, psychoanalysis itself has to be situated in time and space and is unable to warrant claims to universal scientific truth.

Psychoanalysis should be treated as a set of poetic, metaphorical and mythological stories with consequences. Its truths lie in its practice and its outcomes. In that sense the obscurity of its language and its phallo-centrism are real problems, particularly when other forms of psychology and therapy can do its job more effectively. Here we begin to move away from the terrain which cultural studies has marked out for itself and into the realm of an emerging 'discursive psychology', which by implication, we are suggesting could be valuably drawn into the accounts which cultural studies gives of subjectivity and identity.

Construct psychology: an alternative to psychoanalysis

Personal construct psychology (Dalton and Dunnett, 1993; Kelly, 1955; Rowe, 1988, 1996; Viney, 1996) offers a useful if less fashionable (within cultural studies) alternative to psychoanalysis. According to Viney (1996: 4), the constructivist assumptions underlying personal construct therapy include the idea that people use linguistic constructs, or personal mean-ings, to make sense of what happens to them. These constructs form a system that is forged through a series of interpretations and predictions which constitute a life-story. Exploring a person's constructs, which are healthy to the degree that they act as useful predictors and guides, enables understanding of their actions. Personal construct systems are 'locked into', indeed constitutive of, emotions, so that confirmation of the useful-ness and validity of one's construct system is intertwined with positive feelings while more negative emotions are implicated in unsuccessful interpretation and prediction.

Thus, Rowe (1996) contends that to become 'depressed' one has to have acquired over the years a set of inter-linked constructs which relate to the particular circumstances of one's life. These are held to be as follows:

1. No matter how good and nice I appear to be, I am really bad, evil, valueless, unacceptable to myself and other people.
2. Other people are such that I must fear, hate and envy them.
3. Life is terrible and death is worse.
4. Only bad things happened to me in the past and only bad things will happen to me in the future.
5. It is wrong to get angry.
6. I must never forgive anyone, least of all myself (adapted from Rowe, 1996: 16).

In order to display and manifest ourselves as intelligible persons we tell stories about ourselves in the context of social relationships. Personal construct psychology stresses that narratives are rationales for courses of action. Meaning is held to be created by people who actively impose their constructs onto life events in the context of their purposes and goals. Therapy involves the retelling of stories about the past along with the generation of a range of alternative narratives about the future in the context of a dynamic relationship between client and therapist. It also involves making reflexively explicit the constructs which are constitutive of ourselves and our actions.

Consequently, in the therapeutic situation persons are in principle able to reconstruct their past – bringing it into line with the requirements of the present – thereby consolidating an emotional narrative with which they feel relatively content. It is a central assumption of therapy that all constructs can be changed so that 'better' interpretations and predictions can be made. 'Better' means the adoption of new stories and new languages which have consequences held to be an improvement in the lives of ourselves and others as measured against cultural values (which themselves may have been modified or re-prioritized).

From personal constructs to social constructionism

Our constructs, however personal we may imagine them to be, are not simply matters of individual interpretation since they are always already a part of the wider cultural repertoire of discursive explanations, resources and maps of meaning available to members of cultures. Language and meaning are always social in character and there can be no private language (Wittgenstein, 1953). Meaning is formed in the 'joint-action' of social relationships, accounting practices and conversations (Shotter, 1993).

Thus do Potter and Wetherell (1987) seek to demonstrate that fundamental psychological notions such as attitudes, emotions and the inner mind could be approached through the examination of shared language. They stress the constitutive and action-orientation of language arguing that we need to study the flexible ways that language is used. Here, any state of affairs can be described in different ways giving rise to a variability of accounts. In other words, events are put 'under description' by a variety of languages which constitute them in different ways (Davidson, 1984).

Potter and Wetherell (1987) suggest that we need to examine the rhetorical organization of the linguistic and cultural repertoires, made up of the figures of speech, recurrent descriptions and metaphors, by which we construct specific accounts of ourselves and the world. Further, we should consider what, in the context of social dialogue, accounts of actions, memories and attributions are designed to do (Edwards and Potter, 1992). That is, accounts of our actions and ourselves are socially produced descriptions which are marshalled for specific ends including defence of one's credibility.

For Gergen, not only are the requirements for telling an intelligible story about ourselves culturally formed, i.e. to possess an intelligible self requires a borrowing from a cultural repository, but what we take to be our most personal feelings and emotions are discursive in character. He argues that one isn't motivated or incited to action by emotions, rather, 'one *does* emotions, or participates in them as he or she would on a stage' (Gergen 1994: 222, original emphasis). Concepts like anger, love, fear, sadness etc. do not have referents in identifiable and discrete mental conditions. The language of emotion gains its meaning not by reference to 'internal' states but by the way it operates within patterns of cultural relationships. We need to remind ourselves that phrases like 'inside the mind' or the 'inner self' are metaphors that guide us in action not references to literal places or entities.

Thus, the narratives which personal construct therapy attributes to individuals are better understood as

> forms of social accounting or public discourse. In this sense, narratives are conversational resources, constructions open to continuous alteration as inter-action progresses. Persons in this case do not consult an internal script, cognitive structure, or apperceptive mass for information or guidance; they do not interpret or 'read the world' through narrative lenses: they do not author their own lives. Rather, the self-narrative is a linguistic implement embedded within conventional sequences of action and employed in relationships in such a way as to sustain, enhance, or impede various forms of action. (Gergen, 1994: 188)

Nevertheless, while analysis should not attribute constructs to individuals as if they were self-originating, unified and self-centred beings, our stories are performative in the sense that they enact and constitute that which they purport to describe. They are actions in the world which are to be evaluated according to their felicity within a procedure or social convention established by patterns of relationship. As such, it remains pragmatically and therapeutically useful to suggest that we can reflexively rewrite our scripts. Subsequently, the validity or pragmatic usefulness of stories is tested through performance in the context of social relationships. That is, different cultural constructions of the world generate divergent consequences.

Re-description as a shift in being

In so far as 'emotion' is taken to be a performance of the cultural dance of language, then re-description of oneself implies, indeed requires, an emotional shift in being. Hall's (1995, 1996a) account of identity as the suturing together of the discursive 'outside' with the 'internal' processes of subjectivity utilizes the concept of 'identification' to argue that the partial stitching together of discourses and psychic forces which comprise identity is formed through the emotional investments of fantasy. Similarly, Butler reads psychoanalysis in a way which opens up a space in which to discuss how regulatory norms are invested with psychic power through processes of identification marking 'the indistinguish-ability of psychic and bodily formation' (Butler, 1993: 22).

Butler combines discourse and speech act theory with psychoanalysis to argue that the 'assumption' (taking on) of sex involves identification with the normative phantasm (idealization) of 'sex'. Sex is a symbolic subject position assumed under threat of punishment (e.g. of symbolic castration or abjection). The symbolic is a series of normative injunctions which secure the borders of sex (what shall constitute a sex) through the threat of psychosis and abjection (an exclusion, a throwing out, a rejection). Identification is understood by Butler as a kind of affiliation and expression of emotional tie with an idealized, fantasized object (person, body part) or normative ideal. It is grounded in fantasy, projection and idealization. However, identification is not an intentional imitation of a model or conscious investment in subject positions. Rather, it is indissoluble from the very formation of subjects and is co-terminus with the emergence of the ego.

Butler argues that identifications are never complete or whole. Since identification is with a *fantasy* or idealization, it can never be co-terminus with 'real' bodies or gendered practices. There is always a gap or slipping away of identification which is never complete. Like Rose (1997), psychoanalysis highlights for Butler the very *instability* of identity. Consequently, Butler is able to theorize a space for change in which the very notions of 'masculinity' and 'femininity' can be rethought.

The forging of 'new languages' of identity whether as individual therapeutic practice or the collective struggles of identity politics can never be a simple matter of casting off one identity and taking on another through an uncomplicated re-description of oneself. Rather, rewriting self-narrative involves an *emotional shift*, a moving of psychic identifications which constitutes a transformation of one's whole being. Personal change is thus much more complex and difficult than the notion of re-description or rewriting sometimes implies. At some level there has to be a displacement in feeling simultaneous with the taking on of new maps of the world.

Yet whether one is involved in Lacanian psychoanalysis, personal construct psychology, discourse psychology or feminist consciousness raising, the means by which we seek to make that alteration in emotional identification remains verbal. Language is the route and the lever by which change takes place. The question is not whether psychoanalysis or discursive psychology are 'true' in the sense of being accurate representations of an independent object-world, but what their respective narratives achieve in practice.

Self-identity as a reflexive project

All forms of therapy, whatever their theoretical sources, share the contemporary concern with identity as a personal project. That is, the ongoing creation of narratives of self-identity that fashion together perceptions of our past, present and future. Here, self-identity is formed by the ability to sustain a narrative of the self that builds up a consistent feeling of biographical continuity and answers the critical questions 'What to do? How to act? Who to be?' (Giddens, 1991: 75). Self-identity then is *'the self as reflexively understood by the person in terms of her or his biography'* (Giddens, 1991: 53, emphasis in original).

On one level 'reflexivity' is constituted by the continual monitoring of action, a process that is intrinsic to being human. For Giddens, 'all human beings continuously monitor the circumstances of their activities as a feature of doing what they do' (Giddens 1991: 35). 'Routine reflexivity' of this type is not always 'held in the mind' during social activities but is a 'taken-for-granted' aspect of 'pragmatic consciousness'. In another, closely related sense, reflexivity is not simply a 'monitoring', but a 'making'. Reflexivity takes on the performative character of bringing into being in the naming, the necessary 'situated reflexivity' of members' knowledge that makes a thing understood as 'what it is' (Garfinkel, 1967).

Since agents are able to give reasons for their actions, reflexivity also has a more discursive meaning. Here, reflexivity refers to the use of knowledge about social life as a constitutive element of it. Thus, reflexivity refers to the constant revision of social activity in the light of new knowledge (Giddens, 1991). Reflexive identities involve reflection on experience and the active construction of identities in the light of those reflections.

For Gergen (1994) there are problems with the idea that we reflect on experience in as much as there are difficulties in determining a referent for the term 'experience'. How, he asks, can we experience our experience and, in any case, are we not referring to the contents of experience rather than experience itself? Given these difficulties, he argues that we attend to the idea that reflexivity can be understood as 'discourse about experience' (Gergen, 1994: 71). To engage in reflexive identity is to partake in a range of discourses and relationships and to construct further discourses about them. This involves a series of discourses so that 'with each reflexive reprise, one moves into an alternative discursive space, which is to say, into yet another domain of relatedness'. Reflexivity is 'a means of recognizing alterior realities, and thus giving voice to still further relationships' (Gergen, 1994: 48).

Gergen contends that the reflexive discourses of the self are not integrated into a unified whole but remain fragmented and de-centred. While Gergen is right to argue that we cannot ground the idea of a self which possesses a God-like vantage point from which to view and integrate itself, nevertheless, this is the way in which, at this specific historical and cultural juncture, we commonly *talk* about ourselves. Thus, Giddens' notion of identity as a narrative of biographical continuity summarizes the most common western cultural view of the self in the late modern dawn of the twenty-first century.

We are touching here on a variant of one of the most enduring and enigmatic paradoxes of human attempts to explore and explain their own social being, i.e. the contrasting languages of structure and action; subject and object; freedom and determination. Within Foucauldian cultural studies this has been expressed in the tension between 'subject-positions' and the 'ethics of self-mastery': holding subjects to be the 'effects' or 'products' of discourse (Foucault, 1972, 1977) contrasted to the capacity of subjects to construct themselves as an ethical project (Foucault, 1986, 1987). We may argue that such dualism is 'false', 'really' the world and consciousness are one. Yet, even if we can 'experience' it as such (as Zen Buddhists claim to do) we are currently stuck with a dualist language.

Languages for purposes

The 'problem' of structure and action is best tackled as a problem of language and purpose rather than one of description and truth. Analytically, the language of determination helps to trace causality home while therapeutically it assists us in accepting our past; things are the way they are because that's the way they are. Equally, the language of the dance helps us to see that we are social animals and that we live in the world together, while the language of agency encourages us to act and to seek improvement of the human condition.

As Wittgenstein argued, we might think of words as 'the tools in a tool-box: there is a hammer, pliers, a screw-driver, a rule, a glue-pot, glue, nails and screws. The functions of words are as diverse as the functions of the objects' (Wittgenstein, 1953: 6). The notion of a tool acts here as a metaphor by which to describe language as use, it should not be read as implying the intentionality of a pre-existent subject. Concepts of human conduct operate much like tools for carrying out relationships that are at one and the same time constituent features of social relationships. According to our purposes, we may wish to put human beings 'under description' as the social products of cultures (where the purposes are solidarity and /or the alleviation of individual responsibility) or as reflexive individuals capable of choice (where the purposes are to help clients take responsibility for their own actions, or where institutions of collectives, e.g. courts, wish to hold persons responsible for specific actions).

To investigate the problem of structure and agency is to enter the realm of metaphor and to inquire about the matter of languages for purposes. The language of the individual subject is valuable when it provides the means to celebrate the cultural power and capacities of persons. However, it is also useful to point to the wider contours of discourse and cultural life that enable some courses of action while disempowering others. Indeed, this capacity to talk about ourselves in a variety of ways for diverse purposes and in a range of contexts, has underpinned the argument that we can usefully be described as fractured subjects or as constituted with multiple identities.

The fracturing of identity

Although the proposition that we are best understood as 'fractured subjects' has multiple sources, Stuart Hall (1992b) was prominent in setting out the case within cultural studies. He identified three different ways of talking about identity that he called the 'enlightenment subject', the 'sociological subject' and the fractured (de-centred) or 'postmodern subject'.

The 'enlightenment' or Cartesian conception of the subject pictures a conscious and unified individual marked by inherently rational capacities that allow her/him to experience and make sense of the world according to the actual properties of that world. Human beings are held to be fully centred and unified individuals with an inner core. Although philosophically associated with Descartes' famous declaration 'I think therefore I am', conceiving of persons in this way is also central to the contemporary everyday western account of the self, wherein both morality talk and the law are primarily concerned with questions of individual responsibility for actions.

In Hall's account of the 'sociological subject' the social and the individual are mutually constituting. Thus, the internalization of social values and roles acquired through the processes of acculturalization stabilizes the individual and ensures that they 'fit' the social structure. Though the self is held to be the possessor of an inner unified core, this is formed interactively between the inner world and the outside social world represented initially by family members from whom we learn 'how to go on' in social life. Through the processes of praise, punishment, imitation and language acquisition we are made up of the values, meanings and symbols of the culture. This conception of the self is represented in the work of Mead (1934) and his division between the 'I' and the 'Me' (the inner self and the outer self) and echoed in Giddens' (1991) conceptualization of 'self-identity' and 'social identity'.

The social subject is not the source of itself nor is it a 'whole' by virtue of taking up a variety of social positions, nevertheless, s/he is held to reflexively co-ordinate herself into a unity. By contrast, the fragmented or 'de-centred' self is, according to Hall, composed not of one, but of several shifting, sometimes contradictory, identities.

> The subject assumes different identities at different times, identities which are not unified around a coherent 'self'. Within us are contradictory identities, pulling in different directions, so that our identifications are continually being

shifted about. If we feel that we have a unified identity from birth to death, it is only because we construct a comforting story or 'narrative of the self' about ourselves. (Hall, 1992b: 277)

For Hall, no single identity can act as an overarching organizing core since identities shift according to how subjects are addressed or represented. Rather, we comprise fractured multiple and contradictory identities which cross-cut or dislocate each other. The apparent 'unity' of identity is better described as the articulation of different and distinct elements that, under alternative historical and cultural circumstances, could be re-articulated in disparate ways. Thus, identities, which our culture generally takes to be unified and eternal, can instead be thought of as the unique historically specific temporary stabilization or arbitrary closure of meaning.

Articulation and identity

Following Laclau (1977), Hall sees no *necessary* links between the discourses that constitute us, rather, connotative or evocative connections are forged through historical custom and practice. Since there is no *automatic* connection between the various discourses of identity; class, gender, race, age etc., they can be articulated together in different ways. By 'articulation' Hall (1996a) means a connection that can (but does not have to) make a unity of two different elements under specific conditions.

Individuals can be understood as the unique, historically specific, articulation of discursive elements that are contingent, but also socially determined or regulated. Consequently, all working class, Australian white men do not necessarily share the same identity and identifications any more than all middle class, African-American women do. Indeed, it is the very plasticity of identity that marks its cultural and political significance, for the shifting and changing character of identities chronicles the way that we think about ourselves and others at a given moment in time and space. Contestation over identity represents political activity centred on the very processes by which we are formed as human subjects and the kinds of people that we are becoming.

Hall illustrates the notion of articulated identities and the range of identifications which flow from this through the case of Clarence Thomas, an African-American, US supreme court judge with conservative political views. Judge Thomas was accused of sexual harassment by Anita Hill, a black woman and former colleague of Judge Thomas. As Hall puts it:

Some blacks supported Thomas on racial grounds; others opposed him on sexual grounds. Black women were divided, depending on whether their 'identities' as blacks or women prevailed. Black men were also divided, depending on whether their sexism overrode their liberalism. White men were divided, depending, not only on their politics, but on how they identified themselves with respect to racism and sexism. White conservative women supported Thomas, not only on political grounds, but because of their opposition to feminism. White feminists, often liberal on race, opposed Thomas on sexual grounds. And because Judge Thomas is a member of the judicial elite and Anita Hall, at the time of the alleged incident, a junior employee, there were issues of social class position at work in these arguments too. (Hall, 1992b: 279–280)

For Hall, Gergen and Rorty the fragmented multiple identities of the 'postmodern' subject are the consequence of the construction of identity in and through the signifying practices of symbolic representation (with an unstable language as the prime example). We cannot have an identity, rather we are a series of descriptions in language. Indeed, given that 'are' implies an objective representation of what it is to be a person, then we must amend our formulation to say that we are 'usefully described' as multiple subjects. Given that language does not mirror the world, we can never say what we 'really are'. We can only go on making what we consider to be better, more useful, descriptions of ourselves. The value of describing ourselves as 'multiple' lies in recognizing the variety of vocabularies, range of purposes and numerous sites of activity and social relationships that are involved in being a person in contemporary society. For example, human beings can be understood as biological creatures, language users and social beings, descriptions that 'picture' us as formed through biochemical and cultural processes that generate a language-based stream of consciousness. Further, the description of persons as 'multiple' has a useful affinity with cultural pluralism, respect for difference and the institutions of democracy.

Language, identities and social practice

Hall's account of the multiple subject draws on Derrida's concept of differance – 'difference and deferral' – by which meanings are continually supplemented or differed. The unceasing substitution and adding of meanings through the play of signifiers challenges the identity of signs with fixed meanings. This includes 'woman', 'class', 'society', 'identities', 'interests' etc., which are no longer conceived of as single unitary objects with fixed meanings or single underlying structures and determinations. For Hall, following Laclau and Mouffe (1985), it is the role of ideology and of hegemonic practices to try to fix difference, to put closure around the unstable meanings of signifiers in the discursive field. That is, to stabilize what, for example, masculinity or American identity means. What we call identity is here understood to be a production, a temporary stabilization or 'cut' in the flow of language and meaning.

The 'cut' in language

Hall (1995) has argued that because discourse is a potentially endless and infinite semiosis of meaning, any sense of self, of identity or of communities of identification (nations, ethnicities, sexualities, classes etc.) and the politics that flow from them are fictions marking a temporary, partial and arbitrary closure of meaning. It is possible, given the instability of language, to go on re-describing what it means to be a 'woman' forever, in an endless process of supplementarity. However, in order to say anything (to mark significance), and in order to take action, a temporary closure of meaning is required.

Consequently, feminist politics needs at least momentary agreement about what constitutes a woman and what is in women's interests under particular circumstances. For Hall, there has to be a full stop – albeit a provisional one – a cut in the flow of meaning, so that while identities and identification are fictions, they are necessary ones:

> Politics, without the arbitrary interposition of power in language, the cut of ideology, the positioning, the crossing of lines, the rupture, is impossible . . . All the social movements which have tried to transform society and have required the constitution of new subjectivities, have had to accept the necessarily fictional, but also the fictional necessity, of the arbitrary closure which is not the end, but which makes both politics and identity possible. [This is] a politics of difference, the politics of self-reflexivity, a politics that is open to contingency but still able to act . . . there has to be a politics of articulation–politics of hegemonic project. (Hall, 1993: 136–137)

Hall is indebted here to the work of Volosinov (1973) and his concept of the 'multi-accentuality' of the sign. For Volosinov, signs do not have one meaning but possess an 'inner dialectical quality' and an 'evaluative accent' which makes them capable of signifying a range of meanings. Signification changes as social conventions and social struggles seek to fix meaning. That is, the meanings of signs are not fixed but negotiable. They are fought over so that the 'sign becomes the arena of class struggle' (Volosinov, 1973: 23). An ideological struggle is one in which there is contestation over the significance of signs and where power attempts to regulate and 'fix' their otherwise shifting meanings.

As Hall (1996b) suggests, the thrust of Volosinov's (1973) writing echoes Bakhtin's (1984) argument that all understanding is dialogic in character. Bakhtin suggested that signs do not have fixed meanings – rather, sense is generated within a two-side relationship between speaker and listener, addressser and addressee. Many critics hold that Bakhtin wrote under the name of Volosinov. In any case, 'both' suggest that meaning cannot be guaranteed, it is not pure but always ambivalent and ambiguous. Meaning is the inherently unstable domain of contestation rather than the product of a finished and secure language.

Pragmatic narratives and the social self

For Giddens (1991) the multiple narratives of the self are not the outcome of the shifting meanings of signification alone, but the consequence of the proliferation and diversification of social relationships, contexts and sites of interaction. Self-identity and social identities may be descriptions in language but they are enunciated by actors in social practices located in time and space. Giddens suggests that debates about essentialism and anti-essentialism are something of a distraction since, after Wittgenstein, he holds that the meanings of language are forged in use with identities always embedded in pragmatic narratives.

For Wittgenstein, language is not a metaphysical presence, nor a coherent system, but a context-specific tool for achieving our purposes. Here, a meaningful expression is one that can be given a use by living human beings within our 'form of life'. While the meanings of language do derive from relations of difference, they are given a degree of regulated stability by the uses we put words to. For example, to know what games are is to be able to play games. The rule-bound character of language is not constituted by the theoretical regulations of grammar, rather, the rules of language are constitutive rules that mark our pragmatic understandings of 'how to go on' in society. Thus, the stabilizing 'cut' in language which Hall, after Derrida, holds to be the production of identity through the operation of hegemonic power, is described by Giddens, after Wittgenstein, as the routine operation of pragmatic narratives in social practice.

Discourse, identities and social practice in time–space form a mutually constituting set implicated in the cultural politics of identity and the constitution of humanity as a form of life. Identities as descriptions in language are achieved in the everyday flow of language and stabilized as categories through their embedding in the pragmatic narratives of our day-to-day social conduct. Thus, the claim that language is constitutive of identity is not simply an abstract philosophical one, but is an argument located in the everyday social conversations of 'ordinary' life. In carrying out rituals and activities within social relationships people use a language that does not acquire its significance from individual mental states. Consequently, 'one participates in the cultural forms of action as in a dance or a game . . . languages are among the resources available for playing the games and participating in the dances of cultural life (Gergen, 1994: 103–104).

In the daily life of speaking subjects the construction of identity is 'a fluid accomplishment, instantiated in the procedural flow of verbal interaction' (Widdicombe and Wooffitt, 1995: 218). Here, identity is achieved as a verbal construction mobilized for particular purposes in the context of social conversations. In particular, talk is formative of identity in the context of constructing and maintaining social relationships in which we respond to others and produce practical–moral resources and activities (Shotter, 1993).

Accounting for agency

If subjects and identities are the product of discursive practices, if they are social and cultural 'all the way down', how can we conceive of persons as able to act and engender change in themselves and the social order? Subjects commonly appear within these poststructuralist arguments to be 'products' rather than 'producers'. This poses the problem of how to account for the human agency required for the cultural politics of change. If we are party to the dance of conversational life do we simply follow preordained steps or can we introduce innovation in language?

In the context of cultural studies, an emblematic debate has centred of late on the figure of Foucault (1972, 1977) whose description of subjects as 'docile bodies' and the 'effect' of discourse appears to deny subjects agency. Yet, in his later work, Foucault (1986, 1987) proposed a form of agency through a discursively constructed ethics centred on the 'care of the self'. Foucault explores how subjects are 'led to focus attention on themselves, to decipher, recognize and acknowledge themselves as subjects of desire' (Foucault, 1987: 5). That is, how the self recognizes herself as a subject involved in practices of self-constitution, recognition and reflection. As such, agency for Foucault can be said to be a subject position within discourse.

Both Rorty and Giddens have been critical of Foucault for effacing agents from the narratives of history. For Rorty, agency is an irreducible facet of human life; we can act and we are original. While we are all subject to the 'impress of history' we are also a 'tissue of contingencies' (Rorty, 1991b). The specific arrangement of discursive elements is unique to each individual for we have all had singular patterns of family relations, of friends, of work and of access to discursive resources. Acculturalization does not reduce human beings to determinations, rather, 'our accultura- tion is what makes certain options live, or momentous, or forced, while leaving others dead, or trivial, or optional' (Rorty, 1991a: 13).

For Giddens (1984), the 'duality of structure' means that structures are not only constraining, but also enabling. While actors are determined by social forces that lie beyond them as individual subjects, social structures enable persons to act. For example, we are all constructed and constrained by language that pre-exists us, yet, language is also the means and medium of self-awareness and creativity. Here, identities are posed as an issue of agency (the individual constructs a project) *and* of social determination (our projects are socially constructed and social identities ascribed to us).

The social production of agency

We need to differentiate between a metaphysical notion of free action in which persons are self-constituting, and a concept of agency as *socially produced* and enabled by differentially distributed social resources, giving rise to a varying ability to act in specific spaces. There is an important difference between conceptions in which acts are made by agents who are free in the sense of 'not determined' and agency as the socially constituted capacity to act. The notion that agents are free in the sense of being undetermined is untenable since it relies on a metaphysic of original creation. However, we might with Giddens consider agency to be the capacity to 'make a difference', the enactment of X rather than Y. The idea of agency as 'could have acted differently' avoids some of the problems of 'free as undetermined' because the pathways of action are themselves socially constituted.

Agency is the socially constructed capacity to act, nobody is free in the sense of undetermined (in which event one could not 'be' at all). Nevertheless, agency is a culturally intelligible way of understanding ourselves and we clearly have the existential experience of facing and making choices. We do act even though those choices and acts are determined by biological and cultural forces, particularly language, that lie beyond the control of individual subjects. The existence of social structures (and of language in particular) is arguably a condition of action; it enables action so that neither human freedom nor human action can consist of an escape from social determinants.

A riddle of reality or a problem of language?

Giddens' conceptualization of the 'duality of structure' is best read as a metaphor and not as a description of an independent object world of material agents and structures. We can never have 'objective' knowledge of the conditions of our own actions because we cannot step outside of those circumstances in order to compare our pristine selves with those conditions. Whatever we have to say about ourselves and the conditions of our existence is always from within our socially constituted selves. The best we can do is to produce another story about ourselves. Knowledge is not a matter of getting a true or objective picture of reality but of creating tools with which to cope with the world. That we produce a variety of descriptions of the world deploying a multiplicity of vocabularies can be said to match our many purposes.

Problems that revolve around binaries like structure and action are not problems of truth and reality, but a case of different languages for different purposes. We could usefully stop inquiring about what structure or agency 'is' (as if it existed as an objective fact outside of representation), and ask instead about how we talk about them and for what purposes. If we want to stress 'inter-relatedness', discipline and the need for structural change, the language of codes, discourse and subject positions is our tool. If we want to stress ethics, action, change and uniqueness, we talk of utterances of persons in social contexts. The language of determination helps to trace causality home. The language of the dance helps us to see that we are social animals and that we live in the world together. The language of agency encourages us to act and to seek improvement of the human condition.

Consequently, it is felicitous to consider freedom and determination as different modes of discourse and discursively constructed experience. We act with the idea of freedom and the notion of determination 'all the way down' has no bearing on this existential experience. Further, since discourses of freedom and discourses of determination are socially produced for different purposes in different realms it makes sense to talk about freedom from political persecution or economic scarcity without the need to say that agents are free in some metaphysical and 'undetermined' way. Rather, such discourses are comparing different social formations and determinations and judging one to be better than another on the basis of our socially determined values.

In this view, innovation does not lie in the qualities of acts but in retrospective judgements on the form and outcomes of action made in relation to other acts in specific historical and cultural conjunctures. Change is possible because we are unique inter-discursive individuals about whom it is possible to say that we can 're-articulate' ourselves, re-create ourselves anew in unique ways by making new languages. We produce new metaphors to describe ourselves with and expand our repertoire of alternative descriptions (Rorty, 1991a).

In so far as this applies to individuals, so it applies also to social formations. Social change becomes possible through rethinking the articulation of the elements of 'societies', of re-describing the social order and possibilities for the future. Since, as Wittgenstein (1953) argued, there is no such thing as a private language, rethinking is a social and political activity. Change occurs through the linkage of rethinking and re-describing with the material practices that are implicated in it. Rethinking ourselves, which emerges through social practice and more often than not through social contradiction and conflict, brings new political subjects and practices into being.

Cultural discourse and biochemical bodies

The argument that language is constitutive of subjectivity, identity and our cultural maps of meaning does not involve saying that no material reality exists or that by dint of being 'trapped' in language we are somehow out of synch with that material reality (as skeptics might claim). Since language is a tool for adapting to and controlling the environment, we are in touch with reality in all areas of culture as long as one takes this to mean 'caused by and causing ' and not 'representing reality'. As Rorty argues:

> We need to make a distinction between the claim that the world is out there and the claim that truth is out there. To say that the world is out there, that it is not our creation, is to say, with common sense, that most things in space and time are the effects of causes which do not include human mental states. To say that truth is not out there is simply to say that where there are no sentences there is not truth, that sentences are elements of human languages, and that human languages are human creations. Truth cannot be out there – cannot exist independently of the human mind – because sentences cannot so exist, or be out there. The world is out there, but descriptions of the world are not. Only descriptions of the world can be true or false. The world on its own – unaided by the describing activities of human beings – cannot. (Rorty, 1989)

The materiality of the world is one of those things which is, in the Wittgensteinian sense, beyond doubt. That is, we cannot function without that assumption. As Wittgenstein argues (1953), we may in principle imagine that every time we open a door there will be a bottomless chasm beneath us. However, it would be unintelligible to do so within our form of life. It is profitable to conceive of language as a series of marks and noises used by human animals to achieve their purposes. Once we drop the idea that language 'represents' the world and adopt the metaphor of language as a tool, then it makes no sense to suggest that language could be out of phase with the environment. Since language does not represent the material world it cannot misrepresent it.

Sexed bodies

These questions can be further explored in relation to debates about sex and gender thought of as biology and identity respectively. Thinkers have ruminated endlessly about nature versus nurture, biology versus culture, asking about what is 'really' the case with the expectation that one day we will find out the truth. However, let us think about this question in a different way. We do not ask about the 'true' way to ride a bike. If I ride my bike from home to my place of work arriving unscathed and on time I have ridden successfully given my objective. It makes no sense to say I have ridden my bike truthfully. If, by contrast, I wobble and fall off and as a consequence I am late for work I have not ridden my bike untruthfully but have done so badly for the aim I had in mind. We should think of language as a tool for problem-solving rather than truth-seeking. Our knife cuts and carves into shapes we find useful and good, it does not reveal the true character of wood. To deploy this mode of thinking in relation to questions of biology, culture and the self is to consider the purposes and consequences of the vocabularies we use rather than their adequacy to the real (i.e. as accurate representations).

Many of the most influential contemporary feminists, in using the language of poststructuralism, (Butler 1990, 1993; Nicholson, 1990; Weedon, 1997) argue that sex and gender are social and cultural constructions which are not to be explained in terms of biology. This anti-essentialist stance suggests that femininity and masculinity are not universal and eternal categories but discursive constructions. That is, femininity and masculinity are ways of describing and disciplining human subjects. Femininity and masculinity are matters of representation and sites of struggles over meaning.

For Kristeva (Moi, 1986), sexual identities as opposites can only come into being after entry into the symbolic order. Consequently, degrees of masculinity and femininity arise across a range of bodies. Femininity is a condition or subject position of marginality which some men, for example, avant-garde artists, can also occupy. Rather than a conflict between two opposing male–female masses, sexual identity concerns the balance of masculinity and femininity within specific men and women. This struggle, she suggests, could result in the deconstruction of sexual and gendered identities understood in terms of marginality within the symbolic order.

Butler (1993) argues that discourse and materiality are indissoluble. Discourse, which is held to construct, define and produce objects of knowledge in an intelligible way, is not only the means by which we understand what material bodies are, but, in a sense, discourse brings material bodies into view. For example, sexed bodies are discursive constructions, but indispensable ones, which form subjects and govern the materialization of bodies such that 'bodies will be indissociable from the regulatory norms that govern their materialization and the signification of those material effects' (Butler, 1993: 2). Discourse is the means by which we understand what bodies are:

> The category of 'sex' is, from the start, normative; it is what Foucault has called a 'regulatory ideal'. In this sense, then, 'sex' not only functions as a norm, but is part of a regulatory practice that produces the bodies it governs, that is, whose regulatory force is made clear as a kind of productive power, the power to produce – demarcate, circulate, differentiate – the bodies it controls. Thus, 'sex' is a regulatory ideal whose materialization is compelled, and this materialization takes place (or fails to take place) through certain highly regulated practices. In other words, 'sex' is an ideal construct which is forcibly materialized through time. It is not a simple fact or static condition of a body, but a process whereby regulatory norms materialize 'sex' and achieve this materialization through a forcible reiteration of those norms. (Butler, 1993: 1–2)

The performativity of sex

Butler conceives of sex and gender in terms of citational performativity. The performative being 'that discursive practice which enacts or produces that which it names' (Butler, 1993: 13). This is achieved through citation and reiteration of the norms or conventions of the symbolic 'law'. A performative is a statement which puts into effect the relation that it names, for example, within a marriage ceremony 'I pronounce you . . .'.

For Butler, 'sex' is produced as a reiteration of hegemonic norms, a performativity which is always derivative. The 'assumption' of sex, which is not a singular act or event but an iterable practice, is secured through being repeatedly performed. Thus, the statement, 'it's a girl' initiates a process by which 'girling' is compelled:

> This is a 'girl', however, who is compelled to 'cite' the norm in order to qualify and remain a viable subject. Femininity is thus not the product of choice, but the forcible citation of a norm, one whose complex historicity is indissociable from relations of discipline, regulation, punishment. Indeed, there is not 'one' who takes on a gender norm. On the contrary, this citation of the gender norm is necessary in order to qualify as a 'one', to become viable as a 'one', where subject-formation is dependent on the prior operation of legitimating gender norms. (Butler, 1993: 232)

Since performativity is not a singular act but a reiteration of a set of norms it should not be understood as a performance given by a self-conscious intentional actor. Rather, the performance of sex is compelled by a regulatory apparatus of heterosexuality which reiterates itself through the forcible production of 'sex'. Indeed, the very idea of an intentional sexed actor is a discursive production of performativity itself. 'Gender is *performative* in the sense that it constitutes as an effect that very subject it appears to express' (Butler, 1991: 24).

Biochemical bodies

In contrast to the claim that sex is *only* a social construction, there is a considerable body of evidence to suggest genetic and biochemical difference between men and women in relation to language ability, spatial judgement, aggression, sex drive, ability to focus on tasks or to make connections across the hemispheres of the brain (Hoyenga and Hoyenga, 1993; LeDoux, 1998; Moir and Moir, 1998). 'Feminist' psychologist Diane Halpern began her review of the literature holding the opinion that socialization practices were solely responsible for apparent sex differences in thinking patterns. However

> After reviewing a pile of journal articles that stood several feet high and numerous books and book chapters that dwarfed the stack of journal articles, I changed my mind . . . there are real, and in some cases sizeable, sex differences with respect to some cognitive abilities. Socialization practices are undoubtedly important, there is also good evidence that biological sex differences play a role in establishing and maintaining cognitive sex differences, a conclusion I wasn't

prepared to make when I began reviewing the relevant literature. (Halpern, 1992: preface xi)

Genetic science and biochemistry suggest that there are material, i.e. chemical, limits to behavioural possibilities. For example, the anxiety and depression which construct theory attributes to our life scripts is more commonly explained by psychiatrists as having biochemical and genetic causes (LeDoux, 1998; Salmans, 1997). Today, few scientists dispute the influence of hormones on the formation of the fetus as male or female. Hormones are the switches that activate the genes which 'instruct' our brains and bodies as to its reproductive organs, testosterone levels, body fat, muscle development, bone structure etc. It is also thought that those same hormones shape our brain structure so that men and women have different patterns of brain activity.

Biology as culture

Yet, biology is a language and cultural classification system while culture is not an entity that can be definitively circumscribed. Thus, it is literally senseless to decide on a final truth of the culture versus biology debate when the central terms have no stable referents and we cannot step outside of our descriptive languages to compare them with a pristine 'reality'. For example, 'culture' is a conceptual tool which is of more or less usefulness to us as a life form so that its usage and meanings change as thinkers have hoped to 'do' different things with it. Cultural studies redefined culture, moving the focus from high arts to popular activities, not because it uncovered the truth about culture but because this re-description served the political purposes of democratization.

Biochemistry and genetics are constituted by a particular type of vocabulary deployed for the achievement of specific purposes. The arguments of these sciences should be understood not as the revelation of objective truth, or the correspondence of language with an independent object world, but as the achievement of agreed procedures. These procedures have enabled us to produce levels of predictability that have underpinned a consensus or solidarity among the scientific community, leading it to call particular statements true. Such truths are always provisional. Science proceeds by error being underpinned by the methodology of doubt. Paradigm shifts in scientific thinking mean that the truths of today's ordinary science are revised and even overturned by tomorrow's conceptual revolution (Kuhn, 1962).

Scientific truths about diet and exercise are intimately connected to questions of sexual and gender identity. The slender body is a gendered body (Bordo, 1993) because slenderness is a contemporary ideal for female attractiveness. The capacity for self-control and the containment of fat is posed in moral as well as physical terms. The choice to diet and

exercise is regarded as an aspect of self-fashioning, requiring the production of a firm body as a symbol of gendered identity and the 'correct'
attitude. Thus do we use our current scientific understanding of diet and
exercise to achieve cultural goals. Yet, not only can the culturally desirable body shape change, but to our intense frustration, the rules and
truths of dietary science are also malleable.

The pragmatic test

We do not have a vocabulary to describe the limits to sexed behaviour
that biochemistry may set, nor how the interface between the biological
brain and consciousness works. Indeed, there is a philosophical case that
the language of biochemistry could never explain causal connections to
the categories of consciousness because, in a more general sense, the
mental can never be reduced to the physical. There can be no causal
laws which explain events under mental descriptions by those under
physical descriptions (Davidson, 1980). There is no way to explain how
electro-chemical activity is experienced by us as consciousness.

Yet, in pragmatic terms, anti-depressant drugs can be successful in
treating depression while hormone treatment is the necessary and
central plank in body sex-change strategies. The test is empirical and
pragmatic related to purposes and values, not one of correspondence
between the language of biochemistry and 'real' bodies. At the same
time, what it *means* to be male or female remains a cultural question of
signification and there is clear evidence that cultural attitudes about
masculinity and femininity have changed over time (Giddens, 1992).

Consequently, we may say that sex as biology and sex as the
discursive-performative are different languages for different purposes.
Both languages are social constructions that enable us to do different
things. The language of biology enables us to make *behavioural* and bodily
predictions and alterations through, for example, the use of drugs. The
language of the discursive-performative helps to recast the *symbolic*, to
rethink the way we talk about and perform 'sex' with consequences which
we deem to be good, i.e. acceptance of a wider range of sexualities. The
problems felt by men who perceive themselves to be trapped in women's
bodies may be usefully approached using the predictions made available
to us through the language of biochemistry and drug therapy. They may
also be advanced through therapeutic talk and the re-description of self in
the symbolic domain (including dress and body movement). In other
words, both the language of biology and the language of culture are
useful to us, though they achieve different ends. In the context of this
book, though behaviour has biological as well as cultural explanations,
descriptions of persons (including actual or potential behaviour) are
taken to be cultural. Thus, though biology plays its part, identity as a
descriptor of persons is cultural in character.

Evolution and the limits of language

Darwin's story and the practice of language

We may usefully deploy Darwin's story to fit the language of biology and the language of language into an evolutionary tale (Dawkins, 1976, 1995; Sterelny and Griffiths, 1999), that is, a naturalistic and holistic description of human beings as animals that walk the earth adapting and changing themselves in the context of their environment.

Evolutionary biology is a useful causal story that explains human organisms in terms of relationships and consequences. Human history has no telos, or inevitable historical point to which it is unfolding. Rather, human 'development' is the outcome of numerous acts of chance and environmental adaptation which make the 'direction' of human evolution accidental and unpredictable. 'Progress' or 'purpose' can only be given meaning as a *retrospectively* told story of which Darwinism is itself an example (we choose evolutionary biology and cosmology, extensions of Darwin's story, over the bible because within the tradition of our acculturalization they have a consensual truth value as better predictor-tools).

We learn language as an integral part of learning how to do things. As Wittgenstein remarks, 'Language did not emerge from reasoning . . . Children do not learn that there are books, that there are arm chairs etc. etc., but they learn to fetch books, sit in arm chairs etc.' (Wittgenstein, 1969: 475–476). Further, immediate expressions of pain are not the result of thought; rather they are instant actions. As a child develops language, so words replace actions like crying; to learn the language of pain is to learn 'new pain behavior' (Wittgenstein, 1953 #244: 89). Viewed in this way, language is not best described as a coherent system or set of structural relations but as an array of marks and noises used to co-ordinate action and to adapt to the environment. Language is a tool used by a human organism through which the 'pairing off the marks and noises it makes with those we make will prove a useful tactic in predicting and controlling its future behavior' (Rorty, 1989).

There is a challenge here to the (cultural) division between culture and nature. Wittgenstein is suggesting that language grew out of pre-linguistic behaviour – an argument that fits well with the Darwinian notion of language as an evolutionary tool. Thus:

> The origin and the primitive form of language-game is a reaction; only from this can the more complicated forms grow. Language – I want to say – is a refinement; 'in the beginning was the deed'. (Wittgenstein, 1980: 31)

Thinking in signs

Wittgenstein's argument against a private language is based on the idea that there can be no personal original sign. He would have agreed that

'We think only in signs' (Derrida, 1976: 50). Since we cannot think about knowledge, truth and culture without signs, writing is, for Derrida, a permanent trace which always exists before perception is aware or conscious of itself. Like Wittgenstein, Derrida 'deconstructs' the opposition of nature and culture, pointing out that nature is already a concept in language (i.e. culture) and not a pure state of being beyond signs. Ultimately, Derrida argues, the very idea of literal meaning is based on the idea of the 'letter', which is writing. Literal meaning is thus underpinned by metaphor – its apparent opposite. As Derrida puts it, 'All that functions as metaphor in these discourses confirms the privilege of the logos and founds the "literal" meaning then given to writing: a sign signifying itself signifying an eternal logos' (Derrida, 1976: 15). All language is metaphorical; that which we take as literal or descriptive language is better regarded as literalized or habitualized metaphors which are used in a widely shared fashion (Davidson, 1984).

Posed in Derridian terms, the origins and meanings of language or the character of the relations between biology and language are undecidable questions because inquiry is always formed within an already existent sign system. However, saying this is of limited usefulness to us in terms of coping with the world. We need to make decisions about how to treat depression or carry out sex changes. The language of genetics has proved more useful to us in dealing with these questions than undecidability or the bible. Adoption of the evolutionary story with the assertion that language flows out of the relations between creatures and the world has proved more, rather than less, useful to us.

The self-conscious human mind is best thought of in terms of language. Yet to describe human beings in terms of a network of signs, i.e. discursive consciousness, may not deal adequately with all the problems of human experience that we may wish to address. For example, Giddens (1984) suggests that in addition to discursive consciousness we should think in terms of the unconscious (which we may take to be constituted by signs that are normally unavailable to the self-conscious mind) and pragmatic consciousness, that state of being in which we carry out taken-for-granted activities in an unreflexive fashion. Or, to put it in Zen Buddhist terms, we are not mindful of what we are doing.

Direct pointing

Zen philosophy (Crook and Fontana, 1990; Watts, 1957, 1968) asserts the possibility of the 'direct pointing at reality'. That is, an awareness outside of signs, an experiential sensation or state of being in which, through meditation, it is possible to shut off the internal dialogue, the linguistic stream of consciousness, and *be* in the world without thinking or reflecting. We might describe this as a state of awareness, yet we might also say, as Zen monks are inclined to do, that it is something of which we cannot speak. Beyond language is the ineffable or sublime which though not expressible can be experienced. In Zen thinking the self is a sign constituted through identification with a symbol of self. Self-consciousness is, as it is for Derrida, nothing but signs. However, for Zen we may *be* in a realm without signs.

Wittgenstein also marks out limits to language arguing for the existence of a domain about which we cannot speak. He discusses the question of that which we know when no one asks us about it, but no longer know when we are supposed to give an account of it (Wittgenstein: 1953; #89: 42e). Further, the experience of nothingness cannot be a matter of discursive knowledge or understanding but must be a state of existence. There is of course irony in the argument that nothingness or the sublime is signed as an experience outside of representation by the sign-systems of language. To speak about the limits of language is to do so in vocabularies that attempt to sign the unsayable. Beyond language is that which we cannot speak.

This is a problem that has also been grappled with by Irigaray (1985a, 1985b) through her endeavour to write the unwritable, to inscribe the feminine through *écriture feminine* (woman's writing) and *le parler femme* (womanspeak). Irigaray theorizes a pre-symbolic 'space' or 'experience' for women that is unavailable to men. This is constituted by a feminine *jouissance* or sexual pleasure, play and joy, which is outside of intelligibility. For Irigaray, woman is outside the specular (visual) economy of the Oedipal moment and thus outside of representation (i.e. of the symbolic order). Here, woman is not so much an essence, as that which is excluded. The feminine is the unthinkable and the unrepresentable (other than as a negative of phallocentric discourse).

Philosophical and cultural analysis does not offer final single resolutions of questions, but the substitution of one form of expression for another. There is no final vocabulary of language that is 'true' in the sense of picturing a thing called language. We cannot say what language *is*. We cannot say what we 'truly are' in any final or metaphysical sense. We do things with marks and noises, we tell constitutive stories of and about ourselves. Our final vocabularies are always contingent on historical and cultural circumstances (Rorty, 1989). Our best bet is to go on telling stories about ourselves that aim to achieve the most valued and most beautiful description and arrangement of human actions and institutions within the conceptual terms of 'our' tradition (through re-description and re-contextualization) while remaining open to the possibility of new vocabularies which persuade us to look at the world differently and introduce a revolution in thinking.

The purposes of our stories cannot lie in the production of a 'true' picture of the world but in the creation of meaning. This includes the creation of empathy and the widening of the circle of human solidarity. Individual identity projects and the cultural politics of collectivities require us to forge new languages, new ways of describing ourselves, which recast our place in the world. The struggle to have new languages accepted in the wider social formation is the realm of cultural politics.

The cultural politics of language and identity

Rortyian pragmatism and poststructuralist cultural studies share a commitment to the politics of re-description where cultural politics involves the struggle over 'naming' and the power to re-describe ourselves. Culture is a zone of contestation in which competing meanings and descriptions of the world have fought for ascendancy and the pragmatic claim to truth within patterns of power. It is in this sense that the 'power to name' and to make particular descriptions stick is a form of cultural politics. Thus, cultural politics is about:

- the power to name
- the power to represent common sense
- the power to create 'official versions'
- the power to represent the legitimate social world. (adapted from Jordan and Weedon, 1995: 13)

Social change becomes possible through rethinking and re-describing the social order and the possibilities for the future. Rethinking ourselves, which emerges through social practice and, more often than not, through social contradiction and conflict, brings new political subjects and practices into being. These questions of cultural power translate into the practical purposes of identity politics when African-Americans challenge their representation as marginal and criminalized; when women re-describe themselves as citizens rather than slaves; when men decline to be tough in favour of being tender; when the 'grey wolves' give voice to the dissatisfactions of marginalized older people and when Gays and Lesbians stage 'Pride'. Hall illustrates cultural politics as re-description or re-signification in the following fashion.

> Rasta was a funny language, borrowed from a text – the Bible – that did not belong to them; they had to turn the text upside-down, to get a meaning which fitted their experience. But in turning the text upside-down they remade themselves; they positioned themselves differently as new political subjects; they reconstructed themselves as blacks in the new world: they *became* what they are. And, positioning themselves in that way, they learned to speak a new language. And they spoke it with a vengeance . . . they only constitute a political force, that is, they *become* a historical force in so far as they are constituted as new political subjects. (Hall in Grossberg, 1996)

Stories with consequences

Issues of identity and cultural representation are 'political' because they are intrinsically bound up with questions of power. Power, as social regulation which is productive of the self, enables some kinds of knowledge and identities to exist while denying it to others. For example, to describe women as full human beings and citizens with equal social rights and obligations is a quite different matter from regarding them as sub-human domestic workers with bodies designed to please men. The language of citizenship legitimates the place of women in business and politics while the language of sexual and domestic servitude denies this place, seeking to confine women to the traditional spheres of domesticity and as objects of the male gaze. Similarly, for men to use the language of emotions and relationships helps them to orientate away from self and stoicism towards interaction with others. Men can constitute themselves as having an 'inner-world' and are enabled to speak about their domestic lives rather than being confined to the public sphere of work and politics.

Rorty argues that continued re-description of our world and the playing off of discourses against each other is a pragmatically desirable thing to do because:

- It encourages the enlargement of the self as 'our minds gradually growing larger and stronger and more interesting by the addition of new options – new candidates for belief and desire, phrased in new vocabularies.' (Rorty, 1991a: 14)
- We are encouraged to listen to the voices of others who may be suffering where the avoidance of suffering is taken to be the paramount political virtue.
- It offers improvement of the human condition where good emerges through comparison between different representations of practices which are judged to have desirable consequences.

The language of cultural politics brings oppression 'into view' and expands the logical space for moral and political deliberation. This does not involve the discovery of truth, or less distorted perception in opposition to ideology, but the forging of a language with consequences which serve particular purposes and values as part of an evolutionary struggle which has no predetermined destiny. Cultural politics does not need essentialism or foundationalism but 'new languages' in which claims for justice do not sound crazy but come to be accepted as 'true' (in the sense of a social commendation). As Rorty argues:

> injustices may not be perceived as injustices, even by those who suffer them, until somebody invents a previously unplayed role. Only if somebody has a dream, a voice, and a voice to describe the dream, does what looked like nature begin to look like culture, what looked like fate begin to look like a moral abomination. For until then only the language of the oppressor is

available, and most oppressors have had the wit to teach the oppressed a language in which the oppressed will sound crazy – *even to themselves* – if they describe themselves as oppressed. (Rorty, 1995: 126, emphasis in original)

Prophetic pragmatism

Rorty regards feminism as fashioning 'women's experience' by creating a language rather than finding what it is to be a woman or 'unmasking' truth and injustice. As such, feminism is a form of prophetic pragmatism that imagines, and seeks to bring into being, an alternative form of community. Feminism forges a moral identity for women as women by gaining semantic authority over themselves and not by assuming that there is a universal essential identity for women waiting to be found.

Fraser (1995) concurs with Rorty's pragmatism but argues that he locates the re-descriptions involved exclusively in individual women. In contrast, she suggests that such re-descriptions are to be seen as a part of a collective feminist politics. We must move, she suggests, from irony and prophecy to politics. Such a politics must involve argument and contestation about which new descriptions will count and which women will be empowered. Fraser links feminism to the best of the democratic tradition and to the creation of a 'feminist counter sphere' of collective debate and practice.

West (1993), like Fraser, a cultural critic sympathetic to pragmatism, worries about Rorty's failure to analyse *power* and to deploy sociological kinds of explanations to identify the realistic and pragmatic collective routes for social change. According to West cultural politics proceeds by way of:

- *Deconstruction*: a reading of texts which challenges the tropes, meta-phors and binaries of rhetorical textual operations.
- *Demythologization*: mapping the social construction of metaphors that regulate descriptions of the world and their possible consequences for politics, values, purposes, interests and prejudices.
- *Demystification*: a partisan analysis of the complexity of institutional and other power structures in order to disclose options for trans-formative praxis where development of critical positions and new theory must be linked to communities, groups, organizations and networks of people who are actively involved in social and cultural change.

West's criticism of Rorty is that he locates his analysis at the level of demythologization rather than demystification. Foucauldians share this concern with the place of power in social life and, in the interpretation of Bennett (1998), this should lead us to giving cultural policy a more prominent place in our vocabulary. Bennett argues that the textual politics with which cultural studies has been engaged ignores the institutional dimensions of cultural power. He is critical of cultural studies for displacing its politics onto the level of signification and text (a criticism that West implicitly makes of Rorty). This, he argues, has been at the expense of a material politics of the institutions and organizations of culture which produce and distribute cultural texts.

Cultural politics and cultural policy

For Bennett, cultural studies has been too much concerned with consciousness and the ideological struggle as conceived through Gramsci and not enough on the material technologies of power and of cultural policy. Consequently, he urges cultural studies to adopt a more pragmatic approach, to work with cultural producers and to 'put policy into cultural studies'. For Bennett, cultural politics centres on *policy* formulation and enactment within the institutions which produce and administer the form and content of cultural products.

Nevertheless, an engagement with cultural policy still requires us to be clear about the values that guide our work and the targets that policy aims to achieve. While the latter is context and technology specific, i.e. what is aimed for depends on the particular kind of cultural technology and organization under consideration, the former suggests a continued role for criticism and the politics of re-signification. As Morris (1992) asserts, cultural politics located in the academy, bureaucracies and policy initiatives (her example is feminism) requires a 'critical outside', an unregulated site from which the actions of professionals can be scrutinized and criticized. This means, she argues, that feminism rarely falls for the binary logic of criticism *or* policy.

Neither does Rorty, for he advocates both a politics of 'new languages', and political action on the level of institutions and policy. The 'Left' Rorty argues 'is the party of hope' (Rorty, 1998: 14) in its struggle for social justice. However, 'In so far as the Left becomes spectorial and retrospective, it ceases to be a Left' (Rorty, 1998: 14). It is Rorty's contention that to a major extent the cultural left has become a spectator left, being more interested in theorizing than in the practical politics of material change. The cultural left, he suggests, prefers knowledge to hope. It imagines that it can somehow 'get it right' on the level of theory and has given up on the practical task of making democratic institutions once again serve social justice.

While there has been little legislative change for social justice in the USA, 'the change in the way we treat one another has been enormous' (Rorty, 1998: 81). For example, 'It is still easy to be humiliated for being a woman in America, but such humiliation is not so frequent as it was thirty years ago' (Rorty, 1998: 81–82). In that sense, 'the cultural Left has extraordinary success' (Rorty, 1998: 80–81).

However, according to Rorty, the contemporary left remains more interested in cultural power than economic, social and political power. Further, it has given up on practical reform in favour of an abstract and wholly theoretical revolutionary desire to overturn the 'system'. For Rorty, Derrida's declarations of impossibility, undecidability and unrepresentability are illuminating philosophical insights (Rorty has said Derrida is the most interesting living philosopher writing today) that are of use to us in our private quests. However, in the public sphere, 'the infinite and the unrepresentable are merely nuisances . . . a stumbling-block to effective political organization' (Rorty, 1998: 96–97).

Shifting the command metaphors of cultural studies

In this respect, Rorty is close to Stuart Cunningham's (1992a, 1992b, 1993) commitment to social democracy and the values of liberty, equality and solidarity as the motor of a new reformism. Cunningham advances a 'social democratic view of citizenship and the trainings necessary to activate and motivate it' (Cunningham, 1993: 134). This would involve a shift in the 'command metaphors' of cultural studies,

> away from the rhetorics of resistance, oppostionalism and anti-commercialism on the one hand, and populism on the other, towards those of access, equity, empowerment and the divination of opportunities to exercise appropriate cultural leadership. (Cunningham, 1993: 137–138)

As Rorty has argued, anti-representationalism, anti-foundationalism and pragmatism do not of necessity support any *particular* political projects, values or strategies. We may thus disagree with some of Rorty, Bennett or Cunningham's programmatic suggestions. Nevertheless, Rorty's pragmatism enables us to embrace the idea that a cultural politics of representation and a cultural policy orientation need not, at least within Liberal Democratic states, be opposed. Rorty combines a commitment to language-based re-descriptions of the world that expand the realm of democratic cultures (what cultural studies calls a politics of difference) with the need for public policy and political action. There is no necessary reason why cultural studies cannot attend to the important pragmatic calls of policy without relinquishing the role that 'critical cultural theory' has to play. Similarly, if it takes politics rather than posturing seriously then cultural criticism does need to engage with questions of more orthodox politics and the formation of cultural policy.

Summary and conclusions

It is not helpful to think of language as picturing the world with its promise to deliver us 'truth' as correspondence between the world and language. Instead we should think of language as made up of the sounds and inscriptions that humans deploy in pursuit of their diverse aspirations. Explanations of any kind can only ever involve the replacement of one way of describing the world with another. Delineation of progress involves telling new stories which we deem to have better consequences, measured against our values, than previous stories. Progress involves a retrospectively told story which makes judgements about the direction and outcomes of actions and events.

Cultural politics concerns the writing of new stories with 'new languages' (or to be more exact, new configurations of old languages or new usages of old words) that embody values with which we concur and that we wish to be taken as true in the sense of a social agreement or commendation. Cultural politics centres on the struggle to define the world and make those definitions stick. Consequently, cultural politics concerns the multi-faceted processes by which particular descriptions of the world are taken as true. This includes forms of cultural and institutional power so that cultural politics concerns both languages and policy.

Contemporary cultural politics, as understood by cultural studies, has centred on questions of subjectivity and identity. Most often, though not exclusively, this has concerned issues of gender and ethnicity. Subjectivity, that is the condition of being a person, is an outcome of cultural processes, notably the acquisition of language, which bring us into being as 'subjects for' ourselves and others. Identity, it is argued, is not best understood as a fixed entity but as an emotionally charged description of ourselves. Identities are discursive-performative, i.e. identity is best understood as discursive practice which enacts or produces that which it names.

The plastic and changeable character of persons marks the cultural politics of subjectivity and identity as being concerned with the power to name and represent what it means to be male, female, black, white, young, old etc. Cultural politics can be conceived of as a series of collective social struggles organized around the nodal points of class, gender, race, sexuality, age, etc. which seeks to re-describe the social in terms of specific values and hoped for consequences.

However, identities are not best understood in terms of philosophic argument or as the signs of dead texts alone, which is the level that cultural studies has tended to operate on. From a discursive psychology we can learn about the constitution of psychological states within language while through the study of language usage (discourse analysis and conversation analysis) we can explore the mechanisms by which identity claims are achieved in day-to-day linguistic encounters. As such we can develop a more finely grained reflexive understanding of how personal and social change are possible. In our next chapter (3), we discuss the linguistic tools made available to us by CDA that can usefully assist cultural studies in this process.

3

Tools for Discourse Analysis

In this chapter we will be outlining a version of CDA with which we have sympathy. This exposition has two main aims. First, and locally within this book, we want to draw up a set of tools for the analysis of the data in Chapters 4, 5 and 6. The discussion aims to generate a discourse-analytic 'tool-kit' that we can draw upon to demonstrate how constructions of realities are achieved within our data. Second, and more globally, this exposition serves one of the main aims of the book: to provide cultural studies practitioners with an analytic template that could be used in studying social life. Cultural studies, while more and more often making claims about the discursive construction of social and cultural life, has only rarely engaged with the detailed analysis of discourse itself.

By saying that we shall provide *a* version of CDA we acknowledge that there is no commonly accepted version of it. Rather, CDA is made up of a number of approaches including: French discourse analysis (e.g. Pecheux, 1982); critical linguistics (Fowler et al., 1979; Fowler, 1991; Hodge and Kress, 1993); social semiotics (Hodge and Kress, 1988; Kress and van Leeuwen, 1996), sociocultural change and change in discourse (Fairclough, 1989, 1992) and socio-cognitive studies (e.g. van Dijk, 1993a, 1998) (for a review of strands within CDA, see Fairclough and Wodak, 1997). However, we are not aiming to review the entirety of CDA, for this has been done elsewhere (van Dijk, 1997). Rather, we intend to set out a model of discourse analysis as we understand it in order to make explicit its form and assumptions. Our template for CDA consists of a tool-kit of analytical categories that we hold to be useful in the analyses of empirical data.

Textually oriented discourse analysis

The first characteristic of discourse analysis is its 'textual orientation' (Fairclough, 1992). That is, CDA's arguments are based on a close analysis of discourse within texts, whether written or spoken. The analysis of the form and content of specific stretches of discourse forms the basis of our subsequent discussions.

To conduct discourse analysis means that the investigation of language is required to go beyond the boundaries of the syntactic or semantic form of the utterance. While aware of the lexico-grammatical resources of the language-system, we shall also be interested in their functions within the utterance as well as the utterance's functions within its context. Moreover, discourse analysis, as van Dijk (1997: 13–14) points out, is not only interested in the formal (phonological or syntactic) aspects of discourse, or language use. Rather, the focus is also on the social actions accomplished by language users communicating within social and cultural contexts. Drawing mainly on van Dijk's (1997: 29ff.) review of the principles of discourse analysis, we offer below those we hold to be the most important.

- Discourse analysis is interested in naturally occurring text (written) and talk (verbal). That is, 'real-world data' which has not been edited or sanitized and which can be studied in ways that come as close as is possible to their actually occurring forms in their 'customary' contexts.
- Discourse is studied within its global and local context, preferably as a constitutive part of that context: i.e. settings, participants and their communicative and social roles, goals, relevant social knowledge, norms and values, institutional or organizational structures.
- Naturally occurring discourse is a form of social practice within a socio-cultural context. Language users are not isolated individuals, rather they are engaged in communicative activities as members of groups, institutions or cultures.
- The accomplishment of discourse is linear and sequential. This means that units of discourse are to be explained in relation to those that precede them. It can also mean that later elements may have particular functions with respect to previous ones (e.g. answers follow questions).
- Constitutive units of discourse may also be productive of larger units, thereby creating hierarchical structures. Moreover, language users are capable of using those units functionally in constructing or understanding the hierarchy of discourse.
- Discourse analysis is interested in levels or layers of discourse and their mutual relations. These levels of discourse represent distinct types of construction units (sounds, words, syntactic forms) and also different dimensions of discourse operation (linguistic actions, forms of interaction).
- Language users and analysts are interested in meaning and in particular in two types of question; namely, 'what does it mean in this situation?' and 'why is this being said or meant in this situation?' (Leech, 1983).
- Language, discourse and communication in general are rule-governed activities. These include both strict 'all-or-nothing'

grammatical rules and the 'softer' negotiable principles of inter-action (Thomas, 1995). Furthermore, the study of actual discourse focuses not only on how certain rules or principles are followed but also how they are violated, ignored and suspended (Brown and Levinson, 1987; Grice, 1975).

Critical discourse analysis

By locating discourse analysis within critical language studies, we make a number of assumptions with regard to the nature of discourse and the character of analysis. First, we follow Wodak (1999) in assuming that analysis should avoid easy, dichotomous explanations of the phenom-ena studied. Second, we aim to uncover contradictions, or dilemmas (Billig et al., 1988) underpinning social life. Third, our analysis is self-reflective. We realize that it is impossible to avoid bringing into research our own values and evaluations. There is no escape from the fact that one of us was born and educated in a communist country, while the other was raised within the so-called 'free West'.

The requirement for reflexivity does not mean that analyses are invalid, but rather that we must be aware of what we have tentatively called 'flexible critical arbitrariness' (Galasiński, 1997b). We, as researchers, must be aware of the analytic choices we make, especially with regard to the backgrounds we invoke in our investigations (Blommaert, 1997; Galasiński 1997a, Verschueren, 1999). We must also make sure that readers are aware of these presuppositions.

Analysis is interpretative: the process is laden with researchers' attitudes and beliefs as well as the assumption that there is no ultimately 'correct' interpretation of texts (Wodak, 1999). Interpretations are open, dynamic and subject to change. Nevertheless, linguistic analysis of dis-course, anchored within systemic-functional linguistics (Halliday, 1978, 1994; Halliday and Hasan, 1985), can help reduce the arbitrariness of interpretation by anchoring it on the discourse form itself.

CDA makes a number of assumptions about discourse that we dis-cuss below. Once again, our discussion is not aimed at presenting a comprehensive view of what CDA research implies – that has been done elsewhere (for a recent review see Chouliaraki and Fairclough, 1999). Here, we are interested only in making manifest those presumptions that we perceive as crucial to our analyses.

Discourse is socially constitutive

CDA perceives discourse, both written and spoken, as a form of social practice. There is an interactive or 'dialectal' relationship between dis-cursive practices and the contexts in which they occur. Discourse is constitutive of and constituted by social and political 'realities' (Fairclough and Wodak, 1997; van Leeuwen and Wodak, 1999). A constructionist view of discourse permeates CDA which holds that it is through discourse that language users constitute social realities: their knowledge of social situations, the interpersonal roles they play, their identities and relations with other interacting social groups (van Leeuwen and Wodak, 1999). Discursive acts are socially constitutive in a number of ways:

- They play a decisive role in the genesis and construction of social conditions.
- They can restore, justify and perpetuate the social status quo.
- They may be instrumental in the transformation of the status quo.

Discourse is a system of options

The socially constitutive view of discourse is closely related to the assumption that discourse is a system of options from which language users make their 'choices' (Chouliaraki, 1998). The construction of any representation of 'reality' is necessarily selective, entailing decisions as to which aspects of that reality to include and how to arrange them. Each selection carries its share of socially ingrained values so that representation is socially constructed (Hall, 1997; Hodge and Kress, 1993: 5). In other words, alternative representations of a supposed extra-linguistic reality are always possible though they carry divergent significance and consequences (Fowler, 1996: 4). Nevertheless, texts seek to impose a 'preferred reading' (Hall, 1981) or 'structure of faith' (Menz, 1989) upon the addressee.

Following work in social semiotics, we hold that representation is a process subject to regimes of production and reception that are implicated in the 'ideological' complexes of social formations. Practices of representation, resting on more or less contested cultural classifications of people and circumstances, are always part of a communicative situation marked by, and indicative of, the power relations between communicators and the subjects of representation (Hall, 1997; Hodge and Kress 1988; Kress and van Leeuwen, 1996).

Discourse is ideological

The selective character of representation leads us to the view that it is through discourse and other semiotic practices that ideologies are formulated, reproduced and reinforced. The term ideology is understood here as the social (general and abstract) representations shared by members of a group and used by them to accomplish everyday social practices: acting and communicating (Billig et al., 1988; Fowler, 1985; van Dijk, 1998). These representations are organized into systems which are deployed by social classes and other groups 'in order to make sense of, figure out and render intelligible the way society works' (Hall, 1996d: 26). Further, Chouliaraki and Fairclough (1999) propose that ideologies form perspectives capable of 'ironing out' the contradictions, dilemmas and antagonisms of practices in ways which accord with the interests and projects of power.

The concept of ideology has been the subject of some debate (Barker, 2000) in relation to its scope (do all groups have ideologies or just the powerful?) and epistemological basis (is ideology opposed by truth?). We hold ideology to be forms of power/knowledge (Foucault, 1980) justifying the actions of *all* groups. In that sense, marginal and sub-ordinate groups also have ideologies in the form of organizing and justifying ideas. We are all, as Foucault argued, implicated in power relations. The difference between the dominant and subordinate groups is one of degrees of power and differing substantive world views not of ideological versus non-ideological ideas.

The concept of ideology has commonly been counterposed to truth and science (Althusser, 1971) and linked to notion of 'mis-recognition'. However, science is itself a mode of thinking and a set of procedures that produces certain kinds of understandings. It is not an elevated god-like form of knowledge that produces universal objective truth. No universally accurate picture of the world is possible, only degrees of agreement about what counts as truth. For this reason, thinkers like Foucault (1980) and Rorty (1989, 1991a, 1991b) have rejected the concept of ideology.

It is epistemologically untenable to counterpoise ideology to truth, so that the concept as we understand it is virtually interchangeable with the Foucauldian notion of power/knowledge. As such, ideology is constituted by discourses that have specific *consequences* for relations of power at all levels of social relationships (including the justification and maintenance of ascendant groups). While in this book we are continuing to use the concept of ideology we mean by it 'world views' of any social groups which justify their actions but which cannot be counterposed to truth. However, they can be subject to re-description and thus do not have to be accepted.

Ideologies are structures of signification which constitute social relations in and through power. If meaning is fluid – a question of difference and deferral – then ideology can be understood as the attempt to fix meaning for specific purposes. Ideologies are discourses which give meaning to material objects and social practices, they define and produce the acceptable and intelligible way of understanding the world while excluding other ways of reasoning as unintelligible. Ideologies provide people with rules of practical conduct and moral behaviour and are thus equivalent 'to a religion understood in the secular sense of a unity of faith between a conception of the world and a corresponding norm of conduct' (Gramsci, 1971: 349).

Though ideology can be presented as a coherent set of ideas, it more often appears as the fragmented meanings of commonsense located intertextually in a variety of representations. Thus, Billig and his associates (1988) make a distinction between 'lived' and 'intellectual' ideologies. While 'lived' ideology is a complex, contradictory and constitutive part of the meaningful practices of everyday life, 'intellectual' ideology is understood as a coherent system of thought: political programmes/ manifestos, philosophical orientations and religious codifications. The discourses we analyse later in the book do not present the participants' coherent, formal systems of belief (i.e. their intellectual ideologies), but rather their 'lived ideologies'. These meet locally defined objectives of self–other presentation and express opinions that represent and satisfy their preferred views of reality. These narratives are not necessarily coherent, in that they juxtapose contradictory ideas that form the 'ideological dilemmas' (Billig et al., 1988) which are part and parcel of informal world views.

For Billig et al. (1988), discourse is a site of power struggle in which the ideologies implicated by discursive choices are the subject of struggles for dominance within and between social groups. One of the ideologically relevant discourse structures pointed to by van Dijk (1998: 209) is interaction, and, more specifically, the realm of interactional control. Who starts the exchange, who ends it, who initiates new topics, who interrupts whom, and so on, may all be indicative of the interlocutor's power and as such are ideologically charged. Highlighting relations of power in societies, CDA, along with cultural studies, argues that ideologies are discursive in character.

We argue below that ideologies are 'carried' by other non-embodied (i.e. textual) layers of discourse. However, that does not mean that ideology can be simply 'read-off' texts by analysts (a criticism frequently made against the critical linguistics strand within CDA; e.g. Fairclough, 1992). Rather, discourse can be seen to accomplish ideologies (Billig et al., 1988; also Billig, 1990a, 1990b) while not being equated with them (van Dijk, 1998).

Text is multifunctional

Texts are the products of speaking or writing so that the discursive practices in which we are engaged in writing this book are presented to readers as 'text'. One of the main assumptions about text that we make is that it is multifunctional. This assumption flows from the direct association of CDA with systemic and functional linguistics, most particularly that of Halliday and Hasan (1985) and Halliday (1994). There are three such functions:

- the ideational
- the interpersonal
- the textual

It is through the *ideational* function of language that texts are able to refer to realities 'outside' of the speaker, enabling her/him to render intelligible their experience of the world. The ideational function also refers to the internal world of speakers, their cognitions, emotions, perceptions and acts of speaking and understanding. In sum, the ideational function is responsible for the texts' 'representational faculties'.

The *interpersonal* function refers to the interaction between the speaker and the addressee by means of the text. Its role is two-fold. First, it alludes to the fact that speakers can express an attitude or evaluation towards their utterances, that is, speakers can distance themselves from the utterances they produce. Alternatively, speakers may adopt particular speech roles with regard to their utterances (e.g. author or mouthpiece). Second, through their utterances, speakers set up social relationships with those they address. Thus, when giving an order, speakers assume the right to do so, when promising, speakers commit themselves to doing things. By enacting 'informing', 'greeting' or 'thanking', speakers position themselves in particular ways towards their audience.

Finally, language serves a *textual* function by which elements of it are responsible for making discourse appear 'as text' while signalling its relevance to the context in which it appears. Through the textual function language forges links with the presumed extra-linguistic conditions of its occurrence as well as with other texts which have occurred or will occur in that context. In sum, the textual function of language makes it intelligible to the addressee precisely as a text that makes sense within itself and within the context of its appearance.

It is important to stress that text as a whole is multifunctional and normally serves all three functions at the same time. Only some of its elements will be geared towards only one particular function at a given moment. Further, the conceptualization of texts in terms of functions serves an analytical purpose by demarcating the categories through which texts will be explored. The kind of analysis we perform can be seen as 'deconstructing' texts in terms of ideational, interpersonal and textual functions.

Text is intertextual

The final assumption made by the CDA that we would like to bring out here is the intertextuality of texts. As Fairclough puts it, 'Intertextuality is basically the property texts have of being full of snatches of other texts, which may be explicitly demarcated or merged in, and which the text may assimilate, contradict, ironically echo, and so forth' (1992: 84).

That is, intertextuality signals the accumulation and generation of meaning across texts where all meanings depend on other meanings. This citation of one text within another is an expression of the relational character of meaning and, where explicitly acknowledged, an enlarged cultural self-consciousness as in the case of the television programmes *The Sopranos* and *The Simpsons*.

Fairclough argues that intertextual analysis is useful in discovering the networks which texts move through including the transformations they undergo as they shift from one site to another (for example, the journey of a political speech or a press release as it becomes a news story). Further, the assumption of intertextuality makes manifest the historicity of texts. Texts are the product of other culturally situated texts combined into a new structure. The exploration of intertextuality helps uncover what Fairclough calls the 'orders of discourse' of a social domain. That is:

> the totality of its discursive practices, and the relationships (of complementarity, inclusion/exclusion, opposition) between them – for instance in schools, the discursive practices of the classroom, of assessed written work, of the playground, and of the staff room. The order of discourse of a society is the set of these more 'local' orders of discourse and the relationships between them. (Fairclough, 1995a: 132)

The linguistic tools of discourse analysis

In this section we explore the fault-lines which discourse analysis searches for during the dissection of texts. We are seeking to achieve an analytic template that could be deployed in the analyses of cultural texts through reviewing the analytic categories by which a discourse analyst is likely to scrutinize texts.

There are two ways in which this task can be achieved. On the one hand, the discussion can be framed in terms of 'levels of language' (Fairclough, 1989, 1992). Thus, a text is approached as vocabulary, grammar and textual structure. On the other hand, an analytical template can be designed in terms of textual functions (Fowler, 1991).

While there are good reasons for discussing the material in either way, we have decided on the latter approach (i.e. discussion in terms of the text functions) in order to keep the problems of representation, interaction and textual form analytically separate. As our interview data are largely non-interactive, and, moreover, it is their representational aspects that we are particularly interested in, a clear distinction between textual functions should make for a more lucid and precise discussion of the data. However, other 'templates' will provide us with a useful cross-checking of our exposition.

We shall start our discussion with the ideational function, followed by the interpersonal, before finishing with the textual. Illustrative material will come mainly from our previous work so that the points we make with respect to the examples can be followed up in the original texts. Rather than refer to Halliday's work at all times, we would like to acknowledge that the discussion below draws upon Halliday (1978, 1994), Halliday and Hasan (1985), as well as Beaugrande's (1991) detailed discussion of Halliday's work. We shall focus on that which we consider to be the most salient aspects of the linguistic form.

The ideational function

Transitivity

The main element of Halliday's category of the ideational function is his notion of transitivity as being at the core of representation. We may note here a terminological problem: namely that, in traditional linguistics, transitivity refers to the syntactic distinction between transitive and intransitive verbs – those that can be used in passive voice (as in 'John kicked the ball' can be transformed to 'The ball was kicked'), and those which cannot (as in 'Mary ran').

However, for Halliday, the notion of transitivity forms the cornerstone of representation. It is transitivity that enables the representation in multiple ways of an implied extra-linguistic reality. The two main elements of transitivity by which 'reality' can be rendered intelligible are 'process' and 'participant'. That is, in terms of what happens or is the case (process) and by or to whom (participant). Halliday makes a distinction between six types of processes:

- *Material* processes refer to doing, happening, creating and changing. The participants in the structures that contain material processes are actors (those who do) or goals (those unto whom things are done).
- *Mental* processes refer to feeling, thinking or seeing. Participants who perform these are said to be 'sensers' while that which is perceived or felt is called the 'phenomenon'.
- *Relational* processes refer to being and having an attribute or identity, with participants as the 'carriers' or 'identified' and attributes as the 'identifiers'.
- *Behavioural* processes refer to behaving (laughing, smiling, signing). Those who perform such processes are called 'behavers'.
- *Verbal* processes are those referring to all those actions that are about saying something (promising, talking, warning). Those who say things are 'sayers', those who are addressed are 'targets'.
- *Existential* processes concern existing and being there, such as in the sentence 'There are lions in Africa'.

The significance of the processes represented in an utterance can be seen if we consider the case of news bulletins which we might expect to be as 'factual' as possible (whatever that may actually mean). As a marker of objectivity and facticity we would normally expect a high level of material clauses e.g. 'Children were dying out there'. However, if we replace material clauses by mental clauses there will be a significant change in the pattern of the text. The speaker no longer talks about actions, what was done, but about what was perceived, felt or sensed, e.g. 'I saw children dying out there'. Instead of 'what happened?' the text addresses what the reporter or others perceived to have happened. Thus, 'I saw children dying out there' makes a journalist's report more dramatic than 'Children were dying out there'.

Consider another example, the politician's typically evasive answer to the interviewer's questioning

> **A**: You will not predict that you will keep it. You're only saying that you aim to keep it?
> **B**: We wish to keep it, we believe that we will keep it, but there is very little margin of room for manoeuvre here. (from Galasiński, 2000: 105)

Using mental clauses, the politician (B) makes a perfectly safe statement in which he has committed himself to nothing problematic by avoiding firm prediction.

The CIA credo

As we have noted, texts can be transformed to represent 'realities' in a variety of ways. As a further example, we shall explore the 'Credo of the Central Intelligence Agency' as it was made available on the Internet in 1995 and 1996, at HYPERLINK http://www.ico.gov (see Connell and Galasiński, 1996). Readers can find out more about the Central Intelligence Agency (CIA) at HYPERLINK http://www.odci.gov. Since our original study the CIA Web site has changed and the Credo itself no longer exists. Below we reproduce the full text of the original Credo.

> We are the Central Intelligence Agency. We produce timely and high quality intelligence for the President and Government of the United States. We provide objective and unbiased evaluations and are always open to new perceptions and ready to challenge conventional wisdom. We perform special intelligence tasks at the request of the President. We conduct our activities and ourselves according to the highest standards of integrity, morality and honor and according to the spirit and letter of our law and Constitution. We measure our success by our contribution to the protection and enhancement of American values, security and national interest. We believe our people are the Agency's most important resource. We seek the best and work to make them

better. We subordinate our desire for public recognition to the need for confidentiality. We strive for continuing professional improvement. We give unfailing loyalty to each other and to our common purpose. We seek through our leaders to stimulate initiative, a commitment to excellence and a propensity for action; to protect and reward Agency personnel for their special responsibilities, contributions, and sacrifices; to promote a sense of mutual trust and shared responsibility. We get our inspiration and commitment to excellence from the inscription in our foyer: And ye shall know the truth and the truth shall make you free.

The first thing we notice about the Credo is that all the sentences are declarative in the present tense and in the active voice, that is, those who do things are the subjects of the sentence. Consequently, the first transformation these sentences could undergo is to put them in passive voice with the objects of processes put in the subject position. Let us imagine that two of the above sentences are so transformed. Thus:

We measure our success by our contribution to the protection and enhancement of American values, security and national interest.

And

We seek the best and work to make them better.

Becomes

Our success is measured by our contribution to the protection and enhancement of American values, security and national interest.

And

The best are sought and made better.

Through 'passivization', what was a clear corporate self-presentation has been transformed into what looks, at least in the first sentence, like a statement about external forces keeping the CIA accountable. The second sentence has become vague, now stopping short of an unequivocal statement that it is the Agency that seeks the 'best people'. The passive voice, unlike its active counterpart, does not have to include the participant-doer so that the source of action is unclear once the actor has been deleted from the sentence.

'Nominalization' is a transformation that changes the way processes are represented. While they are normally rendered intelligible by verbs, nominalization involves representing them in terms of nouns so that actions become things.

Thus, we can change

> We provide objective and unbiased evaluations and are always open to new perceptions and ready to challenge conventional wisdom.

into

> Our provision is that of objective and unbiased evaluations and ours is openness to new perceptions and readiness to challenge conventional wisdom.

The dynamic, clearly iterative (i.e. recurrent) actions of the company have been transformed into a static provision that one can avail oneself of. As with passivization, nominalization makes it unclear who it is that actually does things. We no longer know who is responsible for the provision identified in the nominalized clause.

We have focused on these two syntactic transformations, leaving aside possible changes of tense or from transitive to intransitive verbs, because of the importance of passivization and nominalization in setting up the structure of action and agency in the text. A crucial question to ask of the text concerns 'who' is represented as 'active' and through which actions. Who is the 'doer' and who is the 'done to' (Galasiński and Marley, 1998).

Finally, with the Credo there is not one single negative sentence. The Credo sends a positive message that tells its readers what the CIA believes in. As such, it cannot tell us that, for example, it doesn't kill people, or it doesn't overthrow governments.

Vocabulary

Thus far, we have focused on the lexico-grammatical level of language. That is, we have been interested in how grammatical structures render reality intelligible to us. In addition, we would like to offer a few comments regarding representation through the lexis. That is, in relation to the vocabulary alone. For example, in the Credo above, saying that the CIA 'spies' rather than 'performs intelligence tasks' would be quite enough to kill the 'feel good' faculty of the text. The connotations, i.e. the association carried by the words or phrases, are quite different. Thus, an espionage organization would never categorize itself as a 'fraternity of spies'.

We may note the relative verbosity of the text: loyalty can be nothing else but unfailing, standards the highest, evaluations objective and unbiased, etc., etc. Further, the values that the CIA subscribes to are American values, which for non-American nations around the world may sound quite ominous. Of course, words such as 'loyalty', 'freedom', and 'highest standards' do not have clear and unequivocal meanings.

Rather, they are ideologically contested phrases that may be decoded differently according to the power, social competencies and cultural knowledge of the groups concerned (Fairclough, 1989; Hall, 1981; Morley, 1992).

We would also like to note the final sentence of the Credo;

> And ye shall know the truth and the truth shall make you free.

Here, the archaic and formal qualities of the language are quite striking. In the Credo words such as 'ye' or 'shall' are 'marked'; in other words, they are used in a way that is extraordinary or unexpected. Here, they are used to make the final sentence more solemn and credible – the CIA is about truth! No doubt the irony would not be lost on the people of Vietnam, Chile, or Grenada.

Some words are more significant to us than others. One of the most interesting categories of vocabulary is the pronoun; words such as 'I' or 'they', or most infamously, 'we'. As we saw in the CIA's Credo, every sentence of the text starts with 'we'. Indeed the text is introduced by the strong:

> We are the Central Intelligence Agency.

Readers would be quite justified in thinking that the author of the text, the one who speaks to us, is the CIA in its entirety. However, as is so often the case with pronouns, matters are a bit more complicated. Let us take a look at the following fragment of the Credo:

> We believe our people are the Agency's most important resource. We seek the best and work to make them better. We subordinate our desire for public recognition to the need for confidentiality. We strive for continuing professional improvement. We give unfailing loyalty to each other and to our common purpose. We seek through our leaders to stimulate initiative, a commitment to excellence and a propensity for action; to protect and reward Agency personnel for their special responsibilities, contributions, and sacrifices; to promote a sense of mutual trust and shared responsibility. We get our inspiration and commitment to excellence from the inscription in our foyer: And ye shall know the truth and the truth shall make you free.

Significantly, for this section of the Credo to make sense the identity of the speaking voice must have changed. The use of the possessive pronoun 'our' in the first sentence connecting the 'people' to the 'we', together with the fact that the people to whom it refers are said to be the 'Agency's most important resource', suggests that the 'we' is constituted by the senior staff of the CIA. The 'we' and the 'people' are not now one. The use of 'our' represents the relation between 'we' and 'people' as one of property ownership; the 'people' (of the CIA) are a resource that 'we' (the senior managers) possess. Further, as senior officers of the CIA, the 'we' is in a position to make statements of belief about other subordinate employees of the organization.

What we observe here is not a mere shift in the reference of the pronoun 'we' (the pronoun most open to manipulation) but, as pronominal analysis shows, it again puts the 'feel good' ambience of the text into question. The text is not a statement of the entire Agency. It is not about all people within the CIA. Rather it is about the 'we' who possess other people making a statement that constitutes them as powerful.

The interpersonal function

Communication is not only about representational effects, for it also encompasses all that language does to constitute and express social and personal relations. We explore aspects of this below.

Mood

In traditional linguistics, mood is normally referred to as a grammatical characteristic of a sentence. In this view there are three moods: declarative, interrogative and imperative. Yet, Halliday contends, this aspect of clauses belongs firmly within the realm of the interpersonal function. For example, the imperative mood is used not merely to construct a certain type of sentence, but to order, command, or request that someone should do something.

To answer questions about the character and composition of an 'order' we must make a brief excursion into what is known as speech act theory. After Wittgenstein, Austin (1962) and Searle (1969) are the founding fathers of a philosophy of language that conceives of it in terms of actions. Hence the title of Austin's book, *How To Do Things With Words*. By saying 'I promise', we are not simply offering information to our audience about promising, rather, we are enacting or performing a promise. In the same way, saying 'I name this ship' or 'I take you as my wedded wife' is performing the action of naming the ship and getting married. In order to name a ship or get married people say words that constitute the acts they name. Thus, a 'performative' is a statement which puts into effect the relation that it names, as in the marriage ceremony's 'I pronounce you . . .'.

For example, Butler (1993) argues that Judges in criminal and civil law do not originate the law or its authority, but through the very practices by which they cite, consult and invoke the conventions of the law, they produce the very authority that is appealed to. The maintenance of the law is a matter of reworking a set of already operative conventions involving iterability, repetition and citationality. Further, for Butler, 'sex' is similarly produced as a reiteration of hegemonic norms, a performativity that is always derivative. The 'assumption' of sex, which is not a singular act or event but an iterable practice, is secured through being repeatedly performed.

In addition, Austin, followed by Searle, introduced the notion of felicity conditions by which speech acts in order to be felicitous, i.e. in order to work, must satisfy certain conditions. Consequently, for an order to be felicitous it must be issued by someone deemed to have the power to do so.

To return to the question of mood; Halliday argues that when issuing an utterance consisting of an imperative sentence we take on a certain 'speaker-role' with regard to the addressee. Orders set up relationships between speakers and audiences which are very different from those constituted by a request or a plea. For example, the tone of the CIA's Credo is one of giving information to an audience, presumably in the first instance Americans, regarding the role of the CIA. The relationship between the CIA and the audience is one in which they tell us and we listen. Through unproblematic and unhesitant declarations, the text presents the CIA as an accountable government agency.

Metalanguage

We now want to inquire about how the text represents what is happening in the Credo. This requires a brief digression back to the ideational function of the text. We might simply say something like:

> In its Credo, the CIA *informed* its audience that they conducted their activities and themselves according to the highest standards of integrity, morality and honour and according to the spirit and letter of our law and Constitution.

But perhaps we might want to say something that would undermine the Credo if only a little. For example:

> In its Credo, the CIA *reassured* its audience that they conducted their activities and themselves according to the highest standards of integrity, morality and honour and according to the spirit and letter of our law and Constitution.

However, we might want to undermine the Credo more severely by saying:

> In its Credo, the CIA *claimed* that they conducted their activities and themselves according to the highest standards of integrity, morality and honour and according to the spirit and letter of our law and Constitution.

The word 'claim' is normally used as a means for speakers to distance themselves from what he or she is reporting. Above, the speaker suggests to us that they do not believe what they are reporting to us.

The problem that we are touching on here is of the representation of language itself, i.e. the question of a metalanguage. A metalanguage is not merely a way of referring to other linguistic expressions, it can and does introduce the speaker's point of view both on the expression itself and, at the same time, on aspects of extra-linguistic reality. This might include the relationships the speaker enters into with their interlocutors (Caldas-Coulthard, 1994; Short, 1989). The act of retelling a narrative involves the speaker's control of what is being retold and how that retelling is structured and organized. Both depend on the speaker's view of the world (Caldas-Coulthard, 1994: 295). Further, the reporting voice (Cook, 1992: 184) may not be one which co-exists with the reported one, rather it may dominate and distort it. Indeed, in his account of voices in media discourse, Fairclough argues that:

> one feature of indirect speech is that although it is expected to be accurate about the propositional content of what was said, it is ambivalent about the actual words that were used – it may simply reproduce them, or it may transform and translate them into discourses which fit more easily with the reporter's voice. An interesting example is: Libyan officials at the UN, faced by the threat of more sanctions, said they wanted more time to sort out the details of the handover. Is the handover the Libyan formulation, or a translation of what the Libyans actually said into another discourse? (Fairclough, 1995b: 81)

The question Fairclough asks refers not so much to the metalinguistic function of the sentence *per se*, but rather to the ideational, or representational function which is concealed within the metalinguistic expression. Caldas-Coulthard (1994: 305–306) seconds this view by arguing that such *verba dicendi* as urge, declare or complain, are not merely metalinguistic, but also metapropositional in that they label and categorize the reported speaker's contribution and as such are highly interpretative.

Modality

Modality concerns the expression of a speaker's attitude towards the proposition(s) that they render in their utterance(s). As such, we shall be asking about whether speakers commit or distance themselves from what they say. The concept that modality deals in is truth, and related to it necessity, possibility, obligation and permission. In other words, modality concerns judgements as to whether something is, might be, or must be the case, and whether one should, ought, or must do something (or alternatively whether s/he may do something).

In the case of the CIA Credo, the text is very low in modality. Not one sentence is modalized, i.e. includes the use of one of the modal auxiliaries. As a consequence, the CIA's representation of reality appears as unproblematic. Of course, if 'must' were to be inserted into the sentence that refers to how the CIA conducts itself to the 'highest standards' the effect is quite different.

> We *must* conduct our activities and ourselves according to the highest standards of integrity . . .

Now, the honesty and integrity of the CIA are put into doubt by questioning whether they would conduct themselves with the highest of standards if they had not been made to. We would also need to ask about *who* it is that requires the CIA to act responsibly.

Forms of address

The final element of the interpersonal function to which we shall refer is that of forms of address. How we address each other is an extremely powerful way of setting up a relationship between interactants. It was Brown and Gilman's (1972) now classic text that first showed that the way we address each other defines interpersonal relationships on the axis of power and solidarity. That is, the choice of the form of address locates speakers in social space constructing the mutual relationships between actors.

For an example of how the system of address forms, sustains and reinforces a particular social institution, one need look no further than western education systems. Pupils normally address their teachers formally by their surnames, i.e. 'Mr Smith', 'Miss Brown' etc. However, this formality is not reciprocated for students, sometimes not much younger than their teachers, are often called by their first names 'Mike' or 'Anna' or in more traditional institutions by surname alone, i.e. Barker or Galasiński! Either way, it is the teachers who have more rights and power than the pupils. These rights are also communicative, for teachers can say things that the pupils cannot.

Nevertheless, life is often more complicated than it might first appear. Thus, the practice within British universities of students and teachers being on first name terms puts the former into a system of solidarity with their tutors. In this way the institutions attempt to empower the students and show tutors to have a 'human face'. Except, that is, until the friendly tutors exercise the right to fail the student, whereupon solidarity collapses in the face of power.

English is one of those languages with a relatively modest repertory of forms of address. Apart from a limited range of titles (Dr, Mr, Ms or perhaps even Your Majesty) there is only the 'you' that serves as a way to address other people. Other languages have more extensive forms of honorifics, such as the polite forms 'vous' (French), 'Sie' (German) or 'pan/pani'(Polish). Thus, in Polish one can be addressed on a spectrum of solidarity and power from *Dareczek* (second-order diminutive of Dariusz), *Darek, Dariusz, pan Darek, pan Dariusz, pan (Galasiński)* which is a default mode of address among adults, *Dr (Galasiński)*, and, finally, *pan Dr (Galasiński)*.

Interaction and control

Though it goes beyond the realm of text, we think it important to mark the place of social interaction in the construction of relationships between social actors. Having already noted above van Dijk's (1998) comments on the ideological potential of interaction, let us reiterate and slightly expand upon those notions.

The main conception that we are addressing here is that of communicative or discursive rights. Though we have already touched upon this when discussing the felicity conditions of speech acts (one who orders must have the right to do so), such rights go much further than the mere right to issue a speech act. They include, for example, the right to start a conversation or a communicative event in general, or, even more importantly, the right to end it. Further, the rights to introduce an agenda during an interaction, or the right to shift the topic, are not merely rights to communicate but rights to exercise power through the control of discursive interaction. More negatively, the right to demand that an appointment be set before seeing someone else is not merely a means of controlling how many people come to our offices, but enacts the right *not* to enter into interaction.

In everyday interactions, especially those that have been institutionalized, we encounter social rules concerning whom we may address and with regard to what matters. Can we interrupt the speaker with impunity or must we ask permission to speak? Do we address the person by their first name or do we maintain formal means of address? Needless to say, there are too many other aspects of communicative exchanges for us to list them all, let alone discuss them at any length. However, our central point is that whatever the interaction, however minute the exchange, it is always constitutive of a social relationship between actors.

The textual function

As we previously stated, the textual function enables the text to become a text, i.e. to be relevant within its context of occurrence as well within itself. We shall discuss this function in terms of cohesion and coherence; theme–rheme structures, and the presentation of information as given or new.

Cohesion

Cohesion is that which enables a text to 'stick' together. It concerns how the various elements of a text are linked to each other to form larger segments. This linkage is achieved through various means including:

- *Reference* (what it is that words refer to). For example, in the CIA Credo, we would normally assume that there is a group of people that the 'we' refers to. The same applies to such pronouns as 'it' or 'I'.
- *Conjunctions* Words such as 'therefore', 'because' and 'but' make quite specific connections. For example, the adding on effect of 'and' between clauses, along with the contrast between them introduced by 'but'.
- *Ellipsis* That is, the deletion of an element in the text structure that is presupposed by the previous text. For example, on hearing 'I love you' we can easily say 'so do I', without explicitly mentioning the processes of love.
- *Lexical cohesion* That is, the use of repetition. For example, we assume that the 'we' in CIA Credo refers to the same group extra-linguistically as it does intra-linguistically. Repetition of the 'we' binds or coheres them together.

Now if we take a possible exchange such as:

A: It's a mystery to me, how the conjuror sawed that woman in half.
B: Well, Jane was the woman he did it to. So presumably she must be Japanese. (Brown and Yule, 1983)

This move seems perfectly cohesive. The first sentence clearly refers to what was said in the first move, the second sentence refers to the first one. However, the text does not make sense. On the other hand, in the exchanges below, there are no cohesive links between the utterances, yet they make perfect sense to us.

A: How old are you?
B: Don't worry, they'll let me into the bar.

A: How old are you?
B: Oh no, I left my headlights on. (Dillon, 1990)

This is where the notion of coherence can be helpful. Coherence describes the text as 'sticking together' not because of formal linguistic units, but as a consequence of social rules of communication and cultural knowledge. A 'coherent' is a text in which there is no violation of conversation rules according to our cultural knowledge of scripts, interaction, dialogue etc. Further, coherence is 'felt' rather than measured. It depends on who it is that we talk to and in what context. Consequently, it is socially and culturally specific.

Theme–rheme structure

A theme is that element of a clause that serves as a point of departure. It is the matter about which the sentence tells us. The theme carries with it the message, 'this is what the clause is telling you about'. As a general rule, in English the theme is that which comes first in the clause. Rheme, on the other hand, is the remainder of the clause, i.e. it is that which we are told about the theme. We may grasp how thematic structure works by realizing that, depending on how the clause is structured, it may serve as an answer to a question other than that which was posed. Let us demonstrate this on the following:

(1) John kissed Mary. – What did John do?

(2) Mary was kissed by John. – What happened to Mary?

(3) It was John who kissed Mary. – Who kissed Mary (presupposing that someone did)

(4) What John did was kiss Mary. – as (1) but with a surprise.

(5) Mary, John kissed her. – Finally, what happened to Mary? (Brown and Yule, 1983: 127)

We have put the notional answers before the questions, not to indicate that different questions demand different answers, but to illustrate the argument that a specific thematic structure has consequences through its provision of particular kinds of information. The questions simply make it clearer what kind of information the sentences are supplying. Let us consider another example:

The rug comes from the village of Shalamazar in the southern Chahar Mahal, but the design is woven in many of the villages. The design is one of those that fit into several possible categories, involving as it does elements of bird, tree, vase and prayer types. The prayer mihrab may be omitted in some cases, but the vase is always present, as are the strikingly drawn birds . . . In rugs of this type excellent natural dyestuffs are very often found, and the quality varies from medium to quite fine. Outstanding examples . . . (Brown and Yule, 1983: 141)

The thematic structure is as follows:

- this rug
- the design
- the prayer mihrab
- the vase
- in rugs of this type
- the quality
- outstanding example

The thematic organization, argue Brown and Yule (1983), gives a clear identification of: (1) the writer's topic area (2) the organization of the paragraph. The latter moves from a particular example of a rug type, through its characteristic design, to generalizations about rugs of this sort. The thematic organization provides a structural framework for the discourse.

In the case of the CIA Credo, the thematic structure is as simple as it is interesting. There is, in fact, only one theme throughout the text, which is the pronoun 'we' and about which we want to make two further points. First, such a tight structure leaves the reader in no doubt about the 'content' of the text. This is a text not only about the CIA, but one in which the CIA is talking about itself. Indeed, this is to be expected given that the text is a Credo, a statement of belief. Second, the repetition of the theme, sentence by sentence, makes it easy for the authors to conceal the shift in identity of the speaking voice that we discussed earlier. There is no linguistic mark that would signal that shift; indeed, the thematic structure of the text helps to disguise it.

Information structure

The information conveyed by a clause can be understood in terms of the 'given' and the 'new'. The given is that which we can assume to be known or recovered by the addressee. The new is that which cannot be so assumed. The information structure of the clause does not need to rely on that which has been said or written in earlier discourse, for the given may also refer to what we can assume to be known within the communicative context.

Even though the theme–rheme structure is speaker-oriented (the speaker chooses it as the point of departure for her or his sentence) and the given–new structure is addressee-oriented (the speaker decides what can be assumed that the addressee already knows), they are not unrelated. Normally, the theme coincides with the given of the clause. In other words, the element that announces what the sentence is all about is normally already known to the addressee. Despite the fact that con-textual features may override the location of the given within the theme,

Halliday (1994) argues that it is still the unmarked way of aligning the information structure with the thematic one.

Let us take a look at the thematic and information structure of the CIA Credo, beginning with the first sentence:

> We are the Central Intelligence Agency.

As we pointed out earlier, the theme of the clause is the recurrent 'we'. However, unless we can actually see a group of people, we cannot simply accept the 'we' as given. Who, we might ask, are the people saying this? There is no way to tell. So why not start by saying 'This is the Credo of the Central Intelligence Agency'. The answer lies precisely in the given status of the theme. The text proposes that we, the readers of the text, know who is talking. This is a strategy quite consistent with opening a Web site and working on an image of legitimacy, law-abidance, and transparency (Connell and Galasiński, 1996).

What follows from this is an interesting exercise in locating the CIA as the given of the text and the rest as the new. In other words, the CIA assumes that its audience knows merely of its existence and nothing about what it does. This is a fascinating finding when one considers that the Credo, like other corporate texts, is displayed for public consumption on the Internet. Yet, we would speculate that this apparent glitch in the form of the Credo is probably well worth it. Thanks to it, the CIA not only establishes itself as a known, taken-for-granted part of American life, but presents itself as a unity defending American values. The average American can sleep peacefully knowing that the CIA is out there making sure that American interests are well-served.

Qualifications and conclusions

In this chapter we have presented what we take to be a 'template' to be used in the linguistic analysis of texts. However, we need to add a few words of qualification starting with the practical use of the template's elements within analytical activities. What exactly do we focus on when we analyse a text? Is this template a kind of checklist of things that one must look for?

The answer to this question is both simple and complicated. We do not mean to say that our model constitutes a 'must' list for the analyst when approaching texts. Their own interests will, at least in part, dictate an analyst's choices. Thus, if I am interested in self-presentation within the text I will focus on the representation of speakers ideationally and interpersonally. Subsequently, it is the data that will drive the analysis. It is the data that are the most crucial aspect of the analysis and they must, as far as is possible, be allowed to 'speak for themselves' (Wodak, 1999).

However, there is a problem here since data do not 'speak for themselves' but are always the subject of interpretation. Further, analysts can fall into the trap of seeing the data only through pre-determined theoretical interests. For example, the assumption that self-presentation is only about the construction of the speaker may well be problematic since the speaking 'I' is constructed in contrast to the Other, non-I.

Discourse analysis is a far from straightforward enterprise. It involves a constant self-reflexive trade-off between the researcher's interests, values and knowledge of the context against the practicalities of a microanalysis that cannot go on indefinitely. This is particularly the case if discourse analysis is to contribute to a better understanding of how social and cultural worlds work, and, if possible, to valued change (van Dijk, 1993b).

We must stress that what we have proposed above is not a finite set of questions that can be asked of a text. Our template, driven by our interests and research backgrounds, necessarily reflects only a part, however substantial, of the analytical possibilities. Equally, the analytical examples that we have presented are not meant to be instances of comprehensive discourse analysis. However, we hope that subsequent chapters, in which we present analysis driven by concrete analytical objectives, will be a useful complement to and extension of our template.

For CDA, analysis is always done in two stages. The first one, the analysis proper, concerns itself with 'hard' data. We ask ourselves about what it is that we shall find in the data themselves. The second stage of the analysis is the interpretation of the findings of stage-one analysis.

The first stage of the analysis is said to be quite independent of the analysts themselves, (providing that one accepts lexico-grammatical analysis as valid and quasi-objective within the cultural context of its use) in that it is repeatable and empirically verifiable. Thus, when we ask ourselves about the thematic structure of the CIA Credo, we cannot, given our cultural-linguistic context, provide any other answer but the one that we gave; namely, that it is the pronoun 'we' that is consistently put in the thematic position in the clauses of the text. Given the grammatical rules of English, this is an argument about the Credo which cannot be reasonably or intelligibly disputed.

However, what we make of the place of the thematic 'we', i.e. the kind of interpretation that we make of the fact of the 'we', is another matter. It is at this second stage of analysis that our ethnic and cultural backgrounds, our values and education, come to the fore. This is, to a considerable extent, when CDA becomes a socially and politically committed affair. Interpretations are likely to be more contentious when the analyses of texts are themselves a part of socially contested discourses or events (see the debate on entextualization of background in discourse analysis between Blommaert (1997) and Galasiński (1997a, 1997b)). That is, when CDA is itself a constitutive part of cultural politics.

Our central point here is that interpretation, however contentious and ideologically motivated, follows on from an empirically verifiable analysis of the text. That is, interpretative analysis comes after the phenomena in the text structure have been observed and analysed linguistically. It is in this culture-bound and context-specific quasi-objectivity that the usefulness of the analyses that we propose is sustained. Thus do we attain one of the important goals of this book; namely, to indicate to practitioners of cultural studies who are concerned with discourse(s) that a formal linguistic and textually-oriented analysis can enrich their investigations and put them on a firmer, more empirically grounded, footing. Thus, we take aspects of established concerns of cultural studies, for example gender (Chapter 4), ethnicity (Chapter 5) and the intersections between these forms of cultural identity (Chapter 6) and explore them with the benefit of CDA.

4

The Name of the Father

Performing Masculine Identities

> I broke his authority; that's what it was. The love from a father to a child has always got that barbed wire of authority on it, always.

> (Interview with 'Joel')

This chapter centres on the performance of masculinity as achieved through men's talk about their fathers. A concentration on fathers as 'the first man' does not imply the relegation of motherhood to the sidelines or an uncritical endorsement of the 'Iron John' (Bly, 1991) mentality. Nor does a focus on talk suggest that analysis of textual representations is now passé. Rather, we take cultural studies' exploration of gender to be multi-faceted and multi-perspectival. Our contribution is to try to cast light on what we hold to be a dark and under-explored alleyway of our cultural consciousness.

The contemporary perception of masculinity as a 'social problem' has put men on the research agenda. If we are to forward the health and well being of men, along with the women who live with them, then we have to comprehend how men perceive the world and their place in it. Exploring the scripts by which men operate in the world (including their implications for action) is necessary if, in the long term, we are to seek ways of changing constructs with negative consequences to more positive ones. This suggests the need for discourse-sensitive ethnographic research into the cultural construction of masculinity.

The research we draw on below is part of a longer project exploring the metaphors and conceptual maps of meaning by which men understand their world, including the processes by which they may come to change themselves. The interviews conducted thus far have been with 30–70 year-old academic and general staff at an Australian university and among 16–25 year-old homeless and 'at risk' men who use Wollongong's (NSW, Australia) CHAIN (Community Health for Adolescents in Need) drop-in centre. Interviews are an appropriate method for exploring the verbal weave that guides men's lives because they offer depth and detail in relation to the meanings deployed by participants in the context of their life-worlds. Linguistic analysis of interview talk, itself a performing of gender, allows us to connect language constructs, the small-scale detail of local life and wider social processes.

The performativity of identity

Identity was the central theme of cultural studies throughout the 1990s. Driven by the cultural politics of feminism, gay rights and multiculturalism, as well by philosophical and linguistic concerns, there was 'a veritable discursive explosion . . . around the concept of "identity", at the same moment as it has been subjected to a searching critique' (Hall, 1996a:1). Hall goes on to detail the 'impossibility' and 'political significance' of identity, that is, on the one hand, the deconstruction of the western notion of the unified subject who possesses a stable identity, and on the other, the continued cultural contestation over the shifting character of identities and the social and political practices in which they are implicated (see Chapter 2).

Identities are not universal, fixed or essential entities, but contingent on historically and culturally specific constructions of language. That is, identities are wholly cultural and cannot 'exist' outside of representations. Specifically, identities are discursive constructions, i.e. descriptions of ourselves with which we identify and in which we have emotionally invested. While identities are matters of culture rather than nature, this does not mean that one can easily replace those ethnic or sexual identities into which one has been acculturalized. While identities are social constructions, they are ones that constitute us through the impositions of power and the identifications of the psyche. This is nowhere more apparent than in relation to gendered subjects, for whom the transformation of sexual identity from 'male' to 'female' and vice versa is an unusually radical procedure.

Sexed and gendered identities are, as argued in Chapter 2, largely a matter of how femininity and masculinity are spoken about, rather than manifestations of universal biological essences (which is not to say that biology does not matter as regards gender difference). We drew attention to the cultural construction of gender using the influential work of Judith Butler (1990, 1993, 1997). Butler's work brings together speech act theory, Foucauldian discourse analysis and linguistically informed psychoanalysis, to argue that sex is a 'regulatory norm' which acts in disciplinary mode to compel 'gendering'. Gender is a social construct, but an indispensable one, formed through discursive discipline and psychic identification. Gender is not a universal of nature or culture but a question of performativity, that is, the re-citation and reiteration of the 'Law' which obliges gendering under the heterosexual imperative. Performativity does not refer to a performance by an intentional actor, but to the impelled performance of regulatory discourses of power.

We accept the argument that gender identities are a matter of discursive-performativity. However, Bulter's is a largely philosophical body of work that does not demonstrate in any empirical way how 'sex' is achieved in the flow of day-to-day life. Specifically, we need to explore the way in which the regulatory discourses of sex are enunciated and identities performed in the social conversations of 'everyday' life. For example, how is masculinity constructed and mobilized for particular purposes in the daily flow of language? This is the kind of detailed investigation that discourse analysis can provide.

Man trouble

The study of gender throughout the history of institutional cultural studies has in practice meant the investigation of women by women within an explicitly feminist framework. However, there is now an increasing body of literature centring on masculinity (Biddulph, 1994; Connell, 1995; Farrell, 1993; Johnson and Meinhof, 1997; Nixon, 1997; Pfeil, 1995; Seidler, 1989). This growing interest in men is signified by the regular appearance of features on various aspects of masculinity in the supplements of the Sunday papers and within 'women's' magazines. Even Susan Faludi, author of a radical critique of masculinity as a 'bedrock of misogyny' (Faludi, 1991), is now giving more sympathetic observance to men's lives (Faludi, 1999).

This new-found attention for men is, as is so often the case in the schoolroom, a result of the apparent destructiveness of contemporary masculinity – from naughty boys to bad men. Real (1998) argues that 48 per cent of men in the USA are at some point in their lives implicated in depression, suicide, alcoholism, drug abuse, violence and crime. In Australia, over 35 per cent of boys in school year 10 had been 'binge drinking' in the previous two weeks and 45 per cent of the male population under 24 drink to a degree hazardous or harmful to them (National Drug Strategy, 1995). The press (*The Sun Herald*, 29.08.99) in Australia reports a government health survey whose findings represent an enormous cost to the state and a human tragedy of vast proportions. The report suggests that men are more likely than women to:

- be obese
- be diagnosed as having 'mental disorders' as a child (e.g. Attention Deficit Disorder)
- be diagnosed as HIV positive (ten times higher)
- have an accident (five times higher)
- engage in high risk behaviour (e.g. dangerous levels of drinking or drug taking)

- be a victim of suicide (six times higher with 80 per cent of suicide victims being male and death rates highest among men aged 20–24 or 80 and above).

Psychotherapeutic work (Rowe, 1996; Mclean et al., 1996) suggests that low self-esteem (itself an outcome of family life), along with the self-perceived failure to meet cultural expectations about masculinity, lie at the root of depression and drug abuse amongst men. Indeed, there is a case to suggest that personal pain, anxiety and depression underpin much male behaviour that appears to the 'outsider' as needless self-destruction. For Real, (1998) men's violence, sex addiction, gambling, alcohol and drug abuse is a form of self-medication, an attempted defence (achieved through 'merging' or self-elevation) against covert depression stemming from shame and 'toxic' family relationships. To give up such bulwarks is to invite a flood of depression to overwhelm the self as the desperate game of propping up self-esteem collapses.

Talk as biochemistry

There is a growing consensus that the best results in the treatment of depression are currently achieved through a combination of anti-depressant drugs and psychotherapy. The roots of depression are planted in genetic and biochemical dispositions intertwined with family trauma. Indeed, one of the most fascinating aspects of current research is the evidence that personal experience, including the way we think, can alter the biochemistry of the brain. Thus, childhood trauma can have 'lifelong psycho-biological consequences' (Real, 1998: 103) with post-traumatic stress syndrome marking the extreme bio-psychological outcomes of dramatic events.

Experiments with primates suggest that separation from the mother promotes changes in serotonin and adrenal enzyme levels. Thus can psychoanalysis be put 'under the description' of biochemistry. There is also evidence that learning or changing our patterns of thinking alters brain biochemistry (LeDoux, 1998). Thus, 'learned pessimism' as an explanatory style, which Seligman (1990) cites as the main cause of depression, and the acquisition of optimism that apparently relieves it, may well be implicated in changing biochemistry. Certainly the evidence which Seligman cites to suggest that pessimism depletes the immune system, while optimistic thinking boosts it, suggests the ability of thought to amend the body (indeed collapses the mind–body distinction).

Seligman's cognitive-behaviourism suggests that patterns of thinking and behaviour are intertwined, just as Wittgenstein suggested that new ways of describing pain involved 'new pain behaviour'. Thus, that rewriting of the self with which psychotherapy is implicated involves not just words, but new conduct, and not just new conduct, but alterations in biochemistry. Further, the emotional identifications described by psychoanalysis, which for Hall (1996a) and Butler (1993) (see Chapter 2) suture discourse to the psyche, or the language which constitutes or 'does' emotion for Gergen (1994), can be put 'under the description' of biochemistry. The emotional shift which is inseparable from rewriting self-narratives and which is sought after through therapeutic talk is implicated in biochemical change. Language digs deep down into the body (LeDoux, 1998; Pinker, 1994).

Toxic parents

It is a bedrock argument of most forms of psychotherapy that adult personal attachments and relationships re-stage aspects of childhood encounters. For many men, life becomes a restless search for love and the overcoming of feelings of inadequacy rooted in the biochemical consequences of family experience. Indeed, the growth of self-identity as the autonomous adult development of self-narrative necessitates the breaking free from parent–child relationships.

Sexual abuse and post-traumatic stress syndrome mark the currently understood outer limits of psychological pain and damage. However, violence comes in many forms and for most men it is the less dramatic childhood injuries of 'petty' violence and neglect that take up residence in their minds. As much as physical violence, it is the lack of nurturing and guidance that leaves its mark. When a child is traumatized within the family the most common reaction is to take responsibility for the failing parent. In order to preserve the emotional attachment to the parent, and in a desperate attempt to maintain the sense of security that derives from being cared for by competent adults (that the person we most rely on as a helpless child is the one causing us pain is a source of acute anxiety), the child will blame himself or herself. 'It was my fault, I caused "him" not to love me, I made "him" angry about something I have done, and there is something wrong with me'. Further, through a process of projective identification or 'carried feeling' (Mellody, 1987) the child may take on the feelings of rage, shame and sadness that have driven the parent.

> All of the abused child's psychological adaptations serve the fundamental purpose of preserving her primary attachment to her parents in the face of daily evidence of their malice. By developing a contaminated, stigmatized identity, the child victim takes the evil of the abuser into herself and thereby preserves her attachment. Because the inner sense of badness (shame) preserves a relationship, it is not readily given up even after the abuse has stopped; rather, it becomes a stable part of the child's personality structure. Similarly, adult survivors who have escaped from abusive situations continue to view themselves with contempt and to take upon themselves the shame and guilt of their abusers. The profound sense of inner badness becomes the

core around which the abused child's identity is formed, and it persists into adult life. (Herman, 1992: 102)

The much-used therapeutic metaphor of the 'inner child' expresses the internalization of emotional language and behavioural maps associated with our early life. On the one hand, children who suffer trauma will take on board feelings of worthlessness and shame, but on the other, through a process of identification, will also internalize the voice of the torturer. Real (1998) describes this with the metaphors of the 'wounded child' and the 'harsh child'. In this context, one of our interviewees, a 22 year-old young man, a former heroin and alcohol user whose mother and stepfather 'abused me physically and emotionally' described an image of himself as:

Jake: But deep down inside, I feel very very very . . . I picture myself in a corner crying a lot, in a dark room; that's the picture that I'm in, with my head in my hands just crying . . . That is the picture of myself in the corner of a room; that's deep down inside. It's all bottled up; I haven't let it out yet because if I do let it out, I'll do damage and I'll go destructive. So I just try not to open the bottle . . . Well, I wish I could cry. I can't cry. I haven't been able to cry for a long time.
Interviewer: Do you think if you remove the top from the bottle the boy would come out and cry?
Jake: Yes, one day he will.

Now, the metaphors that place emotion 'inside' and as a consequence are able to be 'bottled up' are themselves constitutive of an interior self. Emotions are not spatially located in the body, nor are they are distinct entities that could be 'let out'. Rather, we might distinguish between emotions as biochemically driven, unconscious bodily responses, and the words that describe various emotions and which are constitutive of what we take emotions to be (Gergen, 1994; LeDoux, 1998).

Thus, what is at stake for Jake is not so much letting the emotional genie out of the bottle, but the need to learn an appropriate and unthreatening language with which to control the bodily responses he has to images of his childhood, which we would normally call fear and anxiety. That is, cognitive language processes located in the cerebral cortex can, up to a point, be used to contain and regulate the brain's emotional fear circuits (located in and around the amygdala and hippocampal systems of the brain) that operate outside of conscious direction (LeDoux, 1998).

There is an indication in the phrase 'one day he will' that suggests Jake is aware of the need to come to terms with his past and that it is within his power to do so. However, he avoids this necessity through identification of the dangerous consequences that would follow from his doing this. 'I haven't let it out yet because if I do let it out, I'll do damage and I'll go destructive. So I just try not to open the bottle'. Jake's

unconscious choice of language allows him to divest himself of responsibility for his own actions since the 'damage' is positioned as caused by
events beyond his control. Further, he is courageously holding in his
responses to avoid the unleashing of destruction. One feels that Jake
both does and does not want to deal with – that is talk about – his past.
To do so places challenges before him that are painful to grasp. Indeed,
in contradiction to his explicit claim, Jake almost certainly could cry if
only he would let himself. Jake requires a language that makes crying
acceptable for men and, more generally, a language that enables him to
talk about emotion.

There is no suggestion that Jake's pain is his own fault. Indeed, the
attribution of blame is generally not useful in this context. Rather, our
argument here points to the critical place of language not only in Jake's
perception of himself and his family, but as a key component of resolving
the legacy of toxic parents. Toxic parents come in many guises; there are
the sexual abusers, the violent bashers, the verbal torturers, the silent
neglectors, the active controllers and the plain incompetent. The outcome
is that 'At the core of every formerly mistreated adult – even high
achievers – is a little child who feels powerless and afraid' (Forward,
1990: 16). The stage is then set for the compulsive re-enactment of
childhood routines that are broken only through a verbal declaration of
emotional independence and responsibility. If the shackles of noxious
parenting are not cast off then further painful relationships and attempts
at self-medication invariably follow.

Men, addiction and intimacy

In his analysis of the transformation of intimacy transpiring in the
western world, Giddens (1992) argues that:

> Men are the laggards in the transitions now occurring – and in a certain sense
> have been so ever since the late eighteenth century. In Western culture at least,
> today is the first period in which men are finding themselves to be men, that is,
> as possessing a problematic 'masculinity'. In previous times, men have
> assumed that their activities constituted 'history', whereas women existed
> almost out of time, doing the same as they always had done. (Giddens, 1992: 59)

Giddens argues that men's predominance in the public domain and
their association with 'reason' has been accomplished at the cost of their
exclusion from the transformation of intimacy. Intimacy is largely a
matter of emotional communication. The difficulties men have talking
about relationships, an activity which requires emotional security and
language skills, is rooted in a culturally constructed and historically
specific form of masculinity. From birth, boys are treated by parents as
independent and outgoing beings leading to a framework of masculinity

which stresses externally oriented activity (e.g. work and sport) at the
price of a masked emotional dependence on women and weak skills of
emotional communication.

What many men fail to acquire is the autonomy necessary for the
development of emotional closeness. In lacking competency in the
vocabulary of intimacy, many men are unable to name and speak about
feelings, or take responsibility for their own emotions. Instead, they seek
to uphold the basic trust that forestalls anxiety and sustains ontological
security through mastery and control of themselves, others (particularly
women) and their environment. Alternatively, self-medication through
violence, drug use or over-work masks the pain. For example, male
violence can be regarded as a hyper-mastery born out of anxiety which
self-assured routine competence and intimacy cannot assuage because
they have not been attained.

Addiction and other forms of compulsive behaviour, including the
'workcoholism' of high achievers, offer a source of comfort and a
defence against anxiety so that failure to engage in them produces an
upsurge of dread and/or depression. For Giddens, 'Every addiction is a
defensive reaction, and an escape, a recognition of lack of autonomy that
casts a shadow over the competence of the self' (Giddens, 1992: 76). He
argues that addictions as compulsive behaviour are narcotic like 'time-
outs' that blunt the pain and anxiety of other needs or longings that
cannot be directly controlled. Addiction is the 'other side' of the choice
and responsibility that goes with the autonomous development of a self-
narrative (or identity). In circumstances in which traditional guidance
has collapsed, these life-style decisions become a potentially 'dread-full'
process of 'making oneself'.

The addictive experience is a search for that 'high', and giving up of
the self, which acts as a release from anxiety marking a temporary
abandonment of the reflexivity generic to contemporary western life.
This suspension of the self is frequently followed by feelings of shame
and remorse. Since addictions signal an incapacity to cope with certain
anxieties, they tend to be functionally interchangeable. That is, one may
overthrow one addiction only to replace it with another. We may use
alcohol to ameliorate the pain of toxic fathers, but unless we deal with
the source of the pain the struggle to stop drinking may only result in a
shift to sex, cannabis, heroin, violence, endorphins or over-work.

My Father, the first man

The sign of our fathers is marked by ambivalence. 'Father' represents an
all-powerful protector but also the omnipotent lawmaker who wields
the rod of punishment. 'Our Father who art in heaven' is the Lord; the
power and the glory, the provider whose will must be done even as he is
the fount of love and forgiveness. In psychoanalytic terms the father is

signed as the symbolic Phallus, the breaker of the mother–child dyad, the castrator, the abjector and the 'transcendental signifier' of the law, culture and language. The power of the father is the authority of patriarchy with all its suggestions of mastery and masculine control. He is the one with whom boys identify and wish to emulate. He is the one whom girls long for in the quest of romance. The very model of what it is to be a man that is already divided at source.

There is currently much discussion of 'lost fathers' (Daniels, 1998). Some commentators argue that the decline of fatherhood in America is the most extraordinary trend of our time and accounts for many of the social problems encountered there. Poverty, rising juvenile crime, eating disorders, suicide, depression, alcohol and drug abuse are all traced back to absent fathers. Children who grow up with one parent are 2.5 times more likely to become teen mothers, twice as likely to drop out of school and 1.4 times as likely to be out of school and out of work. In America, 60 per cent of rapists, 72 per cent of adolescent murders and 70 per cent of long-term prison inmates are said to come from fatherless homes (Popenoe, 1996).

Other critics suggest that it is primarily the parental conflict and poverty which accompanies single parenthood that accounts for these figures rather than absent fathers *per se* (McLanahan and Sandfur, 1994). It is argued that there is little evidence that children need a male parent so much as they need loving nurturing caring adults, a condition that can occur in a variety of family forms (Stacey, 1996). Indeed, some children are better off without the presence of an abusive father.

While many would argue that it is desirable for children to be actively parented by a man and a woman in a loving partnership, the 'conservative' anxiety about children living in one parent families – which does have a basis in research evidence – has forgotten that there are many roads to happiness. Not only are there a variety of kinship forms across the planet, but much of the family literature has been critical of the nuclear family. In particular, it has been suggested that the 'standard' two-parent family can be the site of violence, the subordination of women, child abuse and the origins of 'mental illness' (Barrett and McIntosh, 1982; Hite, 1994; Laing, 1976; Leach, 1974). Indeed, much contemporary male anxiety and depression is rooted in the father–son relationship and a version of masculinity situated within two-parent families. In any case, we are more concerned here with how men construct an account of their father and his legacy irrespective of the latter's spatial location.

All men are sons

For many men their fathers are not thought of as complex human beings but symbols of virtue, 'what it is to be a man', and/or the very manifestation of abusive power, cruelty and lovelessness. For men, comprehension of their fathers, and if necessary a coming to a peace with them, is a necessary aspect of mental health and autonomous self-development. 'All men are sons and, whether they know it or not, most sons are loyal' (Real, 1998: 21). Consequently, sons internalize their father's voice as the representation of 'true' manhood even as he may also be the hand that wields the stick beating them for their alleged failings. One way or another our fathers are a part of us and, it is argued, if we are at war with him we are divided against ourselves and feel ourselves to be inadequate as a human being (Biddulph, 1994).

> As other fathers have done to their sons, my father – through the look in his eyes, the tone of his voice, the quality of his touch – passed the depression he did not know he had on to me just as surely as his father had passed it on to him – a chain of pain, linking parent to child across generations, a toxic legacy. (Real, 1998: 21)

As Forward (1990) suggests, we are not responsible for what is done to us as a defenceless child, but, if we are to 'recover', then we must take responsibility for positive actions to rectify the damage. To take self-responsibility is to accept 'an end to innocence' (Kopp, 1978); the giving up of a fairy-tale vision of life in which the enemy is clear and the 'good guys' win, or the sense that justice will prevail and we will 'get what we deserve'. If we have been the victim of childhood neglect we may grow up feeling that it should not have happened to us and that we are entitled to be recompensed by the world. Alternatively, we blame our-selves for having lost our parents' acceptance and set out to be 'good' (for example, being work or sporting achievers) in the vain hope that someone will now care for us. We must give up the fantasy that we can control our lives or that we are somehow special, even as we try to accept responsibility for our own actions. A start is to enter into dialogue with the figure of the father.

Talking of my father

The following discussion does not make claims to be a statistically valid representation of the relationship between men and their fathers. First, it is clear that there is no single entity called 'men' who share a set of intrinsic properties in common. Second, fathers and sons go through a series of qualitatively different kinds of relationship during various stages of their lives (Sheedy, 1998). Third, the number of men involved in the interviews cited below is too small to make generalized pro-nouncements about behavioural patterns. Instead, our concern here is with how specific men's personal constructs are constituted and enacted by the nuts and bolts of language as they give an account of their father and his enduring influence on their lives.

Having said that, the majority of the interviews completed thus far (40 and growing at the time of writing) and much of the literature cited in this chapter do suggest patterns of problematic father–son relationships. For example, *The Hite Report on the Family* (Hite, 1994) surveyed 1,047 boys and men (and 2,161 girls and women) to conclude that distance, a sense of forever unattainable 'otherness', and even fear, were the emotions marking the majority of sons' feelings about their fathers. Only 18 per cent of boys said that they had a close relationship with their father and 41 per cent of boys described their father as having an 'explosive temper'.

Case Study: *Daniel*

Aged 35, English born, now living in Australia

> I think the worst realization is that you react in that way because you are like your dad. That's got to be the worst – Daniel.

Daniel is the son of what he described as English middle-class parents. He left school and home at 16 to work on the docks. At 20 he was serving a year in jail for possessing and dealing in heroin. On completion of his sentence, and after a short delay thinking through his life, Daniel went to college and university, finally completing a PhD before taking up employment as a researcher in an Australian university.

A number of themes emerged from this interview including identification of 'control' and 'order' with the 'middle-class' and with his father in particular. Daniel has an ambivalent attitude towards order and control. He disparages these characteristics, resisting them through a lifestyle at odds with his father's expectations and by keeping women who he feels are encroaching into his personal space at arms length. On the other hand, he has a respect for his father's career achievements and accepts that his own accomplishments are the outcome of the self-control and imposition of order onto a somewhat chaotic life. Daniel's self-narrative is noteworthy for the number of occasions on which he describes himself as lacking in confidence as a young man. There is also a component of his personality that constantly seeks after a 'high'. Daniel's need for excitement and continual change may be contrasted with his perception of the stagnant routines he associates with the middle-class life of his parents.

The Fisher King thing

Daniel: I was really under-confident when I left home. I think everyone has a crisis of confidence at some stage, they call it the Fisher King thing. So like everybody else I had that and drugs were . . . .I found them and they were a nice little refuge for me; I didn't have to think because I had to organize all this stuff. You know how when you live at home and your parents have done a lot – you don't realize how much organizing your parents have done for you and then you leave home and all of a sudden you have to do it all yourself. So I got pretty heavily into drugs . . . [Edit] . . . It seems like there are certain things in your life, certain major things that happen in your life that cause you to have this crisis of confidence. I can remember being very confident as a little kid and just thinking that I was the best thing. Life was very easy and everything I did seemed to go well and everybody loved me. My dad was a real control freak so when I left home . . . [pause] . . . 'cause he always used to do stuff and he was always telling me what to do and how to do it and stuff like that, I hadn't got that sense of independence; the sense that I could just go out on my own and do stuff, because I hadn't been allowed to do all that stuff so I was a bit under-confident from that point of view. Then I moved in with this guy about four years after I left home and he was mad. This fellow had a few screws loose and he was paranoid; he loved [name] and she convinced him . . . [pause] . . . I realized later, that I was trying to have an affair with her and he tried to kill me one day and that freaked me out too. I couldn't work out how because I didn't know what it was all about at that stage and I interpreted it as meaning that there must be something bad about me for somebody to dislike me that much to want to try and kill me and that freaked me out too. I think at school I got bullied; my parents were always moving around and I always stuck out at school. [Edit]

Interviewer: You mentioned your dad, how would you describe your relationship with your father?

Daniel: Pretty good now; he still pisses me off because he's a bit too anal for my liking; he worries about things that I don't think people should worry about. But I've reached the stage where I can appreciate what he is and I think he appreciates what I am; we sort of grate against each other a bit now. I always respected him. When I was young I always thought he was an amazing guy and I wanted to be like him. But it started off where I struck out on my own. To some extent I started off doing stuff completely different to him. I think more when I came back and I think that's when I started on my own and I decided to be completely different and when I came out of prison, I really needed some kind of structure to hold onto to get myself back in the land of the living; it's difficult to describe unless you've done it. I decided to adopt his rigid disciplined approach and the immediate thing was that I wanted to make myself do it the way he did it because he has made something of himself. And now it's changed again. It was useful for the short-term because I needed that rigid discipline to get me going.

Interviewer: In a sense of wanting to do something, to make something of yourself?

Daniel: Yeah.

Interviewer: What would you do to make something of yourself?

Daniel: Well, it was kind of making something of yourself in society's terms, you know, getting qualifications, doing something that other people recognize, I suppose. The drug thing was an under-confidence thing. I was propping myself up and the under-confidence was just related to how people view me or how I thought people view me. So getting out of prison and getting qualified, I think was probably a way of getting society's respect or something like that. He was society as far as I was concerned.

Interviewer: Have you always felt under-confident?

Daniel: Yes, I've always been under-confident except when I was a kid; I remember when I was a kid I was so confident. I'm a lot better now but there's still something there that freaks me out. Relationships don't happen for a long time. I get really freaked out by intense relationships.

Interviewer: How does that feel? What is it about intense relationships?

Daniel: Something about the responsibility of having somebody there all the time; the responsibility of entertaining them and living up to their expectations; maybe that's it . . .

Daniel describes himself as being 'under-confident' as a young man, attributing this to relationships with men and most specifically his father, who is held to be a 'control freak'. As a consequence of his father 'always telling me what to do and how to do it' he didn't gain the skills for living which generate confidence in one's own abilities. This was compounded by bullying at school and a threatening relationship with a man whom we might reasonably see as out of control (in contrast with the controlled and controlling father).

However, Daniel's 'lack-of-confidence' narrative is a bit more complicated at the level of language than it may first appear. It reveals a number of tensions that the interviewee does not explicitly acknowledge. While Daniel clearly constitutes himself as under-confident, this construction is far from being straightforward. Daniel's first sentence in the quoted extract is not a simple attribution of under-confidence. He mitigates it with the hedge 'really'.

Hedges

Brown and Levinson (1987: 145) define hedges as particles, words, or phrases that modify the degree of membership of a predicate or noun phrase in a set. They say of that membership that it is partial, or true only in certain respects, or that it is more true and complete than might be expected. Such expressions as 'sort of', 'rather', 'technically' (as in 'Technically, it is linguistics') are referred to as 'hedges'. Brown and Levinson (1987) point out that some hedges cover the entire force of an utterance. In this way, words such as 'sincerely' or expressions like 'I wonder' mitigate or qualify the force such acts have as statements. In other words, the statements become weaker, or, to put it differently, they are licensed not to be fully sincere, truthful or entirely covering the state of affairs referred to (see also Mura, 1983).

But Daniel's mitigated (by 'really'), and thus not fully espoused, admission of under-confidence is juxtaposed with its being constructed as something normal and typical. He says: 'everyone has a crisis'. Both devices could be seen as face-saving (on the notion of face, see Brown and Levinson, 1987), yet from different points of view. While the mitigation undermines the admission – the statement is constructed as potentially not true, or going too far – the typification re-affirms it and positions it as something normal, and thus not necessarily dramatic.

The tensions in Daniel's narrative go further still. While clearly speaking about his own experiences, he casts them as dissociated from himself. He continues the narrative switching between his own perspective ('I didn't have to think') and the generic form ('You know how when you live at home and your parents have done a lot . . .'). Interestingly, the latter statement solicits the interviewer's perspective ('you know') and positions him as appreciating what Daniel is talking about. The choice of pronouns introduces a number of perspectives to the narrative, ranging from references to self through to 'everyone'.

As Meinhof (1997) points out in her discussion of male narratives that refer to 'the most important event of my life', such pronoun shifts might be suggestive of some *unease* in the way the speaker is perceived. In other words, Daniel's talk of his family relationships is far from direct and ordered. Indeed, the full espousal of his experiences returns only when Daniel starts talking about his relationship with the man he lived with and his girlfriend. That is, when he stops talking about his life in his family home.

Taking the blame

In the context of this style of analysis it is important to stress that what matters here is not what was 'really the case', but how Daniel interpreted events and continues to do so now (Rowe, 1996). Once, 'everybody loved me' but then things started to go wrong. According to Daniel, the incident with a 'mad' man led him to conclude that there was 'something bad about me'. However, most child psychology literature suggests that the low self-esteem and lack of confidence he describes would have taken shape at a much younger age. That is, he had already concluded as a child that there was badness at his core, most likely as a result of problematic relations with his parents, notably an austere father. This badness leads Daniel to take the blame for things done to him by others. Bullying is not held to be the consequence of problems other boys have but of the fact that 'I always stuck out'. Note here that the choice of the word 'I' describes a condition of being different in terms of an action and thus enables a more full acceptance of responsibility for what happened. The violence of an unstable man is taken as a result of his unconscious 'trying to have an affair' with the man's girlfriend, again constructed unequivocally with Daniel in an agentive position.

Blame is shared with a father whose work meant moving around a lot and a man who 'had a few screws loose'. That is, Daniel vacillates between reproaching himself and pointing the finger at others. This is a common form of generalized 'blame behaviour', which seeks to attribute causality for 'bad things' within oneself or in others, rather than accept the contingency of events with its implicit loss of control. This is also well evidenced in the unconscious 'linguistic tensions' within the narrative which point to the still troubled character of Daniel's family relationships. His initial account of his family life and relationship with his father is full of contradictions and is far from an undeviating or 'historical' account of what happened.

Through Daniel's eyes

Daniel 'respects' his father and can now 'appreciate what he is' but does not say that he loves him. Nowhere in an interview of over two hours does he say he loves his parents and only once that he felt loved (without naming his parents). Rather, he speaks of feeling 'disappointed that I wasn't able to relate to them on their level' #[1] and 'I'd like to feel more of an affinity with them than I do' #. He describes himself as 'indebted' to his parents who 'have given me the best upbringing that I could have really' #. Indeed, he seems to take sole responsibility upon himself for relationships in which other parties are implicated.

Also noteworthy is that Daniel's account of his father is accomplished entirely through his own eyes. Almost all the description of his father is executed through Daniel's mental processes. Daniel *appreciates* what his father is and *thinks* that his father appreciates him, he *thought* his father was amazing. It almost seems that Daniel's father has no qualities of his own. They only surface when he is represented as on a par with Daniel – when he refers to himself and his father as *we*. However, this is yet another twist in the narrative as Daniel, someone who has started anew, reclaims his independence and symbolically shakes off his father's influence.

The threat of the Other

Daniel expresses the more general view that 'loving someone is just needing them' #. This scares him because 'once you need somebody, then you worry that they are going to go away #'. Not only does love threaten a loss of control – a theme of the interview – but also demands that 'I should be as giving as possible to them so that they can love me' #. Love is not something he deserves unconditionally for being himself but must be earned. He has a 'fear of upsetting people' and feels a 'pressure to be interesting' and popular with the consequent sense that 'I am giving a lot more than I am getting' #.

These feelings are an echo of being 'freaked out by intense relationships' in which he feels the pressure of 'living up to their expectations'. Living up to other people's expectations – his internalized father's expectations – is dangerous because he feels he is doomed to failure. This was a lesson learned through previous experience with his father that had taught him he was of little value. These feelings express a lack of unqualified self-regard at the core of his being. In this he is not alone. Hite (1994) recounts her finding that 'respect', not 'love', is the word used by most sons in relation to their fathers and that 'respect' was virtually a synonym for fear. Real (1998), Rowe (1996), Biddulph (1994), Sheedy (1998) and others all relate male depression and drug use to a family-originated sense of low self-worth.

For Daniel, 'it started off where I struck out on my own' and he started to do things 'completely different' (said twice). 'It', we may say, is a sequence of troublesome events leading to drug addiction and prison that are held to be a consequence of forging his independence, i.e. his difference from his father. Conclusion: independence from father is dangerous. Solution: copy Dad and his ways. Daniel's lack of confidence, allied to an identification with his father as an 'amazing guy' to be imitated, lays the foundation for the adoption of 'his rigid disciplined approach' and 'making something of yourself in society's terms' as at least a partial solution to 'the drug thing (which) was an under-confidence thing'.

Daniel accounts for his post-prison acquisition of academic qualifications as a way of getting society's respect and, at least symbolically, that of his father, since, 'He was society as far as I was concerned'. Bearing in mind that he 'respects' his father, we may also impute that to get his father's respect is to gain self-worth and self-confidence. Failing to do so is what Bly calls a 'soul wound' or what Daniel describes as his 'Fisher King thing':

> Not receiving any blessing from your father is an injury . . . Not seeing your father when you are small, never being with him, having a remote father, an absent father, a workaholic father, is an injury . . . having a critical judgmental father. (Bly cited in Biddulph, 1994: 206)

The fear and attraction of control

Interviewer: Do you find that controlling environments or ordered environments, do you find them comforting, because you know how things are, or do you find them horrendous and you have to kick against them?

Daniel: Yes, I really hate them. In fact the thing that pisses me off most in the whole world is people trying to control me and people telling me what to do. I have a very irrational dislike of it. Even when people tell me stuff that I should be doing, like my housemate will tell me 'can you please wash the toilet or clean the verandah today 'cause I'm fed up with doing it'; even then my first reaction is to say 'f-off, don't tell me what to do'. Even though it's perfectly reasonable; but controlling environments are something that really freak me out . . . [edit] . . . So really it's just a respect thing, you know. I reckon everybody has their individual boundaries between people and they expect people to respect those boundaries and if they're not doing it, it just grates against you.

Interviewer: Do you feel the need to control other people or to be in control? Do you like yourself to be in control of circumstances like work, do you like always to be on top of it? Do you like always to know what you are doing or are you fairly relaxed and you just get on with things?

Daniel: That's usually how I work, the latter, letting things happen. If they piss me off then I just ignore them. I guess I do like to be in control too. I like to be in control of the things that freak me out, the things that make me nervous, things I'm not sure about. So when I'm not sure of myself, I guess I like to feel like I've got control. But most things in life don't freak me out anymore, so I'm quite happy to let things happen as they happen and I'm confident that I can deal with them. I guess it's going back to what we were talking about before, about knowing that you can get into a situation and deal with it. I guess I've got experience in that now to feel relaxed, even in new situations.

Interviewer: So you sound like you've grown in confidence really.

Daniel: Yes, a lot, and I still think because of that problem with relationships that there's something missing. A lot of the confidence and the way I tried to deal with it was just by getting good at stuff. I taught myself how to play music and I did the science thing and I did art. I can do all this stuff and I thought that was it, that I'd be confident after that.

Interviewer: Because you could do things.

Daniel: Yes. But there's something missing still in my confidence; it hasn't [*inaudible word*] but it has improved immeasurably, yeah.

The sequence above follows a discussion about prison, surely the ordered environment *par excellence*. Daniel had described the little scams that he was involved in, in which 'you reclaim some of your life as well . . . asserting the fact that you are an individual and not just a number and part of this machine' #. This sequence returned the conversation to the recurrent theme of order and control. Daniel suggests that 'the thing that pisses me off most in the whole world is people trying to control me' (as his father had done) and that 'controlling environments . . . really freak me out'. Daniel expresses hostility to the feeling that 'people aren't respecting my space' # or, as he puts it above, the boundaries between people that he argues we all have. Both in the sequence above, and elsewhere, he expresses a fear that relationships with women become too intense and encroach upon his space. In such circumstances he feels a loss of control and of confidence. Indeed, it is in having control that Daniel is able to boost his confidence; 'I like to be in control of the things that freak me out, the things that make me nervous, things I'm not sure about'. This he has achieved 'just by getting good at stuff'.

The language of mental states

The claim that people 'do not respect his space', as we quoted him above, introduces an interesting trait in his narratives. The controlling people are those who do not have a certain mental attitude (respect) towards Daniel. This construction is more one of a fear of control, or perhaps, of a possibility of control. In Daniel's narratives, the control he refers to does not belong to the physical world and only partly to the social world of relationships between people. It is predominantly the realm of perceptions and mental states.

Daniel starts his first turn by describing the people who attempt to control him in terms of verbal processes: they are people who *tell* him to do things. The first reaction that he has to these attempts is also verbal.

After all, telling someone to do things does not preclude declining. What 'pisses' Daniel off, again, is not so much the actual control, but his perception of it.

Later on, these constructions are confirmed – Daniel is not so much talking about some 'real', or 'actual' control, or influence over how things are. He is talking about 'liking', 'feeling', 'being confident', or 'having experience' – all these expressions refer to mental processes, to the way things are perceived and experienced. Being in control, again, is not associated with certain actions, or, as one might suspect, the effects of such actions, but with the way he looks at things.

What emerges from this analysis is that, for Daniel, control goes beyond being a relational concept situating him with regard to others. It is also a concept within which he can situate himself and in terms of which he can describe himself. It is the feeling and perception of being in control, along with the confidence that one can be so, rather than actual influence over things, that is important to Daniel. The control theme is used more to develop Daniel's self, rather than to position himself in relation to others. Thus, Daniel's mental world is constituted, at least in part, by verbal constructs that classify the world into those in control of themselves, those who are under the control of others and those who do the controlling. Further, it is likely that Daniel's intertwined psychic and biochemical history make situations that feature themes of control particularly pertinent to him. His 'defence' systems are especially prepared to react to control-related stimuli and produce anxiety in the face of them (LeDoux, 1998). Hence his own feeling that he has 'a very irrational dislike of it' and that 'controlling environments are something that really freak me out'.

The pleasures of mastery

Daniel has trained in the skills of the artist, achieved a high level of academic qualification in science and learned to play and write music. Like many men, including his father the 'control freak', Daniel hoped that 'mastery' of knowledge and skills in externally established domains of work and culture would give him the confidence he felt he lacked. To some extent this strategy has worked, for he has achieved a great deal. However, it has not solved 'that problem with relationships' which includes the fear that 'she's decided that she likes me and wants to hang on to me' #. Nor has achievement proved entirely satisfactory in relation to self-esteem, for he later suggests that once he had gained his Doctorate 'it failed to impress me' #. Even with his new found musical skills Daniel felt that once attained, and the mystery of how it is done mastered, 'I have a fundamental thought that I am not impressed with me . . . it's just the fact that I really don't value myself that much and I think if I can do it then anybody can do it' #.

Daniel feels the need for the control which gives him confidence and self-respect; a strategy similar to that of his father whose achievements he admires but from under whose authority he tried to escape through the 'wild-child' lifestyle. In a replay of the father–son relationship where affectionate demonstrations of love were apparently absent, 'distance' and 'space' are markers of Daniel's personal relationships with women. Yet, in a disavowal of the father-control-achievement matrix, Daniel argues that he prefers 'to let things happen'. His projected self-image is one of the happy-go-lucky guy who is unimpressed by public achievement, including his own, having gained enough confidence through experience to 'feel relaxed, even in new situations'.

Chasing the high

Interviewer: Do you chase after some kind of high? You need some kind of high? If it's not drugs it's playing music or whatever?

Daniel: Yeah. I can get really quite low when I'm not doing something, anything. It gives me that experience, the same kind of high. Maybe that's what I'm doing, constantly changing my job and stuff like that; it's the same pattern that I'm just . . . [*pause*] . . . it no longer does it for you . . . [*pause*] . . . it's like going from speed to smack and you just get fed up with speed after a while. If you are desperate for that high, then you just go on to some other kind of drug or whatever it is and maybe it's the same about work – after a while I get fed up with it and don't relate the effort to go on to that next stage that I was talking about earlier when you really have to get intensely into that one thing.

Interviewer: And partners perhaps?

Daniel: Yeah, it's true. You do get that very intense first stage, it's just beautiful; when you know you are in love and then after a while . . .

Interviewer: And the sex is great.

Daniel: Yeah, a lot of sex stays the same but I start seeing . . . [*pause*] . . . once I start to get to know people more; if I start getting pissed off with them it's because they've let me into some secret of their personality that I don't like and then I just start seeing them . . . [*pause*] . . . so every time I look at them – whereas before I'd look at them and think 'oh how beautiful, just lovely'. Then I start thinking [*laughs*] that I can see something behind their eyes; everything I see then just clouds my judgement. But yes, sometimes physical attraction goes after a while. The first couple of months it's very exciting and then after it's just boring.

Interviewer: The highs begin to decline.

Daniel: Maybe that's more important than I thought.

Daniel gave expression to the sense that his life was now about 'discovering exciting new things about myself . . . like I'm getting bored with science now just because I've done it. It's always like I have to find new things' #. He saw little permanency in his life. Moving on from one interest to another (science to music), from one place to another (migration from England to Australia) and from one woman to another (marriage, divorce and transient girlfriends) in search of the next thing to capture his imagination. As he suggests above, Daniel needs to keep doing things to avoid getting 'low' and bored. He makes the analogy between his seeking of highs from various drugs to his moving from job to job when 'it no longer does it for you'. Indeed, elsewhere in the interview he speculates, not without reason, that he is an 'addictive personality' #.

However, this lack of permanency does not sit entirely comfortably within Daniel's narrative. Observation of the shifts in pronouns tells us another story. Here, it is noteworthy that the shift occurs after a sentence, 'it's the same pattern', in which Daniel seems to acknowledge lack of change or improvement in his ways, i.e. that he is stuck in the same pattern. The pause after this disclosure is also significant, as it is marked – longer than expected in a 'smooth' narration. This, as we said, registers a transition moment when, linguistically, he stops talking about himself. Using the pronoun 'you' he dissociates the narrated experiences from himself at the linguistic surface of what he says. This dissociation continues when he talks about drugs – something perhaps unlikely to be fully espoused at this stage of his life. Getting high in this particular manner must be constructed as a 'general way', a practice no longer associated with himself.

Note also that the shift back to talking about himself comes at the moment when he changes the topic and starts talking about work, admittedly, an activity normally evaluated positively. So even if his relationship with his professional activities is explicitly troubled, this life sphere can be taken on and related directly to him.

Intimacy and boredom

Prompted, Daniel connects his search for excitement with a loss of interest in his lovers that is only partly a matter of sex and more a matter of intimacy. The buzz comes from that feeling of being 'in love', a high which begins to decline as 'they've let me into some secret of their personality that I don't like'. As the psycho–physiological lift of being 'in love' gives way after a couple of months or so to the potential intimacy of emotional communication, routine and building a longer-term relationship (including his fear that they wish to control him and invade his space), Daniel's interest wanes. Given what we already know, we may feel that his lack of confidence in relationships is a flight from intimacy based on a fear of control rooted in his childhood experience of a controlling father.

Moreover, this time Daniel constructs his 'getting pissed off' explicitly in causal terms with his partners. He gets pissed off *because* they let him in on some personality aspect. Thus, his attitude is not attributable solely to himself but is caused externally by others, which helps relieve him of full responsibility. Further, what we postulate as his fear of control and lack of confidence in relationships can also be found in the linguistic structure. Note that his account of relationships is carried out predominantly in terms of processes that refer to sensory perceptions. His relationship with women is about 'seeing' them rather than anything else, a process presupposing unidirectionality and not requiring reciprocity or mutual responsibility.

Highs represent a pleasurable 'time-out' from the demands of other people and the responsibilities that relationships bring with them. In some spheres of his life Daniel is a distinguished achiever displaying elevated self-discipline. On the other hand, he likes to move on from one activity or person to another rather than stick with it as the high declines. As we noted earlier, one of his father's characteristics that he dislikes is that he is 'a bit too anal for my liking'. Getting away and getting high is an escape from fatherly discipline, hopes and expectations.

The fear of failure

Daniel: What they [the heroin crowd] shared in common is the inability to handle and organize their life in a way that fulfils them; instead of making the effort, they have just chosen to use the drugs as an anaesthetic because life is not going the way they want it to, so block it out rather than do something about it. Lazy, maybe like me. I am eternally lazy [*laughs*].

Interviewer: Is that what you think drugs did for you, anaesthetize yourself?

Daniel: Yes, I didn't want to make the effort or I wanted to make the effort but I didn't for whatever reason. Too scared probably to get out there; too scared to fail I think was one of my problems. I didn't want to try because I was worried about failure, probably my father being such an oppressive guy and he was a model for me, that sort of freaked me out a bit, I don't know why. So I didn't want to fail maybe for that reason.

Interviewer: So here's your father a big success and you admired him in some respects anyway. He was a role model of big success so you wanted to be a big success too perhaps. It's a frightening prospect if you don't think that you are gonna make it.

Daniel: That's right. You don't want to know, that's the real thing isn't it, being able to have the courage to get out there and know that you might fail; because it's always worse knowing that you have failed. That's what a lot of junkies share, that thing, 'I could have done this, I could have done that'. You hear a lot of junkie stories like that and to me that means that what they are thinking is what I was thinking probably. It's better to not try at all than to try and then fail; to know that you are a failure. At least if you could convince yourself that if you haven't tried it then you could have done it. [*laughs*] So those people were locked in and I had to get away. It's the old story about drug abuse and [*inaudible word*] and one of the best ways to get yourself off it is to just leave all your old habits and your friends behind. I sort of miss some of them . . .

According to Daniel, the heroin crowd 'use the drugs as an anaesthetic because life is not going the way they want it to'. He and they shared the inability to organize their lives and to make the necessary effort to move it in the desired direction. To organize is to be disciplined, to have self-control. To get high is to remove this demand by flouting it. As he comments, to get high is to avoid the self-discipline required to try and the pain of having tried and failed. But this admission is weakened by Daniel's linguistic constructions. By explicitly constructing the 'heroin crowd' as 'they', a pronoun that in all its potential meanings (see e.g. Mühlhaüsler and Harré, 1990) does not include the speaking 'I', Daniel distances himself from the heroin users. His eventual admission that he might have done the same is cushioned in its assertion by his 'maybe' and subsequent laughter. This distancing has a 'happy ending' when he refers to the heroin users as being locked into a situation that, he, Daniel, had to get away from. Interestingly, he both justifies and typifies his actions by re-casting his experience as a general truth – 'It's the old story . . .'.

Daniel, we would suggest, sought to avoid having failed in the eyes of his high achieving and controlling father. 'It's better to not try at all than to try and then fail; to know that you are a failure'. Lacking confidence in the face of 'my father being such an oppressive guy and he was a model for me', and not wishing to disappoint his father, Daniel attempted to by-pass the pressure through getting high. Ironically, he delivered himself into what he had tried to avoid, since it is unlikely that a heroin habit and a prison sentence were deemed to be a success by his father. These are the twisted things we do for love.

Subsequently, we castigate ourselves for the tortuous route we take to gain our fathers' approval. In this case, Daniel blames himself for being 'eternally lazy', not a characteristic which normally leads to the attainment of a PhD. Indeed, in having to abandon the path of avoiding failure though evasion, Daniel subsequently adopts the 'rigid disciplined approach' required for public achievement that would impress his Dad and himself. Daniel was to find pleasure in the process of getting a Doctorate and learning music, but not in the final moment of achievement when that which was hoped for (personal validation via father's approval) failed to materialize. Nevertheless, Daniel is telling a success story of having kicked a heroin habit. This requires not just the overcoming of physical withdrawal symptoms but a complete change in lifestyle since 'one of the best ways to get yourself off it is to just leave all your old habits and your friends behind'.

Time for a change

Daniel: I was just fundamentally lacking in confidence to take control of my own life, I think, which came from my father. So the thing that really used to freak me out and make me depressed was looking at life and thinking 'well there it is, but I don't dare try and grab it' and so the change I guess was just getting so low that I thought it can't be that bad, just get out and give it a go and see what you think. And I kind of rediscovered what I think I'd found when I was really young that things were really quite easy, that I could do a lot of things that I saw other people do. I didn't have to be scared and I think it was just the 'scared' aspect that was making me see everything so negatively. You know you have a lot of people slagging things off and that's just stupid and what they really mean is that they're too scared to give it a go and they just shrink back into this negative, critical approach to everything that they're not doing, as if to pretend they're not doing it [not] because they're too scared to try, they're [not] doing it because they think it's stupid. I had that kind of mindset and I think the change was just getting so low that I thought I didn't know the way to go so I might as well just try this and it can't get any worse. So I tried it and I kept going.

Daniel's statement that he was 'just fundamentally lacking in confidence to take control of my own life, I think, which came from my father' is an apt summary of those aspects of his life-story analysed here (and there are, of course, others, for Daniel cannot be reduced to his relationship with his father). In this instance his lack of confidence is related to feeling depressed at his inability to grasp life as he felt he should.

Change for a drug user commonly needs to encompass more than overcoming physical addiction, requiring in addition the subduing of compulsive behaviour, that is, the habits and routines of the drug using lifestyle. In turn, it is a truism of the therapeutic literature that addicts must want to stop before they can have any chance of success. Daniel is not unusual in getting to a point where he felt it could not get much worse; 'the change I guess was just getting so low that I thought it can't be that bad, just get out and give it a go' (a turn of phrase he repeats towards the end of the sequence above).

Personal change for Daniel involved a shift of 'mindset', that is, a way of thinking or set of personal constructs. Prison seems to have played a significant role in this, quite apart from the fact that 'only a madman shoots up in prison' #, it gave him time to 'just sit down and think and try and work out what was wrong and what I had to do to sort it out and I suppose I have to think about how I related with other people there, cause that's a kind of intense situation' #. Daniel had to find a way to re-describe himself, indeed he had to develop a willingness to talk about himself, requiring the acquisition and deployment of an appropriate language of the self. Although he still expresses some resistance to talking about his feelings, this is an aspect of his identity that he describes as significantly improved.

Daniel: a typical bloke when he responds to problems – keep it in, don't say anything about it for a while and apparently I keep it in because I feel like it's something I should be able to deal with on my own. I shouldn't have to say 'look, I'm feeling like this' because I don't think I should be feeling like this. So I just ignore it and I'll try and deal with it on my own and it doesn't work and it all comes out.
Interviewer: And then you feel terrible afterwards.

Daniel: I feel pretty bad afterwards but I talk about it now when I've calmed down; I'm quite happy to sit down and talk about it; so it doesn't become a deep festering wound that it used to.

Today Daniel describes his life as 'full of optimism', so that even those occasions when he is feeling down he regards as positive introspective moments used to consider the direction of his life. He has learned to talk positive talk to himself so that 'it will start off negative and then eventually I'll think that's good and that's good and that's good' #. He recognizes that some of the anal qualities of his father that he has acquired are also the basis for achievements in his life. 'It's interesting how the negative influences in your life can end up being quite positive' #. Further, there is in the extract below some acknowledgment that his father's need for control has its foundation in the chaos of a childhood without structure and the need to impose order on his life.

Daniel: And his [*Daniel's father*] background is pretty freaky. She [*Daniel's grandmother, i.e. his father's mother*] should never have stayed married for very long and she was unable to relate to anybody; she spent her whole life moving around from one place to another, never really making friends. He's had that; he had so little control in his life so [*pause*] she didn't produce any structure for him to hang on to at all and it just freaked him out. It was a way of controlling his own environment so he never had to worry about other people's influence, because I think he learnt that he couldn't trust anybody and it freaked him out as well so he had to control the experience.

The carried feelings about order, chaos and mastery which mark the male side of the family have manifested themselves for Daniel in his desire for release into the control free environment of the high *and* his disciplined drive for achievement. Overall, the narrative is constructed as one in which the moves are from chaos to order for the father and from control to chaos and back again for the son. Further, there are the ambiguities of the oscillation between acceptance–rejection that marks Daniel's construction of his relationship with his father and which he implies was mutual. According to much of the therapeutic literature, and as evidenced also in our interview with Maurice below, this is a common state of affairs for men.

Along with control, 'distance' was a recurrent metaphor deployed by our interviewees when talking about their relationships with their fathers. Some men who have had troubled and detached relations with their father self-medicate themselves with drugs (e.g. Daniel and Jake), others set out on a road of public 'achievement' to prove themselves worthy (including Daniel). This was certainly the case for Maurice.

Case Study: *Maurice*

Aged 67, New Zealand born, now living in Australia.

Maurice has had a successful academic career rising to the status of Professor and Dean. Subsequently, retirement came hard to a man for whom work was a central force in his life.

The horizons of work

Maurice: I suddenly saw that I wasn't anybody because I had always been what I was at work and I suppose maybe my father felt the same when he retired . . . I had not realized how much my work and me were synonymous, that I was what I did, not what I was as a person and again I know that's not an original perception but I had never realized that until very recently . . . I guess I was always encouraged to do, test yourself, push your self, you'll never know how far you can go until you try. Don't say, I'm gonna fail . . . We moved internationally, we moved within Australia and I suppose every time I moved was to achieve some kind of promotion. So I suppose that makes it very clear that achievement orientation was a pretty important part of what I'm doing.

At the heart of Maurice's discussion is a contradiction. On the one hand, he is not a person – 'I wasn't anybody' – because he overly identified with work. However, on the other hand, the phrase 'my work and me were synonymous, that I was what I did, not what I was as a person' makes a distinction between work and personhood. He is making the claim that he was a person after all, it was just being covered over by work. Maurice acknowledges the by now widespread contemporary cultural criticism that many men work too hard – 'that's not an original perception' – while simultaneously distancing himself from that claim by constructing himself as a person all along. That is, on a self-reflective level, the intellectual in Maurice understands that he has overly devoted himself to work and thus replicated his own father. On a more unconscious level, indicated by his unreflective choice of words, Maurice wants to deny this shortcoming on behalf of himself and his father.

When Maurice speculates that his father might have 'felt the same' he is sympathetically identifying with his father while at the same time pointing the finger at him since we may assume that it was his father who pushed him to test himself. As we shall see, this ambivalence characterizes the whole of Maurice's discourse about his father.

My father and me

Maurice's father had been a schoolteacher and the importance of education was impressed upon him so that:

Maurice: For my father and me, education was the driving force in our lives. My mother said regretfully, late in life, that the worst thing that ever happened to me was that I went to university – the reason being that it took me away from the family. [*Edit*] But I don't remember him [*his father*] being very oriented towards his own children. He was oriented towards his job which was other people's children and many of the things we did with him were the things that he wanted to do for himself.

Maurice's mother was regretful of her son's educational and work-motivated flight from the family. Yet, this emotional distance from relationships in favour of work was one modelled to Maurice by his own father. Indeed, this educational and work-inspired male distance from family, specifically women and children, was to be a marker of the lives of father and son. Maurice identifies with his father even as he goes on to criticize him for neglecting his family. Later, we shall see that Maurice fears that he is subject to the same accusation from one of his own sons. This may underpin the oscillation between identification and distance that is imprinted on Maurice's discourse about his father.

Interviewer: How would you describe your relationship with your father?

Maurice: Uncomfortable. I think I wanted to like him but I don't think I ever really loved him . . . He was a schoolteacher who never really stopped being a schoolteacher even when he was retired. I was always a small boy to him. I was always someone to be told what to do and how to do it and if you didn't do it to his satisfaction, then you always felt that there was likely to be a penalty at the end. He was a man who could never leave his work behind him at the office . . . I don't think he ever said that he was proud of what I had done and he didn't live long enough to see me finish a doctorate or anything of that kind, but I am sure that he told his friends at the bowling club or whatever, with great gusto and really puff his chest out with the achievements of his son and his daughter and so on. But he could never really tell his children how he felt about them and I don't know what he would have said if I had been around his death bed. I suppose I always respected him but it was the very much the respect of a schoolboy for a schoolteacher rather than the love of a son for a father – and I find that rather distressing to think about that in those terms. It makes me ask the question, what the hell are my children going to be thinking about me now that I'm approaching that same stage in my life. It makes you work a little harder on human relations too I think than was the case there.

In his desire to assert his control, Maurice's father inspired fear and respect but not love. Committed to his work, and always the school-teacher, this was a father who was unable to express his feelings of love – if he had them – for his family and specifically his son. Again, we find the word 'respect' substituted for 'love'. Respect is conditional, distant, and humourless, involving duty, honour and deference. By contrast, the language of love characterizes relationships of affection, closeness and unconditional cherishing, where emotional proximity is signalled and engendered by gentle physical touch. According to Maurice, 'I don't recall my father ever kissing me, I don't recall my father ever hugging me' #. However, he does remember his father as being 'by my standards quite violent'. 'One of my most vivid memories' is of father 'chasing me around the lemon tree in the backyard with a lump of wood in his hands' #.

Mitigators

Perhaps because Maurice now sees himself in parallel with his father in terms of age, his negative account is substantially mitigated. Maurice does not say his father never said that he was proud, or that he never kissed him etc. This negatively perceived lack of action is, as was the case with Daniel, filtered through mental processes. In this case, negated mental processes. Maurice *doesn't think* his father told him he was proud, Maurice *doesn't recall* his father kissing him. These linguistic devices are mitigators.

Mitigating devices are those expressions that are used to soften the intention behind the unwelcome action (Ng and Bradac, 1993: 92; see also Brown and Levinson, 1987). They render violation of a rule less harmful than it might otherwise have been perceived. Here, the mitigation is used to soften the potential 'untruthfulness' of the categorical statements about Maurice's father. Maurice does not want to simply say: 'My father has never kissed me', he prefers to say he did not recall that, and thus should he be mistaken, the error would be his own fault. Further, since there is no way of establishing the 'truth' of the father's kissing behaviour, Maurice's unconscious choice of language casts doubt on the validity of his own perceptions and memory, signalling a desire to shift reproach away from his father and onto himself. This, as we observed earlier (Herman, 1992; Mellody, 1987), is a way of reducing the threat to the father–son relationship that is manifested here as image and memory. It would appear hard for Maurice, even as he is critical of his father, to accept that Dad was 'really' at fault. Thus do men try to preserve their idealizations of fatherhood.

The use of mitigating phrases signals other contradictory dimensions of Maurice's life-story. For example, Maurice's construction clearly positions the father's actions through the son's perspective so that the character of the relationship is a matter of perception. What 'really happened', what the father did or did not do, is not significant – what *is* important is how Maurice sees it now and with which personal constructs. As with Daniel, it is through his use of language that Maurice asserts himself in the relationship and gains control over it. However, at the same time Maurice constructs himself in negative terms. He says: 'I don't think he ever said that he was proud of what I had done'. The linguistic choice Maurice makes is quite interesting. He could as easily have said: 'I think he never kissed me' or 'he was never proud of me'. Yet Maurice decides to negate his father's actions in his own mental process and represent him in more positive terms.

Linguistically then, there is a tension within Maurice's account of his relationship with his father. Maurice describes the relationship in his own terms, yet constructs his father positively. For all the anxiety that surrounds his relationship with his father, Maurice is reluctant to cast the shadow of blame over his father, preferring to maintain the phantasm of the 'Father' by doubting his own perceptions and judgements. We would note that this process occurs in a context in which Maurice is about to say that he has entered a stage in his life, following the death of his father, that causes him to be concerned about his own children's perception of him as their dad. Indeed, immediately following on from this sequence he makes an observation about such situations causing one to think about human relations in general. He is clearly afraid that the relationship he had with his father is being recast and replayed with his own children. He realizes that his children have the power to *think* something of him.

Fathers and sons

During the interview, Maurice became reflexive about his relationships with his own sons. One son 'breezed through' university and is 'sufficiently well adjusted to be able to live in the house next door to us with very good personal relationships . . . we are a mutually supportive group' #. However:

> *Maurice*: The son that I am particularly concerned about had a few years when he was mixed up with the drug scene and it was very difficult to talk to him about anything at all and that was the time when we really should have been talking about these things but couldn't, because he was so touchy, so difficult, so obnoxious and unpleasant . . . I don't really understand what happened. He left school here; he was a very well-adjusted, highly achieving young man. He could have got into medical school in those days if he had wanted to, but he wanted to be a natural scientist.

High achievement and an ability to get along with himself mark the state of being 'well-adjusted' for Maurice. It is noteworthy that at one stage he says that 'I wanted very much to be a Doctor . . . but my mother said 'no, people of our social class, people of our kind don't become doctors' #. We may ponder the frustration Maurice felt when his son, who he felt was capable of being a doctor, and who we may assume was encouraged to do this by his father, decided not to pursue this route. While Maurice maintains a tone of reason and control, his son is cast as 'so touchy, so difficult, so obnoxious and unpleasant' and thus explicitly constructed as the party to blame. Today:

> *Maurice*: My youngest son, in occupational terms, is something of a 'dropout'. He has a lifestyle centred life . . . He does some teaching at the youth centre. He administers and tutors in there, but he doesn't do it on a full-time basis. He is happy to spend part of his weekly life looking after his children. So I admire and respect what he does but I can't help worrying about what the hell is gonna happen when he is another ten years older.

For Maurice, existence as a 'dropout' is one based on 'lifestyle' rather than work (even though paid employment cultivates its own kind of lifestyle), for what is it one drops out from if it is not the achievement-oriented career route valued by Maurice, his father and one son? The distance that appeared between Maurice and his father, which he attributed in part to a commitment to work, rather than family, appears to be 'carried over' into his relationship with one of his sons. However, Maurice denies this:

Maurice: I know that my youngest son would blame my involvement in my work because getting through the university system took me a bit more effort than some people who got to be heads of departments and professors and so on. I think he blames his own years of unhappiness after he left university, probably on me, but I think that is a pretty normal child–son situation. Fathers can't win, can they – at least I don't think they can . . .

Interviewer: Do you think that your son feels that your achievement at work somehow contributed to his drug habits?

Maurice: I've had that impression given to me very forcibly but I think people in that situation are usually looking for excuses.

Maurice explains, or excuses, his own strong commitment to achievement at work on the (here unjustified) grounds that he had it harder than some. Further, rather than accept what he feels to be his son's blame, he turns the tables by suggesting that such a rebuke is not only 'normal' but that it is his son who is looking for excuses. After telling the story of his own father in some detail, he now proclaims that 'fathers can't win'. Later he suggests somewhat bitterly that 'After I've gone he [*the son*] can worry about the relationship he has with his own son' #.

In-different space

The emotional distance which marked Maurice's relationship with a 'workaholic' father appears not only to have been reproduced between himself and his 'dropout' son, but to have characterized all his relationships. Maurice suggested that he had lots of acquaintances and colleagues but 'I don't have any bosom pals . . . I don't have very many people that I can talk to, hardly any' #. Tellingly, his wife 'doesn't think I talk to her enough, but then I think that's a male–female distinction'. That is, not talking enough to one's wife is a generalizable facet of all men and thus not his personal failing.

Interviewer: Do you think you ought to talk to her more often?

Maurice: Yes, but that's one of the areas that I really think men and women differ. She talks a lot with her friends. I am not sure that I've got any friends. They talk about all sorts of things, but if I talk with people I want to talk about something, not just anything and I wonder whether the women's groups can sit down and talk about their innermost feelings, is something that is intrinsic with females. Certainly my wife can talk to her friends about those things I guess [*more*] than she can with me and I simply

don't find . . . I don't want to sit down and talk about my emotions . . . [*edit*] . . . But
the way I was raised and the other part of the masculinity thing is that you keep these
things to yourself; you put on a strong man image and so on. All very stereotyped I
suppose.

Interviewer: So are feelings difficult things to talk about?

Maurice: Yes, I think they are. My parents never talked about feelings and I had no
exposure to that sort of thing when I was a child and I grew up with Dad as a sort of
implicit underpinning to my own social relationships and men of my vintage, the ones I
mixed with, whether at university or outside of university, again, didn't sit down over
a beer and talk about how they were feeling . . .

Maurice's account is shot through with irony. He is aware that he has not
been trained in the language of emotional intimacy by his parents and
that his father acted as a model for social relationships. He is, as we have
already seen, willing to describe his father as a work-oriented man who
experienced difficulty in expressing his emotions. Further, with an ironic
lilt he acknowledges that men's unwillingness to talk about emotions is
'all very stereotyped I suppose'. Yet, despite his clear recognition of the
learned cultural source of his own and other men's reluctance to talk
about emotion he argues that this represents a fundamental male–female
distinction. Further, he suggests that emotional talk is not substantial
enough for men. Maurice wants to talk about 'something, not just anything', implying that in women's relationships talk is the latter. Talking
about feelings is said to be intrinsic to women and something he does not
want to do. From the 'outside' we might speculate that Maurice's imput-
ing of intrinsic relationship skills to women is a defence mechanism
designed to justify his own avoidance. If so, it is not so much a defence as
a father-to-son self-inflicted wound for it leads to having no close male
friends, a situation which the literature reports is the norm among men
(Biddulph, 1994; Hite, 1994; Real, 1998), not to mention a loss of relational
dialogue with women partners.

Taking stock

Maurice pondered the balance sheet of his relative commitments to
work and family relationships, what he called the 'opportunity costs', a
concept drawn not uncoincidentally from a rationalist discourse of
economic behaviour.

Maurice: I can't say that I am unhappy with the outcome because I've had the kind of life
which has enabled me to do pretty much what I wanted in many ways. It has given me
a wide exposure to travel. I have experienced situations that would never have come
to me in any other way except through work. I have been offered opportunities to be
professionally responsible that I'm glad I took, even though they might not have been
all that much fun at the time.

Maurice is not unhappy with his life since it 'has enabled me to do pretty much what I wanted' including the acquisition of new experiences. This is a classically modernist and masculine description of the self. First, he praises doing as one wants, rather than acting in the context of negotiated relationships with all their necessary give and take. This strikes one as the culturally formed position of many contemporary men and indeed representative of the pressure put on men to prioritize their paid work. Second, the self is constructed as formed through a variety of experiences that are to be collected like trophies, reminiscent of the modernist flâneur.

The figure of the flâneur, or stroller, is one who walks the anonymous spaces of the modern city experiencing the complexity, disturbances and confusions of the streets with their shops, displays, images and variety of persons. For Baudelaire (1964), the flâneur was one of the heroes of modern life, taking in the fleeting beauty and vivid, if transitory, impressions of the crowds, seeing everything anew in its immediacy, yet with a certain detachment. Further, the flâneur is marked as peculiarly modern by the rapid change and plurality of styles that form a blueprint for the stylization of the self as a project.

Massey (1994) argues that this modernist experience was and is deeply gendered. The experience of the flâneur and of modernism was one of male-coded public spaces from which women were excluded (e.g. the boulevards and cafés) or entered only as objects for male consumption (e.g. as prostitutes and models). Thus, the flâneur was a male figure who walked spaces from which women were largely excluded and whose gaze was frequently erotic, with women forming the object of the look. Indeed, modernist paintings are often of women and spatially organized in such a way as to privilege a male-coded sense of a 'distance' and 'detachment' (but not disinterest).

Happy families

One might wonder why Maurice should retrospectively be pleased to have taken a course of action involving professional responsibility when it 'might not have been all that much fun at the time'. If something was not fun at the time, it can't really be fun later either. However, these situations are cast by Maurice not as painful obligations, but more positively as 'opportunities'. Maurice is a man who, like many others, and consistent with the expectations of men in the western world deriving from a puritan ethic, puts the trophies of work before emotional happiness.

Maurice does not say that he was, or is, happy. Rather, he expresses his condition in the phrase 'I can't say that I am unhappy'. The stoicism involved in the acceptance that the best one can hope for is to be 'not unhappy' is characteristic of work-oriented men of his age. Further, the phrase 'I can't say' does not mean that he is not unhappy, but that he is unable to speak about it. Nevertheless, he is aware that there have been losses as well as gains. He has few friends, no hobbies or pastimes, a restricted conversation with his wife and an estranged son. Many might think this a heavy price to pay for being 'not unhappy'. Indeed, Maurice himself seems to be partly aware of this (while simultaneously denying it), since now that work is no longer the spine of his life he is seeking to re-establish his family relationships.

> *Maurice*: I think trying to resolve in that period that is left to me, the difficulty is relationships, trying to ensure that my wife feels better with me and about me than perhaps she has at previous times; trying to be sure that my sons don't think I was an unmitigated disaster. Trying to ensure that my grandson . . . he's probably the most important thing to me. I spend a lot of time with him each week now; that when I've gone he will remember me . . .
>
> *Interviewer*: Do you think now that you are looking at relationships with other people as a more significant part of your life than they have been in the past?
>
> *Maurice*: Much more in focus, something that needs to be done than they have ever been before, yes, indeed. My wife would say it's a pity you left it so late . . .

The phrase 'in that period that is left to me' invokes the spectre of death, the inevitable coming of which commonly prompts us to take stock of our lives and to 'resolve' problems. Here 'the difficulty is relationships'. We may note that the distanced abstraction 'relationships' is the problem and not Maurice's own attitudes to, or actions within, relationships. On the face of it, Maurice's project of 'trying to ensure' or 'trying to be sure' about the feelings of his wife and sons signify the positive acknowledgement of their feelings and his responsibilities. Yet, wife and sons are cast here as objects of his corrective actions rather than recipients of his unconditional love. Further, the use of 'perhaps' qualifies his wife's experiences and casts doubt on her negative feelings towards him (which the interview as a whole indicates that Maurice knows all about). In addition, who could think a professor and a man of many experiences to be an 'unmitigated disaster'? That is, Maurice does not believe that he was an unmitigated disaster as a father and wants to deny such a suggestion and in doing so to turn the tables once again on his 'wayward' son. Finally, despite his proclaimed desire to reconstitute his relationships with wife and sons, he seems willing to discard them as a lost cause. He has found a new experience to add to his repertoire that displaces them, namely his grandson, who is 'probably the most important thing to me'. It is easier to start again in new pastures than to say sorry in the context of established relationships.

Conclusions: Our Fathers . . .

In Andrew O'Hagen's (1999) Booker nominated novel *Our Fathers*, a recurrent motif is that 'Our Fathers were made for grief'. O'Hagen's fathers are the post-war generation of toughened Scottish men schooled in poverty, war and industrial graft. Hard-drinking and hard-hitting, some of these men sought solutions in collective unionism and socialist housing, others at the bottom of a liquor bottle. Our fathers share aspects of a modernist masculinity forged under specific historical, social and cultural circumstances. This includes the language of men and the metaphors of masculinity with which we have been concerned in this chapter.

Metaphors have both historical specificity and widespread cultural circulation so that much of what we argued to be central to Daniel and Maurice's narratives, including their relationships with their fathers and the concern with metaphors of control and distance, are instantiations of wider discourses of masculinity. In Foucault's terms, Daniel and Maurice are subjects who have been constituted in a particular 'discursive formation' of masculinity, work, intimacy, etc.

Structuring masculinity

In an alternative formulation to that of Foucault, Giddens, drawing from the ethnomethodology of Garfinkel (1967), argues that social order is constructed in and through the everyday activities and accounts (in language) of skilful and knowledgeable actors or members. The resources that actors draw on, and are constituted by, are social in character and indeed social structure (or regular patterns of activity), distributes resources and competencies unevenly between actors. That is, regularities or structural properties of social systems, which are distinct from any given individual, operate to structure what an actor is. Patterns of expectations about what it means to be a man or a woman, and the practices associated with gender, construct men and women differently as subjects. Gendered subjectivity then enables us to act in specifically gendered ways, for example as a mother or father.

Structuration theory (Giddens, 1984) centres on the way agents produce and reproduce social structure through their own actions. Regularized human activity is not brought into being by individual actors as such, but is continually recreated by them via the very means whereby they express themselves as actors. That is, in and through their activities, agents reproduce the conditions that make those activities possible. Having been constituted as a man or woman by gendered expectations and practices, having learned to be a father or mother, we then act in accordance with those rules, reproducing them again.

This 'duality of structure', by which structures are not only constraining but enabling, means that while individual actors are determined and constrained by social forces that lie beyond them, it is those very social structures which enable subjects to act. For example, we are all constructed and constrained by language that pre-exists us, yet, language is also the means and medium of self-awareness and creativity. In other words, we can only say what is sayable in language, yet language is the medium by which we can say anything at all. In this case, it is the structures of masculinity, the patterned language constructs of men, which both constrain men and make them masculine in a specific way.

Metaphors of masculinity are constitutive of our reality, forming powerful ways of thinking about the world. Indeed, masculinity (or masculinities) is not an entity but a discursive construction. Thus, it is the very talk of Daniel, Maurice and other men, that brings masculinity into being, even as they draw off the linguistic resources of their culture to do so. Metaphors guide our actions and highlight some aspects of experience over others (Lakoff and Johnson, 1980). All language is metaphorical in form, but some metaphors are so embedded in our ways of being that they are literalized and invisible. Others offer new ways of thinking and being, by deploying words in strange and innovative ways that are striking in their originality. While the development of self-conscious 'new languages' is associated with change, it is the 'invisible' assumptions of metaphor which maintain, govern and constitute masculinity in daily life.

Metaphors of reason

As Seidler (1989) has argued, since the enlightenment, men have traditionally associated themselves and masculinity with metaphors of reason. Enlightenment philosophy and the discourses of modernity have championed 'reason' as the source of progress and knowledge, manifested in science and increased levels of material production. The price of industrial growth, the spread of secular rationality and the rise of rational decision-making procedures based on calculability, rules and expert knowledge, was that people submitted to a rigorous discipline and urban anonymity. Enlightenment reason was spectacularly successful, or appeared to be in the first instance, in controlling and adapting the environment in the form of the factories, cities and transport systems of the industrial revolution.

The new society required new forms of subjectivity. Factories ran by clock time rather than seasonal time, demanding discipline and control. The division of labour gave men the role of providing the wages of survival and women the domestic duties of child rearing and housekeeping. Managers and bureaucrats, mainly men, were to operate with impersonal task-oriented hierarchical rules. Modernity is an epoch not just of external domination, but of self-control. Thus, 'As men it is difficult not to be "control freaks". This is the history we inherit' (Seidler, 1989: 63).

Control and distance, as manifested in the talk of Daniel and Maurice, are central metaphors of contemporary masculinity. Control over others and control over ourselves. Distance from others, distance from ourselves. In particular, the association of rationality with masculinity involves the self-discipline of, and distance from, the language of emotions. While it is part of contemporary 'common sense' that men 'suppress' feelings, this is better put as the failure to learn a productive language of emotion. Instead, men's relationships are often inscribed by spatial metaphors including emotional 'distance' and 'controlling their own space' that mark a lack of communication. The male imperative to control emotion, allied to men's lack of experience with the language of emotions, their inability to name emotions and recognize them as such, can, ironically, lead to confrontational incidents. Emotions like anger can be controlled, metaphorically held within, only to burst out in an explosive moment.

The language of modernity stresses the gulf between the masculine public world and the feminine private world. Men are acculturalized to seek esteem through public performance and recognition of achievement. This can take many forms – from violence through sport to educational qualifications and occupational status. It also lends itself to hyper-individualism, competitiveness and separation from the relational. It is 'I' who must perform and 'I' who will take the prize and public accolades. Performance orientation of this kind – from work to sexuality – is manifested in grandiosity on the one hand, and deep feelings of inadequacy and depression on the other, (for the performances are never outstanding enough to satisfy the internal father). The other side of performance-achievement is the need to take flight from the pressure of constant reflexivity and self-interrogation. As we have seen, this is commonly sought after through compulsive behaviours (addictions) centred on work and drugs. That is, the achievement orientation of 'successful' men and the drug abuse of social 'failures' are two sides of the same coin. Both have their roots in the scripts of contemporary masculinity and familial relations.

Finally, we have frequently noted the tensions and/or contradictions within the narratives that Jake, Daniel and Maurice have provided us with. This is not to be read as personal criticism. First, we intend no censure of our subjects, for we are more concerned with the consequences of verbal actions than the pointless attribution of individual blame. Second, the stories we present highlight the multiple identities that constitute actors within contemporary western culture. Not only are we fabricated with unconscious linguistic choices and biochemical responses (retrospectively verbalized as motivations), but our surface discourses are also inconsistent with each other. As was argued in Chapter two, no single identity acts as an overarching organizing core since identities shift according to how subjects are addressed or represented. Further, it is not that we *have* multiple identities (which would imply a subject who possesses) but that we *are* a verbal weave constituted as multiple and contradictory identities which cross-cut or dislocate each other.

Note

1 Where the quotation is taken from a part of the interview not reproduced more fully here it is marked with a # sign.

5

The Language of Ethnicity
The Unbearable Lightness of Being Polish?

This chapter is concerned with ethnicity and nationality as discursive–performative constructions manifested through the achievements of speaking subjects. That is, ethnic and national identities are unpredictable and unstable cultural productions with which we identify. They are not universal or absolute existent 'things'. Rather, ethnicity is a cultural accomplishment. In particular, we set out to demonstrate that ethnic identification is attained through the linguistic action and interaction of specifically located speaking subjects.

Consequently, following a brief discussion of ethnicity as a concept understood from within cultural studies, we devote the substantive part of the chapter to an analysis of empirical data gathered from elderly Poles. Our claim is that these subjects construct ethnicity as a mobile and plastic category constructed through everyday language usage in specific contexts. That said, ethnic categories are commonly stabilized, at least temporarily, by social practice within particular socio-cultural contexts. Thus, what it is to be Polish in the village of Korzeniec is flexible and variable, as we demonstrate below, while at the same time being subject to regulation through the specificities of Polish history and culture.

The concept of ethnicity

Traditionally, the concept of ethnicity has stressed the sharing of norms, values, beliefs, cultural symbols and practices. The formation of 'ethnic groups' relies on common cultural signifiers which have developed under specific historical, social and political contexts and which encourage a sense of belonging based, at least in part, on a common mythological ancestry. As Hall writes:

> The term ethnicity acknowledges the place of history, language and culture in the construction of subjectivity and identity, as well as the fact that all discourse is placed, positioned, situated, and all knowledge is contextual. (Hall, 1996c: 446)

However, ethnicity is not based on primordial ties or universal cultural characteristics *possessed* by a specific group for identities are unpredictable productions of a specific history and culture. What it *means* to be a person is a social and cultural construction 'all the way down'. As our data below suggest, there is no universal 'essence' of ethnicity, rather, what it means to be Polish, English, Australian, Ukrainian, etc. changes over time and from place to place. Consequently, we hold to an anti-essentialist concept of ethnicity (see Chapter 2). Whereas essentialism takes verbal descriptions of ethnic groups to be reflecting a stable underlying identity as its referent, anti-essentialism takes words to be constitutive of the categories they represent to us so that ethnicity is a malleable discursive construction. That is, ethnicity is formed by the way we speak about group identities and identify with the signs and symbols that constitute ethnicity for us.

Ethnicity is a *relational* concept concerned with categories of self-identification and social ascription. What we think of as our identity is dependent on what we think we are *not*. The Scots are not the English, who are not Americans, who are not Russians, who are not Ukrainians, who are not Poles. Consequently, ethnicity is best understood as a process of boundary formation constructed and maintained under specific socio-historical conditions (Barth, 1969). Further, ethnicity is constituted through power relations between groups. It signals relations of marginality, of the centre and the periphery, in the context of changing historical forms and circumstances. Here, the centre and the margin are to be grasped through the politics of representation, for as Brah argues:

> It is necessary for it to become axiomatic that what is *represented* as the 'margin' is not marginal at all but is a *constitutive effect of the representation itself*. The 'centre' is no more a centre than is the 'margin'. (Brah, 1996: 226, emphasis in original)

Discourses of ethnic centrality and marginality are commonly articulated with those of nationality. History is strewn with examples of how one ethnic group has been defined as central and superior to a marginal 'other'. Nazi Germany, apartheid South Africa and 'ethnic cleansing' in Bosnia are among the most clear-cut examples of this phenomenon. However, the metaphor of superiority and subordination is also applicable to contemporary Britain, America and Australia. Thus, ethnicity has been closely allied to nationalisms that conceive of the 'nation' as sharing a culture and requiring that ethnic boundaries should not cut across political ones (though of course they do).

National identities

The nation-state is a political concept that refers to an administrative apparatus deemed to have sovereignty over a specific space or territory within the nation-state system. By contrast, national-identity is a form of imaginative identification with the symbols and discourses of the nation-state. Thus, nations are not simply political formations but systems of cultural representation through which national identity is continually reproduced as discursive action.

The symbolic and discursive dimension of national identity narrates and creates the idea of origins, continuity and tradition. This process does not necessarily attach ethnicity or national identity to the nation-state as various global Diaspora – African, Jewish, Indian, Chinese, Polish, English, Irish, etc. – attest. Further, few states have ethnically homogeneous populations. Smith (1990) not only distinguishes between *civic*/political conceptions of nations and *ethnic* ones, but also lists over 60 states that are constituted by more than one national or ethnic culture. Consequently, ethnicity and nationality are different concepts, so that one may be ethnically Polish, but of British nationality. However, for most of the informants in our study the two concepts were conflated. Being Polish was a matrix of cultural, linguistic and religious identifications and practices as well as a political and territorial concept (though the national soil concerned was more likely to be that of the village than of the nation-state).

Narratives of unity

Cultures are not static entities but are constituted by changing practices and meanings that operate at different social levels. Any given national culture is understood and acted upon by different social groups so that governments, ethnic groups and classes may perceive it in divergent ways. Representations of national culture are snapshots of the symbols and practices that have come to the fore at specific historical conjunctures. They are generated by distinctive groups of people and deployed for specific purposes. That ethnic and/or national identities appear to be unified is the product of those stories that through images, symbols and rituals represent to us the 'shared' meanings of nationhood (Bhabha, 1990). National identity is a way of unifying cultural diversity so that, as Hall argues:

> Instead of thinking of national cultures as unified, we should think of them as a discursive device which represents difference as unity or identity. They are cross-cut by deep internal divisions and differences, and 'unified' only through the exercise of different forms of cultural power. (Hall, 1992b: 297)

National identity is a form of identification with representations of shared experiences and history told through stories, literature, popular culture and the media. It is in this sense that the 'nation' is an 'imagined community' with national identity a construction assembled through symbols and rituals in relation to territorial and administrative categories (Anderson, 1983). Narratives of nationhood emphasize the traditions and continuity of the nation as being 'in the nature of things' together with a foundational myth of collective origin. This in turn both assumes and produces the linkage between national identity and a pure, original people or 'folk' tradition.

Language, identity and identification

Ethnic identity is not a fixed universal essence, but an ordered way of speaking about persons. Ethnicity is always already constituted by representations formed through regulatory discourses of power. Thus, the language of ethnicity does not reflect a pre-given reality but constitutes the parameters of ethnicity and establishes pertinent subject positions from which to speak about what it means to be Polish, Ukrainian, American, etc. In this way, ethnicity is performative; a citation and reiteration of regulatory discourses of identity (see Butler, 1993 and Chapters 2 and 4, this volume).

It is important to note that the regulatory aspects of discourse involve an element of identification or emotional investment that partially suture or stitch together discourses and psychic forces (Hall, 1996a). Identification is understood as an affiliation or emotional tie with an idealized and fantasized object. Further, identification constitutes an exclusionary matrix by which identification with one form of identity frequently involves the repudiation of another (as we shall see below, being Polish for our informants meant repudiating Ukrainians). Consequently, though identity is constituted in and through language, subjects cannot simply cast off one self-description and adopt another at will. Ethnic identities may be social constructions, but they are regulated and show a marked tendency towards sedimentation. Poles and Ukrainians cannot in one overnight decision stop being the subjects that history and cultures have forged of them. Change is possible but, as most psychologists and therapists argue, it is a slow and difficult process.

Nevertheless, emotional identification with any given form of identity is only ever partial. There is always a gap between fantasy and materiality leaving Butler (1993) and Rose (1997) to argue for the instability of identity. As we noted in Chapter 2, the speaking subject, as contrasted with an unproblematic adoption of subject positions, is capable of inventive and creative use of language. Ethnicity remains an achievement of language users, not a crude reflection of one-dimensional discursive subject positions.

Further, identifications can be multiple and need not involve the repudiation of all other positions. People are composed of not one, but several, sometimes contradictory identities, enabling subjects to assume a variety of shifting identities at different times and places. Indeed, it is

not so much that we possess multiple identities, as that we are constituted as a weave of different accounts of the self – we are inter-
discursive. That self-identity commonly takes the form of a unity is yet
another story of our times. Thus, not only may a given subject enact
apparently contradictory identities, but also, ethnic identities are articulated with those of class, gender, nation and age. Subjects cannot legiti-
mately be reduced to ethnicity, nor can ethnicity be represented in a
pure form, set apart from other facets of our acculturated selves.

Polish identity: an achievement of everyday language

The data-analytical aspects of this chapter have two central purposes.
First, we shall buttress the theoretical understanding of discourse analysis put forward in Chapter 2 by showing how this methodology, which
focuses on the structures of language, can provide evidence for an anti-
essentialist understanding of ethnic and national identity. Second, we
shall indicate how the specificities of the socio-political and cultural
contexts in which our narratives were collected contribute to the construction of Polishness as a form of ethnicity.

Given the significance of context, the questions we ask are not about
what it means to be Polish *per se*, but rather what it means to be Polish
for a particular set of informants located at a specific conjuncture of time
and space. Further, we shall be exploring ethnicity as a relational concept constructed through reference to an 'out-group' who do not maintain the specified form of ethnic identification. Finally, we seek to
illustrate through the presentation of empirical evidence, the shifting
and changeable character of the ethnicity with which the informants
identify.

Markers of ethnicity

To support the claim that ethnicity is a category constructed in and
through discourse, we shall first identify those linguistic resources that
are particularly evident in its construction. Thus, Wodak and her
associates (1999) focus on those linguistic means that serve to construct
unity, sameness, difference and origin. The following are said to be of
particular significance:

- *Personal reference*. For example, anthroponymic generic terms (e.g.
  ethnic labels) and personal pronouns (e.g. 'we' and 'they')
- *Spatial reference*. For example, toponyms/geonyms (i.e. names of
  places) and spatial reference constructed through persons (e.g. 'with
  us')

- *Temporal reference.* For example, temporal prepositions (e.g. 'then') and adverbs of time (e.g. 'long ago'). (adapted from Wodak et al., 1999: 35)

In addition, Wodak et al. propose vagueness, euphemisms, linguistic hesitation and disruption, slips, allusion, rhetorical questions and modes of discursive representation (whether what is said is reported as said by someone else or not) as linguistic devices deployed in the construction of ethnicity. While we acknowledge the usefulness of this approach, we seek to complement it with an alternative technique for studying narratives advanced by Meinhof and Galasiński (2000) in their exploration of conflicting identities on the former East–West German border. They propose to look for indications of conflicting voices in the narratives of informants. That is, they anticipate evidence of 'competing' perspectives in the world views that informants' narratives put forward. Subjects are constituted with multiple and potentially contradictory identities.

Meinhof and Galasiński argue that the explicit presence of conflicting voices in the discourse of informants (e.g. through named roles, labelling of groups, direct quotations of what others say, or said) represents a distancing of actors from views which they have already acknowledged as alternative perspectives to their own. Clear and cohesive expression in the discourse is indicative, write Meinhof and Galasiński (2000), of tension and ambivalence that have, to some extent, either been already resolved or coped with by a hardening of their attitudes against them. The less explicit presence of these other voices (as in changes of pronouns) indicates a potential threat to the construction of a coherent identity. These are accompanied by other linguistic phenomena such as dis-cohesion (e.g. long pauses or breaks in the grammar).

We are not of course suggesting that it is only the elements discussed above that have ethnicity-construction potential. On the contrary, these are simply the means that are of particular importance in the specific project at hand. However, we shall be drawing upon the entire 'tool-kit' described in Chapter 3. In particular, we shall argue that it is the configuration of agency structures in the narratives that contribute in a major way to the construction of Polishness.

The data

The analysis in this chapter is based on seven interviews collected during the summer of 1999 in the village of Korzeniec, located in the South-east of Poland. Administratively, it belongs to the community (*gmina*) of Bircza, within the county of Przemyśl. The Polish-Ukrainian border is situated approximately 12 km to the South-east and 30 km to the East. All the interviewees have lived locally since at least before the Second World War and all were aged over 70. The interviews were open-ended and, in so far as it was possible, the interviewees topically controlled them. The interviewees were informed that the purpose of the interview was to learn something about 'how life was in their youth'. All interviewees knew the interviewer as someone who spent his holidays in the area and some knew him by name.

The historical context

Although the agenda of each interview was set up in a different way, all lingered around the events of the Second World War and its immediate aftermath. Indeed, historical context is required to fully appreciate the significance of the data, including the preoccupation with wartime events.

It must be stressed that we do not seek to attain a universal 'historical truth' in our account, nor do we wish to make judgements about 'factual' accuracy. Rather, we are interested in relating events as interviewees and local publications see them. Certainly the accuracy of such accounts is likely to be challenged by those constructed in these stories as 'enemies'. Indeed, one of our interviewees told us of a visit to Canada where 'her' story was challenged by alternative accounts. In short, we are only concerned with the local Polish perspective on the historical events in question, for they form the context of our data.

Our account is largely based upon publications that were made available by the community council in Bircza (Włodek, 1981; Zatwarnicki, 1997) along with an historical debate in the local newspaper (Kotlarczyk, 1997). A striking aspect of the recently published pamphlet (Zatwarnicki, 1997) about the Bircza community, is that the chapter devoted to its history apportions about the same space to the events of 1945 and 1946 as it does to the previous six centuries. Further, the account ended in 1946, as if the 51 years between 1946 and 1997 had not occurred.

According to the aforementioned pamphlet (and the other sources mentioned above), 1945 and 1946 saw three major attacks by Ukrainian separatist troops (Ukrainian Uprising Army – UPA) on Bircza with a resultant heavy loss of life. Witnesses described the most appalling atrocities committed on the inhabitants, including setting surrounding villages on fire and torturing civilians as well as Polish military personnel. The hostilities ended when a major force of the Polish army moved into the area and defeated the UPA.

These events are still very much present in the living memory not only of those who experienced them (such as our interviewees), but also the younger generations. Quite clearly they are formative of the identities of people living in Bircza. All our interviewees spent a long time talking about them and all of them struggled to control their emotions as they did so. As we shall show later, there was no hesitation in apportioning blame in the narratives of our informants, for whom responsibility clearly rested with the Ukrainian side.

The dark memories of these events were rekindled when in 1996 Bircza community council received a request for permission to erect a monument to the Ukrainian soldiers 'murdered by Poles'. This petition resulted in an open meeting of the council where the project was rejected. Further, the local newspaper unequivocally cast aside any possibility of Poles taking responsibility for starting the events that led to the killing of Ukrainian troops.

When we set out to obtain the interviews we were aware of the implicit enmity against Ukrainians present in the area. However, we sought to obtain information mostly about pre-Second World War times, speculating that the time elapsed between then and the present would result in a certain 'romanticization' of the narratives that we heard. However, what we received were, for the most part, stories centred on 1945 and 1946. They were narratives of ordeal, fear, hatred and anger. They were stories of surviving the worst possible nightmare.

As expected, the main groups of actors who featured in the collected narratives were Poles and Ukrainians and it was through the relationship between these two groups that ethnicity, or more particularly what it means to be Polish, was achieved. There was one other group against which Poles and Ukrainians were positioned: the Jewish community that lived in Bircza before the war, during which time they were either killed or deported by the Nazis.

The anti-essentialist view from Bircza

In the discussion that follows we shall demonstrate that even though ethnicity is commonly held to have clear characteristics, these are represented at one and the same time as being marked by unchanging criteria *and* as being fluid and problematic. Furthermore, we shall show that ethnicity is constructed not so much as 'something' a particular group possesses, but rather as a set of characteristics that differentiates groups from one another. Ethnicity is relational and context-bound so that it cannot be separated from the contingent circumstances of the people 'claiming' it. In other words, we shall argue that the constructions of ethnicity encountered in our interviews are carried out through the construction of the 'Other'. We shall focus particularly upon the 'structures of agency' enacted within the narratives that systematically position ethnic groups in similar agentive positions in relation to each other.

A view through the Other

To observe that ethnicity is predominantly constructed through the presence of an 'Other', leads investigation not to the question 'who are Poles?', but rather to the issue of how Poles are different. That is, we must ask about the relationship of Poles to the 'out-group'. Ethnicity in our narratives is a relational concept, it is not a condition people are in, or set of traits people possess, but a relationship between groups of people. Witness the following two examples.

For the ease of probably most of our readers, when quoting from the data in the main body of our exposition we shall only provide the translation of the extracts. We have put their Polish originals in the Appendix. In the translations we attempted to render the style and the content of the originals, thus we left all their unclearness, ambiguities and (grammatical) inconsistencies of the originals, and have not attempted to impose an interpretation of them through our translations.

Extract 1

BT, male, aged 76[1]

BT: Only Korzeniec was Polish and Bircza was Polish. And such was the villages there Wygon over there Hominskie but they were mixed and Ukrainians were mixed they lived there in the households and they hated Poles.
DG: And Poles liked them?
BT: Pardon?
DG: And Poles liked them?
BT: No.
DG: No?
BT: Of course they didn't like [them]. No. It spoke Ukrainian and in Polish they even didn't want to speak to the Poles.

This extract, typical of what we heard in the interviews, clearly positions the two ethnic groups, Poles and Ukrainians, against each other (note that the interviewee uses an ethnic term 'Rusin' in reference to Ukrainians – it is not, to our knowledge, marked). By constructing the two groups as hating each other, the speaker positions these two ethnicities in stark opposition, an action that simultaneously draws out the clear distinction between them.

Particularly noteworthy is the speaker's use of the generic, unmitigated form of utterance. The interviewee talks about *all* Ukrainians and responds to the interviewer's question by referring to *all* Poles. Further, he refers to Ukrainians as 'it' (in the Polish original the interviewer uses the impersonal form of the verb) by which the genericness of this representation of Ukrainians is taken to a higher level of abstraction. There are no longer individual Ukrainians who all hate Poles, but a mass entity that does so. It is, of course, as the history of ethnic conflict tells us again and again, so much easier to abuse an inanimate object or undifferentiated 'lump' than an individual person.

The form of the verb used in the context above is quite unusual in Polish although it is used locally, mostly when the speaker does not want to assign responsibility to whoever did something. In this respect it is similar to the passive voice in English, in which agency can be deleted from the structure of the sentence (see Chapter 3). However, in this case the identity of the social actor is clear and as such the form must be seen as marked. We would suggest that the explanation for this usage is the drive to provide a further distinction between the two ethnic groups. Note that the interviewee constructs the hate relationship as unidirectional, it is the Ukrainians who hate Poles. The bi-directionality of the hate relationship is introduced by the interviewer in such a way as to position the two groups on a par in espousing negative feelings towards each other. However, the interviewee undermines this apparent equality by introducing the impersonal form of the verb.

The distinction between the two groups is further reinforced by the frequent use of the pronoun 'we' in the narratives. Consider the extract below in which the interviewee is describing religious practices from before the war.

Extract 2

BT, male, aged 76

BT: Because there were Ukrainians here. They spoke Ukrainian. Oh, this is the way they spoke [*imitates Ukrainian*].
DG: They spoke? [*imitates Ukrainian*]
BT: They spoke. They spoke in Ukrainian everything [*imitates Ukrainian*]. So you could tell them by their language but everything was in Ukrainian.
DG: I see.
BT: Poles were Polish but there were more Ukrainians.
DG: Mmm.
BT: So Ukrainian that they had separate [church, religious] holidays. Other [church, religious] holidays they had and we had Polish other [church, religious] holidays.

In addition to exhibiting religion as one dimension of ethnicity (which we discuss later in the chapter), this extract demonstrates once again the linguistic effort that has been made by the speaker to set apart the two ethnic groups. The central mechanism of interest to us is the use of the pronoun 'we', reputed to be one of the most manipulative words in the lexicon.

The speaker's 'we' is interesting because, while possibly being inclusive of the interviewer, it certainly sets Poles apart from the Ukrainian out-group (on the inclusivity and exclusivity of 'we' see Mühlhaüsler and Harré, 1990; also Wilson, 1990). Moreover, the 'we' that refers to Poles cannot sensibly be used without the implied out-group. That is, 'we' Poles are defined by being other than Ukrainians. In such a way *BT* defines the holidays he celebrated as simultaneously 'ours' and Polish, as opposed to those celebrated by Ukrainians, whose holidays were simply 'other', being not of the Polish in-group. Thus does the empirical evidence give support to the theoretical point that ethnicity is a relational concept in which it is only through the implied or explicit presence of the Other that one can identify oneself in ethnic terms.

This theoretical argument finds further support in our data when Poles and Ukrainians are defined as those being in a particular relationship (hating each other), or as engaged in different religious practices (having different holidays). Such constructions are typical of the narratives we have elicited, and, in fact, we have not found statements in which the speakers would describe themselves as Poles, i.e. people having certain characteristics. If Polishness has certain features they are normally described in terms of not being Ukrainian. Ethnicity is always constructed through difference and opposition, rather than a timeless characteristic of a particular group of people.

Language and religion

As the extracts below suggest, being Polish, Ukrainian or Jewish means having certain religious practices and speaking different languages. However, we shall argue that this ethnicity-defining view of language is not an easy and unambiguous one. Rather, the relationship between language and ethnicity is fundamentally dilemmatic. We follow here the work of Billig and his associates (Billig et al., 1988) in adopting the view that the ideologies underpinning discourses are not free of contradictions. For example, language can be used as a means of identifying someone's identity, only for it to be denied that it constitutes such an indication.

Let us begin by exploring the ways in which language and religion are deployed to circumscribe ethnicity. For example, we have already shown in Extract 2 a description of Ukrainians that defines them in terms of their language and church holidays. Indeed, the description of the two nations in terms of their different religious holidays was the most frequent way in which Poles and Ukrainians were distinguished. Note the following extract:

Extract 3

KA, female, aged 82

KA: And there was such harmony, you know, and there were several [over ten] Ukrainian families and when there were Polish religious holidays they would come to visit us for the Polish holidays. Parents, children would come and be happy. And when there were their holidays we would go to visit them. Such was the harmony. Later you know something happened there was such strong hatred.
DG: Mmm.

KA: Slaughter. They would beat.
DG: So what happened?
KA: How would I know?
DG: How did it come to that?
KA: They say it was priests that incited them.
DG: Polish or Ukrainian?
KA: Ukrainian priests.

Of particular interest here is the unequivocal positioning of blame upon the shoulders of the Ukrainians for the hatred and, more generally, the loss of harmony, in the relationship between them and Poles. Later we shall show that this is part of a pattern of discursive representations in which Poles are more often than not represented as merely the recipients of Ukrainians' (negative) actions, while being themselves passive and thus blameless. In the next extract the speaker's story explicitly points to the significance of speaking a language and being able to say a prayer in it as a test of ethnicity.

Extract 4

KZ, male, aged 83

Talking about his survival strategies during the war

KZ: And so when I got there with a Jew. A Jew and I. We walked together. So the Jew went to Jews' [houses] to get something to eat and I went to Ukrainians.
DG: Mmm.
KZ: And it caught me and is chasing me and I say I am Ukrainian.
DG: Mmm.
KZ: What do you want of me? [*speaks Ukrainian*]
DG: Mmm.
KZ: He says we'll see whether you are Ukrainian or not [*part Polish, part Ukrainian*]. And I went to the house and say the prayer [*imperative*]. So I make the sign of cross and the Father and the Son and the Holy Ghost [*part Polish, part Ukrainian*] three times, you know [*recites 'Our Father' in Ukrainian*] and only then when I said 'Our Father'.
DG: And did they believe?
KZ: Oh immediately Hantka give him some bread and milk [*imitates Ukrainian*]
DG: I see [*laughs*] and they would not have given to a Pole?
KZ: If I could not [say the prayer] they would have killed [me] immediately [literally 'cut'].

Language and religion revisited

Academic research confirms *KZ*'s popular anthropology in that local language and religion (together with occupation) are considered to be the main cultural criteria identifying Polish peasants of the 19th and early 20th centuries (see Stomma, 1986). However, the problem is that these criteria are undermined in the very same narratives that set them up as indicators of ethnic belonging. Language and religion as markers of ethnic difference are put into question when they are also deployed to confirm similarities between ethnicities. Simply speaking, the Polish or Ukrainian languages are no longer a sufficient characteristic of ethnic identity as the following examples suggest.

Extract 5

PT, female, aged 72 and ZT, male aged 79

DG: You say that Poles married Ukrainians, I mean Poles [male] to Ukrainians [female] or Poles [female] to Ukrainians [male]. And did they get married to Jews?
ZT: No no.
DG: Why not?
[. . .]
PT: It's a different faith.
ZT: It had to be a Jew.
DG: But Ukrainians it's also a different faith, isn't it?
PT: It doesn't matter it was only in the Ukrainian language and Polish.
DG: I see.
PT: And Jews have a completely different creed.

Here, those who had earlier been described in very distinct terms are now united to form a contrast with a third group with the magical result that previous differences disappear. Apparently, religious difference no longer matters, for it has become the same practice spoken in a different language. When contrasted with the Jews, Ukrainians and Poles are seen to be of the same faith set apart only by language. Indeed, language as a marker of ethnicity is itself capable of being undermined as in the following two extracts where Ukrainians are constructed as speaking Polish.

Extract 6

MD, female, aged 81

MD: And [Ukrainians] came to your house and took a cow or a piglet or a hen or whatever. They came because they needed to eat. And they spoke Polish, because Ukrainians also spoke Polish.

Extract 7

BT, male, aged 76

BT: Now there are only Poles. And occasionally there are still Ukrainians still there are some Ukrainians when you to Kalwaria [and] Wola Ruska there are some Ukrainians but they don't speak Ukrainian any more but Polish.
DG: Why not?
BT: Because there are more Poles so who will he speak to?

In both extracts the speakers make the assumption that Ukrainians speak Ukrainian. Although *MD* refers to Ukrainians as speaking Polish, there is a clear presupposing that it is a second language. Similarly, the contrasting use of 'but' in *BT*'s response also presupposes that Ukrainians would speak Ukrainian. Yet, both interviewees use generic terms to refer to the Polish speaking Ukrainians: 'they' do it and still 'they' are Ukrainian. Speaking Polish is no guarantee of being identified as Polish.

We think that these representations are significant in understanding discursive constructions of ethnicity. We would argue that what the speaker does here is to construct ethnicity not only as a relational concept, but also one which is context-bound. Whether language and religion are taken as a marker of difference and ethnicity depends on the context and what is at stake in each case. Thus, where Poles are not a clear ethnic majority (as in pre-war times), it is the paramount task to make sure that Ukrainians are clearly distinguished from Poles. However, under the different circumstances of a later era differentiation between Christians and Jews supersedes this priority. Consequently, Polish and Ukrainian ethnic opposition is put aside so that these former enemies come to occupy common ground that differentiates them from a third group.

The context-bound character of ethnicity is not only associated with the ambiguities of language and religion. There are other ways in which ethnicity is associated with the here and now, or here and then, of the lives of our interviewees. Thus, in the next section we shall demonstrate that being Polish or Ukrainian is inextricably bound to the socio-economic circumstances of the village in question. However, our interviewees go even further than that suggesting that the contexts in which people live allow them to 'pick and choose' their ethnicity. The interviewees appear to make an ultimate assault on the notion that ethnicity is something stable and unchangeable; but then, in a paradoxical circle this view is itself eroded.

Ethnicity and working practices

We begin our discussion of the context-bound character of ethnicity by showing that its construction is clearly associated with the everyday practices of the people concerned. In other words, for our interviewees, to be Polish means to be Polish in the community of Bircza. Witness the following examples:

Extract 8

GkT, male, aged 80

DG: So did Poles marry Jews?

GkT: Here they didn't because there was more field. And the Jew will not go to the field to the cows.

DG: I see.

GkT: So why would he get married?

DG: Sure.

GkT: He felt in love and the Jewish girl wept later so even one Ukrainian had a Jewish girl in his neighbourhood, but so what? They liked each other but he will not get married because crops would be cut by sickle, scythe.

Extract 9

KA, female, aged 82

DG: So the Ukrainians also went like this [with bare feet]? They were so poor?

KA: All. All like that.

DG: Jew as well?

KA: Jews are Jews. They had some shoes because they every Jew had to have a business.

DG: Mmm.

KA: I mean it's called business. A little shop here with soap here with something and here with something here with cloth everything they had there. Always every week he had to have such [shoes?] for Friday as we for religious holidays [Christmas] once a year. They had them every week.

DG: Mmm.

KA: And Sabbath they baked rolls and a hen had to be there and broth and little rolls and they lit up lights and Poles went there and washed cleaned for them a few pennies he gave or something to eat. That's the way it was.

In these two extracts, ethnicity is marked out by the occupations performed by members of the in-group and out-group. For example, Jews do not farm the land but have businesses, while Poles help clean for them when they are barred by religious belief from doing so themselves. Crucially, such constructions are only possible in a community context in which Jews actually live and there are people who are farmers. We would speculate that such descriptions of Jews and Poles are no longer possible among the younger generations for there are no longer any Jews in Bircza and the surrounding villages. Nor would they be likely to be possible within urban communities where there are no farmers. Thus do we see the way that ethnicity is articulated with social class and consequently that Polishness must be redefined according to the context.

Polishness is further localized when the interviewer asks about the movement of Poland's national territorial borders. Before the Second World War, Bircza was just about in the middle of Poland and about 500 km away from the eastern boundary. The movement of Poland's borders, combined with the incorporation of the entire Ukraine into the Soviet Union, led to the village becoming a mere 12 km from the frontier on foot and about 30 km from a car crossing. We were interested in finding out whether these facts were significant in the consciousness of our interviewees. In exploring this issue, we were mindful of Billig's (1995) argument that nation-states are celebrated in their entirety. This is why there cannot be two Macedonias, a reference to the recent attempt to create a new state called Macedonia which resulted in a fierce diplomatic row. Billig writes:

> America is not beautiful because it offers a stunning waterfall near Buffalo or a canyon a couple of thousand miles away in Arizona. The country as a totality is praised as special, as 'the beautiful'. (Billig, 1995: 75)

Following this argument, the movement of a border and the loss of a substantial part of the realm should feature extremely significantly in the consciousness of those whose country was being taken apart. Yet, in fact, our interviewees barely noticed the change and did not really know what the interviewer was talking about. The only attempt to engage with the question was the following:

Extract 10

KA, female, aged 82

DG: Do you remember how it was when the border suddenly got moved with Bircza well, not right on, but almost on the border. How was it?

KA: How am I supposed to know? Well, somehow we were not interested. Perhaps I won't say so accurately because we did know that it was moved but there was no radio or television nothing. Nobody was interested and one did not read newspapers.

The claims of 'knowing' about the border movement could, in our view, be no more than an attempt to fend off the potentially face-threatening act of admitting ignorance (on positive face, see Brown and Levinson, 1987). Throughout the interview, the interviewee constructed an image of an enlightened person who travelled outside Poland. To admit ignorance would be damaging to this persona. In any case, along with her fellow villagers, she claims to be uninterested in the movement of the border.

For us, *KA*'s words are akin to *BT*'s expression of uncertainty about the national belonging of the main town in the region, Przemyśl, situated approximately 30 km away and a safe haven for a lot of the inhabitants of Bircza during the conflict with the Ukrainian troops. *BT* says:

Extract 11

BT, male, aged 76

BT: Yes, and we fled to Przemyśl.
DG: But to Przemyśl it's towards the Ukraine.
BT: But Przemyśl was not Ukrainian was it?
DG: No Przemyśl is Polish.

Even though *BT* only asks for confirmation of what he already suspects, it is significant in our opinion that such a question could be asked at all in the light of Billig's aforementioned argument regarding the unity of national identification. Certainly Billig (1995) offers a persuasive description of banal nationalism. However, Billig was largely concerned with the presence of nationalism in the public sphere: the media, official historical accounts, or within political discourse. By contrast, we are dealing with semi-private accounts of ethnicity and ethnic belonging. These, as we hope to have shown above, are more localized and cut off from the celebration of the national realm in its entirety. The Poles in our interviews are not Poles from Warsaw or Kraków, they are Poles from Bircza. We would also posit that the question of what constitutes Poles from Warsaw or Kraków does not arise in Bircza.

Finally, on this point, following years of holiday presence in the community of Korzeniec, the interviewer, after being someone from Kraków, which is far enough away, became someone from England and was often asked about his new country. One of the questions asked was about what people sow in England. This question clearly illustrates the local perspective on a different country. In other words, England was constructed in the same way that Poland is constructed; as the 'Heimat' (to use the German word) around us.

Ethnicities to choose from . . .

In this section of the chapter we want to explore further our informants' 'naïve' anti-essentialist view of ethnicity. First, we shall explore the way in which the adoption of ethnic identification is justified; second, we shall suggest that our informants' ethnicity is flexible enough to allow for a degree of 'choice' over the form in which it is embraced.

The first extract we discuss refers again to the hate relationship between Poles and Ukrainians. However, this time the generic statement about Poles is not left alone for the interviewer to interpret, but, rather, it is offered with a justification. Polishness in this extract is constructed through a burden of authenticated and legitimated hate. It is noteworthy that the interviewer is challenged during the exchange and his non-confrontational style is used to support the interviewee's argument.

Extract 12

KZ, male, aged 83

KZ: If you had come I was in [the village of] Borownica. Borownica screamed that that they [Ukrainian troops] press them strongly because all the villages around were Ukrainian. Borownica was Polish. So we went to Borownica. We were in Borownica. There once you know Ukrainians went to a house and cut [killed] everything and brought to the well.

DG: Mmmm.

KZ: And they threw into the well. And we came and only one child only a girl escaped and to Borownica and told [us] about it. So when we came to that house and that papers everything blood on the ground. Papers, everything strewn all over in the house.

DG: Mmm.

KZ: We went looking we saw it in the well that all is thrown into the well. What would you say?

DG: I would not like to have seen it. There are no words.

KZ: Well, what would you say?

DG: There are no words.

KZ: So then when a Pole saw such a thing he would take the skin off him as well.

DG: Yes, yes, and you think this hatred has been there till today?

KZ: Now I am past it because you know it was 50 years ago.

Here, KZ's repetition of the question 'What would you say?', despite the interviewer's response that he cannot find words to respond to the atrocity, seeks to confirm the interviewer's inability to talk about it, and, at the same time, underscores the horror of the experience. The entire narrative leads to a statement of what Poles would do and serves as a justification for a hostile attitude towards Ukrainians. Thus, one of the most frequent elements in the description of Poles and Ukrainians, namely their relationship of hatred, is legitimated. If Polish ethnicity is defined by hating Ukrainians, then, or so it is argued, such antipathy is legitimated through its roots in experience.

The important point for us is that this 'naïve' or popular view of ethnicity is once again anti-essentialist in its construction, for ethnicity is not an *a priori* given set of characteristics but is negotiated through experience. If ethnicity requires justification, then it cannot be treated as a universal and essential part of self. Rather, it is a changeable and negotiable characteristic that is subject to the self's reflexive capabilities.

This form of ethnicity has some affinity with Bourdieu's (1984, 1991) notion of habitus (for a discussion of national identity in terms of habitus, see Wodak et al., 1999). That is, ethnicity can be understood as dispositions or internalized group norms whose task is to regulate and generate the actions (practices), perceptions and representations of individuals. As such, ethnicity mediates the social structures which speakers inhabit.

Of course, dispositions are not unchangeable. Rather, they are historically dynamic and articulated with the socio-economic and cultural configurations of the community that is characterized by them. Thus, the changes that were engendered by the Second World War and the subsequent hostilities between the Polish and the Ukrainian communities, influenced or 'modified' that set of dispositions associated with what it is to be Polish. In the extract above, what we see is a popular account of that change taking place (for an account of change in the economic habitus, see Bourdieu, 2000).

As a final piece of evidence for the plasticity of ethnicity, we would like to discuss extracts in which our interviewees construct ethnicity as something that can be chosen, picked from a range of options.

Extract 13

PT, female, aged 72 and ZT, male aged 79

PT: And Jews have a completely different creed. And . . .
ZT: In Bircza there even was one family such that he had to convert.
DG: I see.
ZT: He had to convert to Polish and she was Polish and he liked her and had to convert from Jewry to . . .
PT: To Polish.
ZT: To Polish.

Extract 14

KZ, male, aged 83

This extract includes interventions from KZ's wife who was present at the interview yet did not take part and thus her demographics are unavailable. Her interventions were limited to a few sentences.

DG: You are saying you told me that Poles [male] married Ukrainians [female]. Was there a lot of it before the war?
KZ: There was a lot everywhere I don't know, in Korzeniec there wasn't there were only three Ukrainians but in Bircza, Stara Bircza and Nowa Wies, there was a little.
DG: Yes?
KZ: Even my [wife]
KZ's wife: Before there wasn't so much difference.
DG: And now the differences are bigger?
KZ's wife: Now I don't know. Now the Ukrainian has not a [Orthodox] church to go to so one doesn't even know whether they are Ukrainian or not.

In Extract 13, ethnicity is constructed as something you can convert from or to; in this case transforming oneself from being a Jew to being a Pole. The interviewees do not describe this occurrence as anything extraordinary, even if it is unusual. Of particular interest is the idea that the metamorphosis in ethnicity is achieved through religious conversion. For our informants, religion was of major significance in the narration of ethnicity so that, in Extract 14, the status of Ukrainian ethnicity is undermined by the non-existence of the Orthodox Church in Bircza. Parenthetically, it is worth adding that the interviewees differed quite significantly in their narratives as to who destroyed the church. In any case, the absence of the church is something that makes Ukrainians stop being Ukrainians and, presumably, become Polish. We shall comment on this change in the next section of the chapter.

We would like to make one other observation with regard to Extract 14. In the first move of the quoted exchange the interviewer asks what for him is a clear question about the phenomenon of Polish men marrying Ukrainian women. The 'it' in the question refers back to the practice of inter-ethnic marriages. Yet, the interviewee interprets the question very differently. He understands it as referring to Ukrainians in general and responds by recounting the fact that there were three such families living in Korzeniec.

This 'misunderstanding' is interesting because of the negative connotations carried by referring to groups of people by the pronoun 'it'. Linguistically speaking, as we commented in relation to Extract 1, the use of the third person singular in reference to a group positions them as a homogeneous whole, thus obscuring the composition of groups by different individuals. This also occurs when the pronoun itself is used without an associated verb form. Yet, in contrast to the verb, the use of the pronouns in reference to a group of people would be marked and this is how it is interpreted by the interviewee.

'It' in Polish is used almost exclusively as referring to objects, very rarely to animals, and almost never humans. Consequently, the inter-viewee's usage of pronouns would have been understood by him as extremely condescending and belittling of the groups of people to whom he referred. And yet the interviewee does not signal any discomfort with this structure and, in fact, takes it up again in the form of *było* (neuter past form of *być* 'to be'; '[it] was'). This 'misunderstanding', or alterna-tive decoding, is indicative, we would suggest, of ethnic relations between Poles and Ukrainians, and, more particularly, the often referred to hatred between the two groups.

The unbearable dilemma of ethnicity

In this section of the chapter our intent is to show that ethnicity takes essentially dilemmatic form. As we have already demonstrated, the construction of ethnicity through language and religion is riddled with 'ideological dilemmas' in which contrasting and incoherent sets of beliefs underpin the same category (Billig et al., 1988). Language and religion are constructed as both indicative and not indicative of ethnicity. However, the dilemmatic character of ethnicity goes beyond specific indicators, for, as the extract below illustrates, the constitution of ethnicity in general is dilemmatic.

Extract 15

KA, female, aged 82

DG: And now those Ukrainians who live here speak Polish or Ukrainian?
KA: There is a lot of them you see but they are Poles. Over there in Wola there is a lot of them. But they are Poles and they keep everything Polish but when Ukrainian religious holidays come then our [people], Poles go to Przemyśl to the Orthodox church to look and whether they over there and there is a lot of them there. They go to their own religious holidays, the Jordan.
DG: I see.
KA: [lit:] The wolf is lured to the forest [a saying meaning that one's true nature can't be changed].
DG: So are they Poles or Ukrainian?
KA: Poles.
DG: Poles?
KA: Poles.
DG: I see.
KA: They are now Polish. And the Jews, you know.
DG: But they used to be Ukrainian.
KA: Yes. And when the religious holidays [come] they keep Polish and Ukrainian.
DG: I see.

Our attention is directed here to the interviewee's insistence, even when challenged, that the people the interviewer called Ukrainians are Polish. The interviewee is adamant that these 'Ukrainians' are now Polish. The evidence she offers in support of this argument is by way of reference to their 'form of life' as being Polish. However, this conviction is undermined by her suggestion that one cannot change the fundamental nature of the universe. The proverbial wolf will always remain a wolf and will want to go to the forest. Or, as the English would say, a leopard cannot change its spots. Apparently it is the same for those Poles who used to be Ukrainian. Despite being Polish they still go to celebrate the Ukrainian holidays, referred to here as Jordan (from the river Jordan).

The interviewee contradicts herself within the space of a couple of moves. Within the exchange she both allows for ethnicity to be changed on the basis of everyday practices, and to be seen as something that does not go away – the wolf will always be lured into the forest. This is precisely what is meant by the dilemmatic character of ethnicity. It is held to be a feature of the groups that is non-essential and changeable, yet at the same time it is claimed as something deeply embedded and universal.

Agents and patients: the unbearable lightness of seeing

In this part of the chapter we are interested not so much in how ethnicity is constructed, i.e. what it means to be Polish or Ukrainian, but in how Poles and Ukrainians are represented as 'doing things' or becoming engaged in events. In particular, we shall focus on how the spectrum of participant – process – circumstance (see Chapter 3) is constructed by the speakers with regard to these ethnic groups. That is, we are concerned with the discursive functions that are ascribed to ethnic groups or their representatives regarding the processes in which they are engaged.

This exercise has two objectives. First, we want to find out whether there are recurring patterns of representation of Poles and Ukrainians that feature in the informants' narratives. Second, we are interested in whether these patterns of representation contribute to the overall image of each ethnic group within our informants' accounts. In other words, we are interested in exploring the relationship between the dilemmatic ideologies of ethnicity exhibited by our analysis and those underpinning the representation of ethnic groups.

Our analysis is driven by the observation that it was ethnicity that constituted the predominant mode of identifying persons and groups within the narratives. The informants did not commonly categorize people in alternative terms, a phenomenon that cannot be explained away by an interview agenda which allowed for these categorizations. The questions in the interviews were designed to be triggers that were taken up by the informants and the content of the responses was to a considerable extent controlled by them. Indeed, the interviews differed quite significantly in terms of their topical repertoire; some inter- viewees were predominantly talking about their experiences as observers or victims of the conflict, some talked about their active participation in it. It was also the interviewees' choice to focus pre- dominantly upon the Polish–Ukrainian conflict of 1945 and 1946, a phenomenon that is indicative of the articulation of ethnicity with age and generation.

Having observed the identifying power of ethnicity within inform- ants' narratives, we would argue that the construction of ethnicity, whether Polish or Ukrainian, is, as Hall (1990, 1996a) argues, always already a matter of representation. There can be no ethnicity outside of representation. This is particularly observable in this case given that both ethnicities were represented as in a clear relationship, i.e. of hating each other. Here, our conception of ethnicity is extended from the relational context-bound characteristics of a group to representations of specific activities that are not positioned as generic attributes of the group as a whole.

The analysis of agency

In our investigation we focused on the agency structures within the narratives, the way in which 'doing things' is represented in discourse, including who is positioned as doing which kind of things, in relation to what, or whom. The main concepts by which to understand this transitivity are process and participant, i.e. who is involved in a particular action or condition (see Chapter 3). In analysing agency structures the focus falls predominantly upon the participant and the roles that she or he are attributed with in relation to a particular process.

In Chapter 3 we discussed the roles of those participants who 'do' the different processes. For example, actors are those performing material processes and 'sayers' are those 'doing' verbal processes (for an accessible discussion of agency structures see Simpson, 1993; for a detailed analysis see Halliday, 1994). However, there are two elements of the agency structure that we have not yet discussed. The first involves the other participant in a process. When an actor is kicking, they are more than likely to be kicking something. The object of kicking is the goal of the process (action). Occasionally, if the goal is a human being it is referred to as 'patient' (Fowler, 1991). Thus, in the sentence 'John kicked the ball', John is the actor, kicking is the material process and the ball is the goal of the process. Material processes are not the only ones that have their other participants: people can say, think or see something. Thus, the product of a verbal process is verbiage and the objects of mental processes are phenomena.

In addition to transitivity analysis, there is another mode of inquiry available to us that focuses on how actions are engendered. This is called the ergative analysis. The need to introduce ergative analysis is accessibly discussed by Simpson (1993: 93) on the following two sentences (in brackets the analysis in terms of transitivity).

(1) I broke the vase (actor – process – goal)
(2) The vase broke (actor – process)

Transitivity analysis does not differentiate between the structures of the two sentences even though in (1) the actor is someone who is engaged in deliberate action while in (2) the actor is an affected participant, i.e. someone or something that has things happen to them. However, this distinction can be achieved by employing ergative analysis, which concerns itself predominantly with the issue of causality in actions. Thus, an agent is the participant that causes things to happen, it is the external agency in the process. This kind of analysis would therefore have the actor in (1) as the agent in the process of breaking while the actor in the second sentence would be called the medium. Halliday (1994: 163) describes the medium as 'the entity through which a process comes into existence'. Ergative analysis offers a complement to the analysis of transitivity, an extra layer that enables us to fine-tune an examination of the discursive representation of 'how things happened'.

For the purpose of agency analysis we have focused only on those parts of the narratives where there could be no obvious expectation of how agency will be distributed with regard to the two main ethnic groups – Poles and Ukrainians. Even though we have taken into consideration the entire corpus, we have decided to prioritize only certain of its aspects. We are predominantly interested in those narratives that were not constituted by highly detailed stories of Polish or Ukrainian actions, or in which only one ethnic group was the main 'character' of the story. Rather, we were more concerned with those accounts that dealt with the overall (generic) relationship between Poles and Ukrainians and particularly with the beginning of the conflict. For example, we have ignored accounts of a Polish military assault on a Ukrainian troop camp since the narrative was told through the eyes of a participant telling a story about how Poles outwitted Ukrainians. Consequently, it was reasonable to expect that it would be the participants of the detachment, and thus Poles, who were positioned in the role of actors or agents, and the Ukrainians in those of goals.

Further, we were not much interested in the explicit ascription of blame, for that was expected to be laid by Poles on the Ukrainians and, as our interviewees claimed, vice versa. Indeed, we found a number of accounts of how Ukrainian priests and lawyers incited the Ukrainian population against Poles. Instead, we were curious about the ascription of responsibility in the linguistic sense. That is, we analysed the narratives to find out in what kind of participant roles the two ethnic groups or their representatives were positioned. While explicit narratives of blame and responsibility are part of the conscious mythology of a group, the choices on the level of syntactic structure are normally unconscious, even though they are ideologically significant.

Agents and patients

Our hypothesis about the patterns of agentivity through which Polish and Ukrainian ethnic groups were constructed was borne out by the data. Thus we found a tendency to fashion the relationship between Poles and Ukrainians in terms of patients and agents. That is, Poles were the goals, the recipients of actions taken by Ukrainian agents. As such, the responsibility for events in the community of Bircza was linguistically placed on the heads of the Ukrainian population. The first two extracts below (16 and 17) are *sui generis* summaries of what happened in Bircza and thus were particularly interesting for us.

Extract 16

BT, male, aged 76

BT: Now there are neither Jews nor Ukrainians. All was swept away. Germans took the Jews to camps and shot them, Ukrainians on the other hand made those gangs against Poles and murdered Poles. And in forests it went and was afraid, the people were hiding. Because it attacked [lit. 'beat']. Until the military came and destroyed and that's it. And they were just about to take over the militia [station] these Ukrainians and all. Militia was here but they were few people and few military. Later they phoned for the military. The military a company came and so these gangs they were millions of these Ukrainians. From all over. All against Bircza the town they wanted to take over and murder the Poles.

Extract 17

KA, female, aged 82

KA: And there are Ukrainians there [referring to a foreign country the interviewee visited] and they don't believe that there are Ukrainians among Poles. What they did with Poles, what they did with us that they always attacked first started they cut [killed], beat, burned and all that in newspapers it says we did with them. The opposite they turned everything around.

Extract 18

KZ, male, aged 83

KZ: It was like that, they [Ukrainians] were persecuting Poles and Poles took big hatred towards them. And this hatred still exists today.

In Extract 16, the interviewee distinguishes between different groups of Poles. In fact he uses the ethnic label 'Poles' only with regard to those that were the target of the Ukrainians' (potential) actions. Ukrainians are the active participants in two processes (making gangs and wanting to murder) explicitly directed against Poles and one implicitly so – 'it attacked'. Interestingly, the actions taken against Ukrainians are constructed as carried out by the military with no ethnic label ascribed to them. The same applies to the action of phoning for the military that was carried out not by 'Poles' but by officials.

These distinctions between the opponents of Ukrainians are not matched by any similar such differentiation among Ukrainians, who are treated generically as those who made 'gangs' (Polish *bandy*, a word used commonly to refer to Ukrainian troops, carrying strong negative connotations of criminal activities). This constitutes a clear position of agency constructed for Ukrainians against the position of goal created for Poles.

In Extract 17, the interviewee also ascribed to Poles the role of target for Ukrainian actions. Yet, she chooses to describe them by using the instrumental case of *Polacy* – 'Poles'. Having used the verb *zrobić* (perfective form of 'to do'; i.e. something similar to 'to have done') she opens up two paradigmatic possibilities. She can use the dative form of 'Poles', and thus construct a sentence akin to 'What they did to Poles', or she can use the instrumental case and end up with the sentence she actually used, i.e. 'What they did with Poles'. In either case the sentence clearly ascribes the role of the goal of a process to Poles.

The choice is significant. The former option, the use of the dative case, is predominantly deployed in reference to activities aimed at human beings. By contrast, the latter, the use of the instrumental case, is principally used with reference to inanimate objects. In this way, the interviewee not only positions Poles as the goal of Ukrainian agents' deliberate actions, but also constructs Poles as objects unable to defend themselves, let alone strike back. Poles are constructed as unable to be an active party in the conflict.

Extract 18 introduces an implicit causal relationship between what the interviewee sees as the two main processes in the conflict. Polish hatred is the upshot of the persecution (rendered by *mścić* and the preposition *nad*) on the part of the Ukrainians. This extract is also interesting because it seemingly introduces symmetry into the relationship. 'They' do something and 'we' do something back. However, there are a number of differences between the representations of the two groups.

First, the Ukrainians are represented as clear agents in what can be seen as a material process with an explicitly determined goal. On the other hand, Poles are represented as 'taking up' (hence the implicit causality) a mental process. Moreover, the rendition of the mental process is carried out by a nominalization, i.e. an action (which is normally rendered by a verb) is constructed as a thing (rendered by a noun). This is significant because what Poles are constructed to do is not actually to hate, but, in fact, 'take up'. A fundamental difference between the representation of the two ethnic groups is therefore between a very negative process (persecuting) and a neutral one (taking up). Furthermore, the causal relationship between the two can then be seen in a different context – something negative results in something neutral.

For our last quotation in this chapter we shall return to Extract 1. Here the interviewee challenges what he probably interprets as the interviewer's attempt to put Poles and Ukrainians on a par with regard to hating each other.

Extract 1

BT, male, aged 76

BT: Only Korzeniec was Polish and Bircza was Polish. And such was the villages there Wygon over there Hominskie but they were mixed and Ukrainians were mixed they lived there in the households and they hated Poles.
DG: And Poles liked them?
BT: Pardon?
DG: And Poles liked them?
BT: No.
DG: No?
BT: Of course they didn't like [them]. No. It spoke Ukrainian and in Polish they even didn't want to speak to the Poles.

The interviewee introduces Ukrainians as hating Poles, upon which the interviewer asks whether Poles reciprocated with liking. What might be interpreted as a surprised 'no?' in the interviewer's last move is answered with a somewhat irritated statement of obviousness – Poles didn't like Ukrainians. And here is the crucial shift in the interviewee's utterance. Even though the interviewer changed the focus of the exchange onto Poles, the interviewee is not prepared to talk about Poles and their likes or dislikes. Rather, he immediately shifts the topic onto Ukrainians, telling the interviewer about their attitude towards Poles in entirely negative terms.

Note also the lack of any marker of the shift. The interviewee continues his utterance as if the interviewer had not asked his question. BT's 'no' is ambiguous in the sense that it could be understood as an answer to the hypothetical question about Ukrainians, with the rest of the move being an elaboration of this 'no'. The point is, that the events of the Polish–Ukrainian conflict are implicitly constructed as being of the type where one talks about what Ukrainians did, rather than what Poles did. Poles are not the main *dramatis personae* in the drama.

This analysis draws attention to a tendency in the narratives to represent the conflict between the Polish and Ukrainian inhabitants of Bircza and its community in terms of agents and patients, with Ukrainians as the former and Poles as the latter. In this way, the conflict is constructed as being of the Ukrainians' doing, not only explicitly, but also on the level of linguistic representation. Poles are reduced to passive participants who merely suffered at the hands of their opponents.

Conclusions

Theorists within the 'discipline' of cultural studies have argued that ethnicity is a discursively constructed relational concept that constitutes and regulates a specific form of cultural identity. As such, an investigation into ethnicity will concern itself with relations between groups, in particular cultural contexts. Further, ethnicity is concerned with power and particularly with relations and representations of centrality and marginality. This is an anti-essentialist stance that holds ethnicity to be a culturally specific naming, constituted in and through discourse, rather than being a universal entity or set of traits possessed by ethnic groups.

In this section of our book, informed by the tool-kit of functional linguistics outlined in Chapter 3, we have demonstrated some of the mechanisms through which ethnicity is achieved by specific culturally located speaking subjects. That is, ethnicity is relational and context-bound so that it cannot be separated from the particular circumstances of the people 'claiming' it. We have shown that anti-essentialism is not simply a philosophical position, but the stance of speaking subjects deploying a specific grammar within their particular pragmatic narratives.

Though regulatory discourses offer us subject positions, particular speakers may or may not 'take-up' (or be interpellated by) a given discourse. Competition in the discursive field, combined with the fantasy characteristics of identification, gives rise to subjects constituted with fluid multiple identities. Consequently, the construction of any given ethnic identity remains the achievement of speaking subjects. It is not enough to assert through generalized theory, that ethnicity is X or Y. Rather, we have to show empirically how ethnicity is performed by definite tangible persons within concrete cultural conditions.

Having said that, it is also the case that speaking subjects deploy language that operates with a grammar of which they are not reflexively aware. That is, a good deal of grammatical 'choice' is performed at an unconscious level with implications and consequences not fully appreciated by individual speakers. It turns out that apparently little words like 'we' and 'they' (personal reference), 'with us' (spatial reference) and 'long ago' (temporal reference) have big consequences. Thus, if human beings are to learn how best to live with difference, rather than resort to violence, then an understanding of, for example, 'structures of agency' that systematically position groups as the doers or the done to, the guilty and the innocent, the human and the 'it', is of crucial significance.

Note

1 We consistently conceal the identity of our interviewees. The initials by which they can be recognized do not correspond to their names though the demographics we provide are correct.

Appendix

Extract 1

BT, male, aged 76

BT: tylko Korzeniec był polski i Bircza była polska. i takie było wioski o Wygon tam Homińskie tego ale i tak mieszane były i tak Rusiny mieszane były tak po domach mieszkali i mieszane były ale Polaków nienawidzili:
DG: a Polacy ich lubili?
BT: proszę?
DG: a Polacy ich lubili?
BT: a nie:
DG: nie?
BT: ale skąd ta gdzie lubili: nie: no jeden po po rusku mówiło a to polsku i oni nie chcieli nawet z Polakami wiele rozmawiać

Extract 2

BT, male, aged 76

BT: no bo tu Rusiny były. po rusku hadały. tak o hadały
DG: hadały?
BT: hadały. hadały po rusku wsio: hadały: tak że że ich poznać było po mowie ale wszystko po rusku było.
DG: acha.
BT: polski byli Polaki byli ale więcej Rusinów było.
DG: mchm
BT: takie Ruskie że że oni mieli święta osobne: inne święta mieli a my polskie mieli inne święta.

Extract 3

KA, female, aged 82

KA: taka zgoda była proszę pana i i Ukraińców bylo kilkanaście rodzin to jak były polskie święta to oni do nas na polskie święta przychodzili rodzice dzieci i cieszyli się. A jak były ich święta my znów do nich szliśmy taka zgoda była. Później proszę pana coś się stało nienawiść taka była okrutna
DG: mmm
KA: Rzeź. Bili.
DG: a co to się stało?
KA: hmm ja wiem?
DG: a jak to się zrobiło?
KA: to to mówią że to tak księża zbuntowali:
DG: polscy czy ukraińscy?
KA: ukraińscy księża

Extract 4

KZ, male, aged 83
Talking about his survival strategies during the war

KZ: no i jak ja tam nadeszedł z Żydem. Żyd i ja. oba my szli. to Żyd szedł po Żydach żeby
coś dostać zjeść a ja szedł po Ukraińcach.
DG: mchm
KZ: o: no i złapało mnie i goni mnie o: ja mówię ja Ukrainiec
DG: mchm
KZ: szczo chocze ty w mene?
DG: mchm
KZ: o: mówi budymy widel czy ty Ukrainiec czy ni? i przyszedłem do domu mów pacież.
no to ja się żegnam i ojca i syna i światowo ducha i ojca i syna trzy razy panie [recites
'Our Father' in Ukrainian] dopiero wtedy jakżem zmówił Ojcze Nasz.
DG: i uwierzyli?
KZ: o: zaraz Hantka daj mu chliba i mołoka:
DG: acha [*laughs*] a Polakowi by nie dali?
KZ: jak by nie umiał achże: rżnęli zaraz: rżnęli panie

Extract 5

PT, female, aged 72 and ZT, male aged 79

DG: mmm a mówicie państwo że że się Polacy żenili z Ukraińcami znaczy Polacy z
Ukrainkami czy tam Polki z Ukraińcami a z Żydami się żenili?
ZT: nie nie.
DG: czemu?
[. . .]
PT: to już jest inna wiara.
ZT: musiał być musiał być Żyd
DG: no ale przecież Ukraińcy to też inna wiara nie?
PT: to nic ale to tylko było w języku ukraińskim a a polskim.
DG: acha
PT: a Żydzi to już mają całkiem inne w ogóle wyznanie.

Extract 6

MD, female, aged 81

MD: no i przychodzili do pana do domu brali se krowę czy prosiaka czy kurę czy co.
Przychodzili brali bo im trzeba jeść. a to oni bardzo po polsku se mówili bo Ukraińcy
po polsku też mówili

Extract 7

BT, male, aged 76

BT: tylko tera Polacy: a gdzie niektóry jeszcze Rusiny są: jeszcze jeszcze jeszcze gdzie niektóre Rusiny tam tam jak się jedzie na Kalwarie ta Wola Wola Ruska Wola to jeszcze gdzie niektóre Rusiny są ale już po rusku nie mówią tylko po polsku.

DG: czemu?

BT: no to bo już Polaków więcej jest aż gdzie będzie do kogo będzie mówił?

Extract 8

GkT, male, aged 80

DG: to żenili się Polacy z Żydami?

GkT: ta tutaj tak się nie żenili bo tu więcej było pola do pola do krów to Żyd nie pójdzie:

DG: acha.

GkT: no to po co będzie się żenił.

DG: no tak

GkT: zakochał się potem Żydowka płakała to nawet jeden Ukrainiec miał tam w sąsiedztwie Żydowkę no ale co z tego? lubieli się no ale żenić się nie będzie bo na pole dawniej sierpem sie rżnęło: kosami:

Extract 9

KA, female, aged 82

DG: i to Ukraińcy też tak chodzili [with bare feet]? tak biedni byli?

KA: wszystkie: to wszyscy tak

DG: Żydzi też?

KA: Żydzi to Żydzi. Tam mieli jakieś buty bo tam oni każden Żyd musiał mieć jakiś interes.

DG: mchm.

KA: No to nazywa się interes. Sklepik. tu ze . . . z mydłem tu z czymś tu z czymś tu z materiałem wszystko no tam mieli. zawsze każden tydzień on musiał mieć na piątek takie jak my na święta byli na rok to oni mieli co tydzień.

DG: mchm

KA: i szabas bułki piekli i kura musiała byc rosół i i bułeczki i świecili swiatła wszystko i Polacy szli tam myli sprzątali im parę groszy tam dał czy co zjeść o tak było.

Extract 10

KA, female, aged 82

DG: pamięta pani jak to było jak nagle granica się przesunęła i Bircza to prawie no na no nie na samej ale prawie na granicy. jak to było?

KA: a ja wiem panie? no jakoś tak proszę pana nie interesowali my się. może nie powiem tak to dokładnie bo to tak wiedziało się o tym ze przesunięta ale ni to radia ni to telewizoru niczego nikt się tym wiele nie zajmywał tym i gazet się nie czytało:

Extract 11

BT, male, aged 76

BT: tak: i my pouciekali do Przemyśla:
DG: no ale to do Przemyśla to w stronę Ukrainy.
BT: no ale Przemyśl to nie był chyba ukraiński?
DG: nie. Przemyśl jest polski.

Extract 12

KZ, male, aged 83

KZ: jak by pan przyszedł ja był w Borownicy. Borownica krzyczała żeby tego że tam ich mocno cisną [Ukrainian troops] bo tam wszystkie wsie były ukraińskie dookoła Borownica polska. no to my poszli do Borownicy. byli my w Borownicy. tam pewnego razu proszę pana Ukraińcy zaszli do jednego domu i wyrżli wszystko do tego i wszystko wynieśli do studni.
DG: mchm
KZ: i w studnię powrzucali. przyszli my tylko jedno dziecko tylko dziewczynka uciekła i do Borownicy powiedziała o tym. to jak my przyszli do takiego domu i że papiery wszystko po ziemi krew papiery wszystko porozrzucane w tym domu.
DG: mchm
KZ: o: poszli my szukać zobaczyli my to w studni ze to wszystko jest powrzucane do studni. co by pan powiedzial?
DG: ja bym nie chciał tego widzieć wie pan. na to nie ma słów.
KZ: no: co by pan powiedział?
DG: nie ma słów.
KZ: to wtenczas Polak jak zobaczył takie coś panie to skórę by z niego ściagał też.
DG: tak tak i myśli pan ze ta nienawiść jest do dzisiaj?
KZ: no: to już to już teraz mi przeszło bo już to to już jest pięćdziesiąt lat jak to było.

Extract 13

PT, female, aged 72 and ZT, male aged 79

PT: a Żydzi to już mają całkiem inne w ogóle wyznanie i
ZT: w Birczy nawet nawet tu jedna rodzina była taka że on musiał się wychrzcić o:
DG: acha
ZT: musiał się wychrzcić na polski a ona była Polka i on ja polubiał i musiał się wychrzcié z żydostwa na
PT: na polski.
ZT: na polski. (. . .)

Extract 14

KZ, male, aged 83

With interventions of KZ's wife who was present at the interview yet did not take part and thus her demographics are unavailable. Her interventions were limited to a few sentences

DG: a niech mi pan mówi pan powiedział że się Polacy żenili z Ukrainkami. dużo tego było przed wojną?

KZ: no dużo było tak wszędzie ja nie wiem bo to i po Korzeńcu po Korzeńcu nie było bo tylko były trzy Ukraińcy ale tu po Birczy po Starej Birczy po Nowej Wsi tu było: trocha

DG: tak?

KZ: nawet moja=

KZ's wife: = przedtem to nie było takiej różnicy

DG: a teraz sa różnice większe?

KZ's wife: to teraz ja wiem? teraz już Ukrainiec cerkwi nie ma to: nawet człowiek nie wie czy są Ukraińcy czy nie:

Extract 15

KA, female, aged 82

DG: (. . .) a teraz ci Ukraińcy co tutaj mieszkają mówią po ukraińsku czy po polsku?

KA: a jest: ich i dużo jest proszę pana ale oni są Polakami. tam na Woli ich dużo jest. ale oni są Polakami polskie wszystko utrzymują ale jak są ruskie święta to nasze Polacy jadą do Przemyśla do cerkwi popatrzeć i czy oni tam i pełno ich tam jest. jadą na te swoje święta na ten Jordan.

DG: acha

KA: no to ciągnie ich zawsze wilka w las ciągnie.

DG: no to to są Polacy czy Ukraińcy?

KA: Polacy:

DG: Polacy?

KA: Polacy.

DG: aha.

KA: oni teraz Polakami są. a Żydzi proszę pana=

DG: = a byli Ukraińcami?

KA: tak. a jak święta to utrzymują polskie i ukraińskie.

DG: ach rozumiem. mchm

Extract 16

BT, male, aged 76

BT: tak tak a tera tak. ani Żydow ni ma ani Ukraińców ni ma. i wszystko to powymiatało. Żydy Niemcy wzięli do obozów tam postrzelało Ukraińcy znów bandy se zrobili na Polaków mordowali i i i tego po lasach chodziło bało się wszystko tak chowali się ludzie te. bo biło. aż wojsko przyszło wyniszczyło wyniszczyło i już. oni chcieli milicję zająć te Ukraińcy i wszystko. milicja tutaj była ale to mało ludzi było wojska mało było później dzwonili po wojsko wojsko kompanię najechało i tak te bandy było miliony było tych Ukraińcow. ze wszystkich stron. wszystko na Birczę na miasto wszystko chcieli zająć a Polaków chcieli wszystko wymordować.

Extract 17

KA, female, aged 82

KA: a tam [referring to foreign country] są Ukraińcy. i oni nie wierzą że tu Ukraińcy między Polakami są. to co robili z Polakami proszę pana to co robili z nami że sami pierwsze napadali zaczęli rżnęli bili palili to wszystko w gazetach i pisze że to robili my z nimi. przeciwnie wszystko odwrócili.

Extract 18

KZ, male, aged 83

KZ: to proszę pana było tak no oni się mścili tak nad Polakami a Polaki wzięli wielkie nienawiść na nich. i do tej pory jest nienawiść.

6

Intersections

It is the man's thing to be far away, it is the woman's thing to faithfully wait

In this concluding chapter we address the motif of intersections. Our first intersection is one that brings together the themes of Chapters 4 and 5, namely masculinity and ethnicity. This directs us to the gendering of ethnicity through their mutual constitution and in particular to the masculinization of Aboriginality. That is, not only do the identities of Aboriginal men lie at the intersection of discourses of Aboriginality and masculinity, but the latter becomes virtually a discursive condition of the former. Our second theme of intersection refers to the dialogue between cultural studies and CDA upon which this book is founded.

The articulation of identities

According to Hall, the end of essentialism 'entails a recognition that the central issues of race always appear historically in articulation, in a formation, with other categories and divisions and are constantly crossed and re-crossed by the categories of class, of gender and ethnicity' (Hall, 1996c: 444). The concept of articulation was developed by Hall to theorize the relationships between various discursive components of a social formation. The notion refers to the formation of a temporary unity between elements that do not have to go together. Articulation suggests both expressing/representing and a 'putting-together'. Thus, representations of masculinity may be 'put-together' with representations of race in context-specific and contingent ways that cannot always be predicted before the fact. Hall expresses this idea thus:

The term [articulation] has a nice double meaning because 'articulate' means to utter, to speak forth, to be articulate. It carries that sense of language-ing, of expressing, etc. But we can also speak of an 'articulated' lorry (truck) where the front (cab) and the back (trailer) can, but need not necessarily, be connected to one another. The two parts are connected to each other, but through a specific linkage that can be broken. An articulation is thus the form of the connection that *can* make a unity of two different elements, under certain conditions. It is the linkage which is not necessary, determined, absolute and essential for all time. You have to ask, under what circumstances can a connection be forged or made? The so-called 'unity' of a discourse is really the articulation of different, distinct elements which can be rearticulated in different ways because they have no necessary 'belongingness'. The 'unity' which matters is a linkage between the articulated discourse and the social forces with which it can, under certain historical conditions, but need not necessarily, be connected. (Hall in Grossberg, 1996: 141, emphasis in original)

In this way we may consider identities to be the unique articulations of specific discursive traces that circulate under definite cultural and historical conditions. One of the tasks of cultural studies then, is to analyse those articulations that have taken place under particular conditions and illustrate how various contingent practices are 'put together' with each other.

Multiple identities: from code switching to hybridity

We may consider the process and resources required for the articulation of identities in a number of different ways. First, we may reflect on the multiple identities of the contemporary subject, that is, the weaving of the patterns of identity from discourses of class, race, gender, etc. We can thus conceive of people as operating across and within multiple subject positions, constituted by the intersections or criss-crossing of discourses of race, gender, age, nation, class, etc. In this sense, we do not *have* a weave of multiple beliefs, attitudes, languages, etc., we *are* such a weave. To abandon an essentialist universal condition called 'race' or 'ethnicity' does not mean that the social and historical construction or racialization of specific groups of human beings need also be lost. On the contrary, the critique of essentialist arguments reveals the radical contingency of identity categories helping to combat the *reduction* of people to race, by encouraging us to see all people as multi-faceted (hooks, 1990). A young singer expresses the range of shifting identity positions available to her:

I rap in Bengali and English. I rap on everything from love to politics. I've always been into rapping . . . it was rebellious, the lyrics were sensational. I could relate to that, I could identify with it. Like living in the ghetto and that . . . It's from the heart. It's: 'I'm Bengali, I'm Asian, I'm a woman, and I'm living here'. (cited in Gardner and Shukur, 1994: 161)

The subject positions of this young woman involve the articulation of positions drawn from a variety of discourses and sites. At the very least she has identifications with being Bengali, English, a woman, with youth culture and with Rap, an American-Caribbean hybrid, now appropriated as Anglo-Bengali.

Second, we may explore the construction of one discourse, e.g. of ethnicity, in terms of metaphors drawn from another discourse, e.g. gender. For example, within discourses of 19th century social Darwinism the idea of 'race' was connected to the notion of the ascent of 'Man', nations are commonly gendered as female and absolute ethnic differences are premised on the idea of blood-lines and thus women's bodies. In Australia, Prime Minister Howard's attempt to include the concept of 'mateship' in the preamble to the constitution, was indicative of the way in which an Australian identity is explicitly coded as male for important sections of the community. Finally, what it is to be considered a 'man' is likely to be different across various ethnic groups, while racism may take the form in which one ethnic group derides another as effeminate.

Third, we have to take into account the capability of persons to move across discursive and spatial sites of activity that address them in different ways. As Rose has argued, people

> live their lives in a constant movement across different practices that address them in different ways . . . the existence of contestation, conflict and opposition in practices which conduct the conduct of persons is no surprise and requires no appeal to the particular qualities of human agency . . . in any one site or locale, humans turn programmes intended for one end to the service of others. One way of relating to oneself comes into conflict with others. (Rose, 1996: 140–141)

For example, British-Asian girls are commonly able to construct for themselves unique identities by virtue of living across cultural boundaries, and, as girls, being somewhat marginalized within male-dominated cultures. In particular, the hybrid identities and apparently contradictory subject positions they take up, are, at least in part, the outcome of the proliferation of discursive resources stemming from different conventions, sites and practices, which are, on the surface, logically inconsistent with each other (Barker, 1999).

The concept of hybridity has proved useful in highlighting cultural mixing and the emergence of new forms of identity. However, we need to differentiate between types of hybridity and to do so with reference to the specific circumstances of particular social groups. Pieterse (1995) has suggested a distinction between structural and cultural hybridization. The former refers to a variety of social and institutional *sites* of hybridity, for example, border zones or cities like Miami or Singapore. The latter distinguishes cultural *responses* that range from assimilation, through forms of separation, to hybrids that destabilize and blur cultural boundaries. He argues that structural hybridization, which increases the range of organizational options to people, and cultural hybridization, which involves the opening up of 'imagined communities', are signs of increased boundary crossing. However, they do not represent the erasure of boundaries so that we need to be sensitive to both cultural *difference* and to forms of identification that involve recognition of *similarity*.

In particular, we need to distinguish between those circumstances where two distinct cultural traditions are juxtaposed in time and/or space leading to situational code switching and the hybridization that occurs from the mixing of difference and the production of the new. The former would see persons described as Asian *and/or* British; Italian *and/or* Australian, while the latter brings forth claims to be 'British-Asian' or 'Italian-Australian'. To be British and Asian requires one to code-switch, from say, the domestic expectations of an Asian household, to the British youth cultural expectations that surround gendered behaviour. By contrast, a hybrid identity involves the development and adoption of the homegrown syncretic cultural forms of 'British Asian-ness' expressed in the musical forms and youth cultural styles of British Banghra-Rap-Hiphop crossovers (e.g. Apache Indian, Cornershop).

The concept of hybridity remains problematic in so far as it assumes or implies the meeting or mixing of completely separate and homogeneous cultural spheres. To think of British-Asian or Italian-Australian hybrid forms as the mixing of two separate traditions is problematic because neither British, Italian nor Australian cultures are bounded and homogeneous. Each category is always already a hybrid form which is also divided along the lines of religion, class, gender, age, nationality and so forth. Hybridization is the mixing of that which is already a hybrid. All cultures are zones of shifting boundaries and hybridization (Bhabha, 1994). Nevertheless, the concept of hybridity has enabled us to recognize the production of new identities and cultural forms, for example 'British-Asians'. Thus, the concept of hybridity is acceptable as a device to capture cultural change by way of a strategic cut or temporary stabilization of cultural categories.

Gendering ethnic identity

In this section we want to consider the gendering of ethnicity by male interviewees with self-designated ethnic identities. For example:

Extract 1

Joel: Well, I was born in what was then called The Netherlands East Indies colony, born in Sumatra, which to me is a very important thing. I don't talk about Sumatra being Indonesian or Dutch or anything. It's just Sumatra which is my mother, because I think that all humans need a backbone and right through the back of Sumatra runs the Bouquet Valley which is like the Himalayas. It's the backbone of Sumatra and I was born there. My mother is from Java, which is not Javanese, it's Dutch, Vietnamese and German.

Our first interest in this extract is the description of Sumatra and Java as ethnically hybrid. Thus, Sumatra is 'The Netherlands East Indies' and potentially 'Indonesian or Dutch' while Java is said to be not 'Javanese, it's Dutch, Vietnamese and German'. Further, since Joel's mother is Javanese and his father of Dutch-Sumatran lineage, then Joel himself could claim a hybrid identity. However, the already acknowledged multi-ethnic character of Sumatra is glossed over into a discursive unity that is 'just Sumatra'. Crucially, Sumatra achieves this unity in Joel's discourse by being 'my mother' and 'a backbone'.

Just as the Bouquet Valley is the backbone of Sumatra, so every human being needs a backbone 'which is mother'. Interestingly, in this context, being without a backbone is to be without direction or identity. Yet, to be without a backbone, or to be spineless, is also taken to be an insult, commonly directed at men, that designates the target as being weak, fearful, and without integrity, resolution, character or principle. Later in the interview Joel describes his mother as 'a very powerful woman; nobody shit on her, you know'. From this direct statement and from numerous other references in the interview, we may conclude that Joel's mother was an important figure in his life. She, like Sumatra, had backbone, and in common with Sumatra, gave Joel backbone. Further, like Java, Sumatra and Joel himself, his mother was an East-West hybrid. Thus, 'my mother was raised a Catholic but also a woman of the East . . . The Pope can say what he likes to her, she knows that already. But when Krishnamurti talks, he became a personal friend of hers, then it's different.'

Aboriginality as masculinity

It is perhaps because Joel's discussion of ethnicity is mediated by the notion of nationality that he feminizes his Sumatran identity. By contrast, for our two informants cited below, Aboriginality is coded as male.

Extract 2

Roger: Everyone just brings the black fellows down, 'cause I'm Aboriginal; it just brings black fellows down like nothing. I think the grog does it. It killed both me uncles. He had it on his twenty-first birthday. He had a shot and he lay down, spewed up, choked on it and died. The other went to Sydney to buy speed and he sniffed it up and it blew his brains out. This only happened in the last five months. They had two days between each other; one died of alcohol and one died of that.

Interviewer: This must put you off.

Roger: It didn't so much put me off. I was sitting with me uncles and he's telling me if I end up going up there, when I get up there, there's something waiting for me. He was just telling me that if I ever touch it, I'm dead, whether I'm dead here or dead up there.

Interviewer: Is heroin a big problem within the Aboriginal community?
Roger: If you go to Canberra you don't see blacks walking around, you see blacks as you
see them. They are all using. The only ones that don't use are the girls and a couple of
the boys that don't hang around town.

Roger makes an explicit identity claim with his 'I'm Aboriginal'. This is
in contrast to Paul (below) who describes himself as Koori, a specific
indigenous Australian people. This, we would suggest, is because Roger
has more or less white skin whereas Paul is clearly black. While Roger
feels the need to identify himself with Aboriginal peoples in general,
Paul takes this for granted and locates himself more specifically on the
map of indigenous peoples as Koori. It may also be significant that
Roger constantly describes indigenous Australians as black, whereas
Paul does not do so across the entire interview. In short, the question of
what does or does not count as Aboriginal (itself a matter of some
debate in Australia), is more of an issue for Roger than it is for Paul.

However, they share in the masculinization of Aboriginality. Twice
in his opening sentence Roger indicates that he is talking about
Aboriginal people with the phrase 'black fellows'. Not only is the
Aboriginal community black, but they are male. We may note that the
term 'black fellows' is a fairly common self-designation among indigenous men. Later, it is his male uncles with whom Paul sits and from
whom he takes advice about the dangers of drug use. Indeed, in
suggesting that heroin use is a widespread part of the Aboriginal
community in Canberra, Paul again locates this as a male community. It
is only 'the girls' who do not use and 'a couple of the boys that don't
hang around town'. The generic 'the girls' suggests that no women are
users and that all women are excluded from the Aboriginal male-user
group. By contrast, the boys who are not part of this community have
more specific designations 'a couple' and moreover they are not really a
part of the town community, i.e. they are not really 'one of us'.

Extract 3

Paul: I started drinking, smoking and I liked the effect of that and when I started drinking I
started hanging around the boys in Redfern and that's where I felt comfortable, 'cause
I'm Koori as well and they taught me how to car thieve and do all sorts of crime,
smash and grabs, armed robbery. But I didn't do an armed robbery 'cause I was the
driver, 'cause I've been driving all my life. I hung around the boys in Redfern and then I
got locked up for car stealing.

Paul's phrase 'I started hanging around the boys in Redfern and that's
where I felt comfortable, 'cause I'm Koori as well' achieves at least two
things. In an Australian setting, Redfern is a suburb of Sydney identifiable within the popular imagination as an Aboriginal area and one

that, in white media thinking at least, is deemed to be dangerous and troublesome. Thus, Redfern functions here as a sign of Aboriginality, with problematic connotations. However, it is not the aboriginal community *per se* in which Paul feels comfortable, but more specifically 'the boys'. In other words, for Paul, the Aboriginal community is essentially male. Further, 'the boys', refers to a specific set of men, those who 'taught me how to car thieve and do all sorts of crime'.

Paul feels comfortable with the boys because 'I'm Koori as well'. This phrase locates both himself and the boys as Koori while at the same time suggesting that Aboriginality is the basis of a shared communality. Nevertheless, we must add the observation that the phrase 'the boys' is one that has connotations of male solidarity and 'wildness' in other sectors of the English-speaking world. For example, readers may recall the *Thin Lizzy* song 'The Boys are Back in Town' or the movie 'The Lost Boys'. Further, in this context, the phrase echoes the wider sense of Australian male solidarity as expressed in 'mateship' and the ritual addressing of each other as 'mate' under almost any circumstances. Although black and white Australian men are in many respects segregated, they share a sense of male solidarity within their own communities.

Thus, Paul recounts meeting the renowned criminal (according to Paul) Darcy Dugan in a half-way house.

Extract 4

Paul: I was seventeen then and that's where Darcy Dugan was living . . . He done thirty three years in jail. I admire this guy; I read up on him and my mum named the horse after him. He's a legend. I got on well with him and he showed me everything; I idolized him for how staunch he was. He wouldn't let anyone make him cry or bash him; he was a hard man.

For Paul, Darcy Dugan is 'a legend' whom he 'idolized' because he encapsulated the rather traditional male virtues of being 'staunch', not crying, resisting other men's violence and generally being a 'hard man'. There is nothing specifically Aboriginal about these characteristics, which would also be admired by a section of the male descendants of the 'European' colonizers of Australia. This is also the case with Roger's declaration that 'I love sport mate, I'm an all-rounder. I love cricket, I love footy, I love soccer, I love netball; any game you throw at me mate'. This is a statement that could have been made by many a white male Australian. Indeed, it is distinctively Australian in its use of the terms 'footy' for rugby league (particularly in New South Wales), 'soccer' for what most Europeans and South Americans would call football, and in its characteristic use of the term 'mate' to address other men. In short, while Aboriginality is encoded as male, so is the wider nationality of Australian-ness.

Masculinity holds together a male aboriginal community, for, as Roger says, 'black fellows stick together'. It also binds other groups of men together, notably Anglo-Australian men, but also Greek-Australian men, Italian-Australian men, etc. However, while 'mateship' may sometimes transcend the differences between Anglo, Greek and Italian men (though the dividing term 'wog' to designate non-Anglo men remains in currency), it rarely does so between the Aboriginal community and others. Thus, there is an ambiguity to 'mateship' in that the solidarity that is claimed to be a facet of Australian masculinity cannot breach this particular ethnic divide, even though certain characteristics of maleness are shared.

The ambiguity of aboriginality

The terms 'Aboriginal' and 'Indigenous Australian' are words that identify a specific *ethnic* grouping. However, we have already noted in Chapter 5 the slippery, shifting nature of such labels. Indeed, we put forward the anti-essentialist case in relation to ethnicity. This makes identification of the characteristics that make up Aboriginality inherently difficult because unstable and context-specific. This presents Australians, black and white, with a 'problem' in that Federal government funding is attached to certain Aboriginal projects and activities. More particularly, the ambiguity of Aboriginality furnishes Roger with a self-nomination dilemma as the following three extracts suggest.

Extract 5

Interviewer: So do you see yourself as Aboriginal?
Roger: Yeah, you have a look at my family; they are as black as the ace of spades, mate. The only reason I'm white is because my father is white. That's the only thing I hate about him is that he has white skin. I wish he had black skin.
Interviewer: So your dad was white and your mother was black.
Roger: Yeah.
Interviewer: And you identify with being black.
Roger: Yeah, I'm classed as a black man. When they ask white or Aboriginal, I put Aboriginal.

As we have already seen, Roger identifies Aboriginal people with 'black fellows', yet his own appearance is on the face of it white. However, Roger wishes to claim an Aboriginal identity for himself by dint of his family being black. The irony of course is that while Roger masculinizes Aboriginality, it was his father who was white and his mother who was black – a fact that leads him to express some resentment towards his dad. Roger wishes that his father had black skin so that, by implication, he would also have a black appearance, thereby eliminating, as far as he is concerned, any doubt about his ethnic identity.

Roger is uncomfortable with hybridity and wants the certainty of ethnic absolutes. Further, whereas the 'traditional' resolution of such ambiguity has been expressed in the idea of 'passing' (for white), Roger wants to be undeniably black. Nevertheless, it remains unclear as to who exactly has the power to authenticate his claims other than himself. While 'I'm classed as a black man', this nomination is carried out by himself in response to classificatory questions which 'they' put to him. However, on some occasions this 'problem' is solved, albeit unpleasantly, by the labels and actions of others.

Extract 6

Roger: I got hunted out because the teachers were fucking racist. I ended up bashing one of them because he called me a black half-caste. The teacher turned around and [*inaudible words*]. We went and had a fight where nobody could see us. I went bang, bang, bang and he started bleeding. After that, I never went back to school because I thought every school has racists. I class myself black as the ace of spades because I didn't grow up with white people, I grew up with blacks. Everyone I went around with was a black . . . They might see me as a white fellow but if they sit down and have a conversation with me, do I sound like a white fellow? I can tell a black fellow the way they talk, the way they go on, what they talk about.

In one sense, the actions of 'the teachers', and one in particular, help to resolve Roger's uncertain ethnic identity since, as he sees it, they label him as 'black' and act in racist ways towards him. However, the term 'half-caste' leaves the ambiguity intact, so that Roger needs to define himself as 'black' which he does by saying that he was brought up within a black family. Indeed his description of himself as black is given emphasis by the designation 'black as the ace of spades'. Further, the term 'black' no longer refers to skin pigmentation as such but has become cultural. Roger is black because he was raised within a black family and one can tell black fellows not by looking, but by listening. In other words, conversational topic and style define being black.

Nevertheless, we may note that the gendering of Aboriginal culture remains unambiguously masculine; we are still talking about 'black fellows' and 'white fellows'. Further, Roger's response to the racism he encounters is not merely one of understandable anger, but of a rather characteristically male resort to violence. Not all men are violent and not all violence is carried out by men. Nevertheless, the evidence is that violence is more commonly the response of men, and certainly western culture encodes it as male. Indeed, Roger does not simply deploy violence but adopts a grandiose tone in boasting about it. 'I went bang, bang, bang and he started bleeding'.

In the final extract (no. 7 below) of this section we can see that Roger's shifting use of small words like 'us', 'my', 'we', 'the', and 'they' betrays his continued unease about his ethnic identity. On the one hand, 'us black fellows', 'my people', 'we own' and 'we can't', all unite Roger with the Aboriginal male community through processes of identification. On the other hand, when he says 'I respect the blacks' and 'they are the best fucking race in the world', he is putting distance between himself and black people, despite his avowed intent to do the opposite, since 'the' and 'they' indicate groups of people of whom he is not a part.

Extract 7

Roger: It's not so much being black, it's just that us black fellows stick together. That's why I brag about my people; we own this fucking place but we don't go around saying that all the time. One thing I realize now is we can't do nothing about it; this is a multicultural land and there's nothing we can do now. But I respect the blacks. I reckon they are the best fucking race in the world.

Aboriginality as Family

We have seen above how Roger's central claim to Aboriginality is his family upbringing. Paul implicitly supports this stance in the following extract.

Extract 8

Paul: This time around, well, you know how I was adopted out, next week I'm heading up there to meet my family for the first time. I'm looking forward to it.

C: Do they know?

P: Yes. There are 17 brothers and sisters in my old family and we're all from [edited] all around up north. After 30 years not knowing who I am, I realize now my identity.

C: So this is really important to you.

P: Yes; if I don't do this my spirit won't rest and I feel like I have to do this or my soul will never rest.

Paul was adopted by a white family at a very young age and has not ever met or known his biological black parents. Since Paul is a black man raised in a white family we can see why it is that he felt comfortable with 'the boys from Redfern' who became his new 'family' – or at least a site of solidarity, analogous to one that one might hope for from a family. Now, meeting his 'old family' will, he hopes, enable him to realize his identity. To be Aboriginal is to be within the family. That, in this context, there is something specifically Aboriginal about the claim to family is indicated by the words 'spirit' and 'soul' which, though not exclusively part of a black vocabulary, are key aspects of an indigenous Australian understanding of the universe that connects them to 'The Dreamtime'.

Simultaneously, the notion of family is extended to all those men who show solidarity with one another. At the age of 18, Paul underwent the first of many stints in jail. Despite the fact that 'it's rough in there', 'I was right in there because 70 per cent were Kooris and they all look after each other, make sure you are comfortable and have got drugs, they'll fix you up'. Later:

Extract 9

Paul: After the eighth year going in and out, you get a bit sick of it and I felt like the world was crumbling around me and I was gonna take my own life. What stopped me was my 11-year-old boy that I've got now and I'm starting to think about him. I got support from other elders, 'cause they saw me down and out and they know when someone is in trouble and they come over and talk to you to see if you are alright . . . I got all better, 'cause the boys gave me strength. This guy gave me a rock and it's carved like a grinding rock and you can see the handprint, it gave me a special feeling, a special power that I could feel the vibes from and I slept with that rock underneath my pillow, to give me strength. It gave me strength and I've still got that rock until this day.

In one way the above is a repetition of the theme of male solidarity – 'the boys gave me strength'. However, the use of the term 'elders' makes that solidarity more specific in that 'elder' is a position located within the family and community. Aboriginality is a matter of family, but family is encoded as male. Further, it was the thought of his son, a symbol of male lines of descent, that helped restore his hope along with the 'grinding rock' that gave him 'a special feeling, a special power'. Now, the giving of this rock is an Aboriginal cultural gesture enacted by 'this guy', i.e. a man.

The double-coding of 'family' as both blood lines and circumstantially generated male solidarity is given a further twist by Roger when he says that:

Extract 10

Roger: I've got family in every jail in Australia. But if I go in there and say I'm someone's grandson, they will know.
Interviewer: Your grandfather spent a lot of time in jail.
Roger: He was respected all over Australia. He used to go out drinking all the time . . . He used to walk around and smoke bongs all day. He lived out in the bush. He had a tent and his fire and that was it.

Thus, Roger has blood family in every jail and as such he feels sure that he would be welcomed as the grandson of a former inmate who was 'respected all over Australia'. It is not unreasonable to assume that Roger is exaggerating here, that his grandfather was known and respected, not all over the country, but among Aboriginal men in a particular geographical place, or who had also been to jail. This leads us to our final point, that the masculinization of Aboriginality ties indigenous cultural identity to a deeply problematic form of manhood. Among the themes of the conversations was alcohol and heroin abuse, taking and driving away, armed robbery, violence, confrontation with the police and doing time in jail. While women no doubt play a part in these activities as well, they remain primarily male pastimes right across the spectrum of Australian ethnic cultures and indeed across the entirety of western culture (see Pfeil,1995).

To this situation we must add the injustices of the structural position of Aboriginal peoples that places them in positions of subordination on every socio-economic and cultural indicator available. Aboriginal people suffer more poverty, more crime, more violence, more alcoholism, more drug abuse, more unemployment and more time in prison than any other group within Australia. Given the discussion so far, it will come as no surprise to readers that in most of these categories it is Aboriginal men who lead the way. We must also note that male on female domestic violence is relatively high within the Aboriginal communities of Australia. Finally, the similarity of the accounts with each other and with reports from Australian government (1992), academic (Poynton, 1994) and journalistic (Pilger, 1994) sources into the condition of Aboriginal people in Australia suggests that the accounts given by Roger and Paul are not isolated ones.

Gendering ethnic identity in context

As might be expected, we have also observed gendering of ethnicity in our Polish data. However, in discussing extracts from our Polish corpus, we do not particularly want to repeat the exercise from the previous section and show that the same kinds of phenomena occur in a different language. Rather, in this section we would like to argue that the masculinization of ethnicity is not best understood as merely another example of male dominance in a patriarchal society (even if it is possible to argue that at some deeper level it is so).

As Rowbotham (1981) has argued, the concept of Patriarchy treats the category of 'woman' in an undifferentiated way, obscuring the differences between individual women and their particularities in favour of an all-embracing universal form of oppression. Not only do all women appear to be oppressed in the same way, but there is a tendency to represent them only as powerless victims. Indeed, the implications of this criticism, i.e. that women are not a mass but are marked by difference, is also applicable to men in that all males are held to be a part of an undifferentiated oppressor class. Indeed, we concur with Kristeva's argument that:

> the very dichotomy man/woman as an opposition between two rival entities may be understood as belonging to *metaphysics*. What can 'identity', even

'sexual identity', mean in a new theoretical and scientific space where the very notion of identity is challenged? . . . What I mean is, first of all, the demassi-fication of the problematic of *difference*. (Kristeva, 1986a: 209, emphasis in original)

For Kristeva, sexual identities as opposites can only come into being after entry into the symbolic order, that is, sexual identity is not an essence, but a matter of representation. According to Kristeva, degrees of masculinity and femininity exist in biological men and women. Femininity is a condition or subject position of marginality which some men, for example, avant-garde artists, can also occupy (Kristeva, 1986b). Indeed, it is the patriarchal symbolic order that tries to fix all women as feminine and all men as masculine, rendering women as the 'second-sex'. Kristeva is suggesting that the struggle over sexual identities takes place within each individual. Rather than a conflict between two opposing male–female masses, sexual identity concerns the balance of masculinity and femininity within specific men and women. This stresses the singularity and multiplicity of persons as well as the rela-tivity of symbolic and biological existence.

The specificities of cultural context

We would like to argue that the construction of Polish ethnicity in masculine terms can be understood as being motivated by certain cultural myths and values that have been present in Polish society for some time. In other words, we would like to demonstrate that just as ethnicity cannot be seen in isolation from the context, nor can its gendering. Our attention is drawn to the specificities of the gendering of ethnicity in a particular cultural context, rather than to a universal and monolithic Patriarchy. Perhaps we could say that we are dealing with the articulation of the specificities of Polish culture with the discourses of Patriarchy.

Before we discuss these points further, we must make explicit a relevant and important difference between the English and Polish languages. Polish, like other languages such as German, French or Spanish, and unlike English, has gender as a grammatical category. It means that in those languages, nouns are catalogued according to gender classification. In other words, nouns such as 'table' or 'car' can be masculine or feminine (as in Spanish or French), or masculine, feminine or neuter (as in Polish and German). It must also be noted that the Polish gender system is more far-reaching than in the case of the other lan-guages mentioned here. In Polish, adjectives, pronouns, as well as certain verb forms, are gendered.

Now, unlike English, whatever the choice of the label describing reality, the Polish language automatically explicates it in terms of gender. Thus, to make the example relevant here, ethnic labels (such as 'Pole', 'Spaniard', 'Russian') are gendered. Thus, words such as *Polak* ('Pole') or *Ukrainiec* ('Ukrainian') are used both to refer to a male person of Polish or Ukrainian nationality, and, especially in plural, generically to people of these nationalities. The feminine equivalents of these labels *Polka* ('Pole', Polish female) or *Ukrainka* ('Ukrainian', Ukrainian female) can only be used in reference to females and unequivocally denote persons of female gender.

This choice, even though historically and culturally motivated, as well as potentially indicative of the patriarchal societal system in which they evolved, is a systemic one. This means that users of language cannot but make these linguistic choices if they want to talk about Ukrainians or Poles. In other words, it is the language system that in dictating certain choices, also genders the representation of reality. To repeat, we do realize that such gendering is not neutral – it is the result of certain social and historic processes. Yet, the linguistic options that have evolved are to a considerable extent beyond the choice of the individual language speakers. Challenging this gendering in language is of course difficult, as utterances appear either odd, or linguistically incompetent, or simply will carry a different and unintended meaning.

By contrast, the kind of gendering that we were talking about in the case of our English language data, is of a different order. Though this gendering is carried out in language, it is not done at the level of the linguistic system, but, rather, at the level of discourse, i.e. grossly over-simplifying language that is used in a certain social and cultural context with a certain communicative and social purpose. In other words, the gendering that was performed in English is not a result of the systemic organization of language – the speakers did not have to say what they said, a different choice would have been, linguistically speaking, possible. Their choices were more actively and contextually ideological than the structural gendering in Polish. Of course, ideology operates at a structural or systemic level and active contextual choices also exist in Polish. However, we are trying to draw attention to different modes of gendering in language use.

Let us give an example that will illustrate the difference between the two levels of gendering of the ethnicity. Subsequently, we shall only be interested in the non-systemic gendering of ethnicity.

Extract 11

KA, female, aged 82

Speaks of Ukrainian priests inciting their flock to turn against Poles

KA: They [Ukrainian priests] did this under the German occupation. And when we were fleeing our houses because there was this war and they were shooting and Germans were in the river beyond the town and they asked what we were. We said a Pole [masculine] and he says Poles [uses the German word] Jew [uses a Russian word] bang bang they will kill.

DG: Mmm.

KA: So only the Ukrainian [masculine, singular] will be left. And they.

Choosing the form *za Niemców* ('under the Germans'), an unmarked form in informal discourse, the interviewee has no choice but to use the plural form of the masculine noun *Niemcy* ('Germans'). The choice is also limited in her final move. Saying that only Ukrainians are going to be left in the region, she cannot but use masculine nouns. Although the use of the singular form is significant here and gives a more distinct impression of masculinity, it is the language that does not allow the interviewee to manoeuvre out of the masculine representation of reality. While there are almost infinite forms the interviewee could have used, they would have been more or less marked (as unusual) given the tenor of the interview and social background of the interviewee.

However, our subject's choice of noun during self-identification cannot simply be put down to the system of language. On being asked who 'we were' the interviewee uses a term which, while not standing out in her discourse, is not dictated by the *system* of language. Being female, she could have used the feminine ethnic label *Polka* or in plural *Polki*, or, alternatively, given that the group could have been mixed, she could have said *Polacy* ('Poles'). This latter term, while masculine, is systemically, as we noted above, used to refer to Polish people generically. The use of *Polak* ('Pole', masculine, rarely used to self-refer by a woman) is precisely the kind of gendering of ethnicity that we have been talking about in the case of our English language data. Using the masculine ethnic designation, *KA* foregrounds the male component of the group and implicitly suggests that Polishness has something to do with masculinity.

The male enemy

The non-systemic gendering of ethnicity always implies constructing it in masculine terms. It is men, or, as the case may be, boys, who are the token representatives of the nation. Witness the following examples:

Extract 12

KA, female, aged 82

KA: No one will tell them this, they don't want to hear that someone might tell them that [they are] a Ukrainian [singular, masculine]. There is one like that up there a Ukrainian, he comes to work for me, [he] says that if I tell him when someone told him [this] he wanted to fight. He doesn't want to know: he is a Pole.

Extract 13

KA, female, aged 82

DG: Only Poles were at school?
KA: Jews were, Ukrainians, Poles.
DG: Mmm. And did you all get along?
KA: Jews were not liked, Poles always teased them.
DG: Poles didn't like?
KA: [Poles] always teased them.
DG: Teased?
KA: That they had these sideburns and they put them behind their ears, so he put it
   behind the ears and behind him in a desk [someone] would pull it [the sideburn].

The use of the singular and masculine term for the generically referred
to Ukrainian population (Extract 12) can be construed in terms of
putting a masculine frame of reference upon the entire population. The
reference to an individual person functions as evidence in the narrative.
On the other hand, in Extract 13, the generic reference to Polish pupils
teasing (the Polish *dokuczać* has more negative connotations than the
English 'tease') their Jewish school mates is exemplified in masculine
terms. To tease Jewish children, in the words of our interviewee, meant
to tease boys.

What we observe is that these instances of masculinization are performed in those parts of the narratives that refer to some form of conflict
between the pertinent ethnicities. In other words, the masculinization of
ethnicity mostly occurred whenever the narrative constructed people of
one ethnicity in opposition to, or in contrast with, people of another
ethnicity.

In both extracts above, the interviewee positions either the Ukrainians
or the Jewish children as members of the out-group, outsiders in some
conflict with the in-group (Poles). The opposition in Extract 12 is
underscored by the reference to the individual Pole/Ukrainian who is
prepared to be violent. Incidentally, this opposition is drawn up on two
levels. On the one hand, this opposition is directed against those Poles
who say that they are not Polish, while on the other hand, its object is the
Polish population in general, for the interviewee constructs the person as
a Ukrainian.

The next extract, which we have already presented in the previous
chapter, demonstrates even more clearly the masculinization of the
enemy who is constructed in ethnic terms.

Extract 14

KZ, male, aged 83

KZ: If you had come I was in [the village of] Borownica. Borownica screamed that that
   they [Ukrainian troops] press them strongly because all the villages around were

Ukrainian Borownica was Polish. So we went to Borownica. We were in Borownica. There once you know Ukrainians went to a house and cut [killed] everything and brought to the well.

DG: Mmmm.

KZ: And they threw into the well. And we came and only one child only a girl escaped and to Borownica and told [us] about it. So when we came to that house and that papers everything blood on the ground. Papers, everything strewn all over in the house.

DG: Mmm.

KZ: We went looking we saw it in the well that all is thrown into the well. What would you say?

DG: I would not like to have seen it. There are no words.

KZ: Well, what would you say?

DG: There are no words.

KZ: So then when a Pole saw such a thing he would take the skin off him as well.

DG: Yes, yes, and you think this hatred has been there till today?

The conflict that the exchange sets up is not merely between Poles and Ukrainians. It is between a masculine Pole and a masculine Ukrainian (referred to in the interviewee's last move by the personal pronoun 'him'). Now, this extract is interesting because it offers the possibility of interpreting masculinization as resulting from the fact that most of the combat soldiers in the Second World War were actually men. It is therefore more than likely that those who committed the atrocities in the interviewee's account were actually male.

However, we do not believe that this is a convincing interpretation. Rather, we would like to argue that the masculinization of conflict that occurs within the Polish data derives from one of the values formative of Polish culture, namely the ethos of the knight/gentleman (see Ossowska, 1986). It is the men who could have been knights, it is 'men's job' to go to war and fight. This ethos of fighting males is not only still present in the Polish popular culture (especially songs and films), but also in the language. For example, men who hit women are scornfully declared to be 'ladies' boxers'.

It is, we are suggesting, this cultural division of labour that is responsible for the masculinization of ethnicity in our Polish data. It draws upon the still-living Romantic tradition in Poland. After Poland's loss of independence at the end of the 18th century, the Romanticist literature of the 19th century not only abounded in themes relating to Poland's loss of statehood, but also featured the mostly lone male romantic hero fighting to bring Poland's independence back. Such literary works, commonly regarded in Poland as the best Polish literature ever written, for example, Mickiewicz's *Dziady, Part III*, or Słowacki's *Kordian*, together with a number of other Romantic works, (including those by Krasinski and Norwid) contain characters who single-handedly want to free Poland from the occupier's yoke. Incidentally, only one of the 'greatest' Polish works (Mickiewicz's *Grazyna*), has a female hero leading the fight, yet she has to dress up as a man, for fighting is becoming only to men.

In her recent study of Polish national identity, Kloskowska (1996) points out that this literature has been very formative of contemporary Polish national identity, with some of today's public figures being constructed as romantic heroes. Traits of the Romanticist tradition can also be found in Polish political discourse (see e.g. Jaworski and Galasiński, 1998). Thus, the masculinization of Polish ethnicity can be, according to us, derived from the long-standing myths of what constituted an honourable fight for independence, one of the most visible topics in Polish public discourse. In our view, the Polish interviewees draw intertextually upon these myths and construct a culturally 'valid' and intelligible image of the enemy. This image requires the enemy to be male.

The main point that we are making here is that just as constructions of ethnic identity cannot be analysed in abstraction from the time and place in which they occur, neither can the analyses of ethnicity's gendering. The masculinization of ethnicity is motivated not only by the overall patriarchal system of the society, but also, more locally, by the historically developed discourses of conflicts, wars, and struggles for independence. These discourses draw intertextually from both the 'fossilized' myths of the nation in the so-called 'patriotic' literature, as well as through the reinforcing public discourses. In such a way, the discourse of the Romanticist tradition of fighting for Poland that developed in the 19th century has subsequently been re-processed and re-located in the public discourses of 20th century Poland, finding its way into the discourses of the general populace. Of course, these semi-private discourses provide those public ones with a base of intertextual reinforcement.

The construction of Polishness in our interviewees' narratives is part of such discursive practice, both context-dependent and context-renewing, in which a fight is necessarily a male thing. As one of the popular Polish songs from more than decade ago had it:

> It is the man's thing to be far away,
> It is the woman's thing to faithfully wait.

In conclusion: reflections on writing this book

When we were discussing the concept of this book during the late spring of 1998 we were drawn to it for different reasons. For Chris Barker, schooled in cultural studies, the attractiveness of the idea lay in the ability to draw upon the tools of micro-linguistic discourse analysis as an addition to his cultural studies workshop. For him the book arose out of the frustration of making claims on linguistic data that, however right they seemed theoretically, lacked the clout of harder linguistic evidence.

For Dariusz Galasiński, trained in linguistics and discourse analysis, the book was a way of tapping into the richness of the cultural studies' theorizations. It was a means by which to leave the restrictive boundaries of micro-analysis in search of a wider perspective on social and cultural life. For him, the book arose out of a fascination with how close his and Chris Barker's interests were, but how distant they also seemed. This fascination extended to include the theoretical depth of cultural studies that discourse analysis on the whole lacks, thus requiring it to go increasingly to other domains for its social and cultural theoretical background (see e.g. Chouliaraki and Fairclough, 1999).

To risk gross oversimplification and make it into a pun, we could say that while cultural studies has the theory but lacks coherent method, discourse analysis has the method but lacks sufficient scope and depth of theoretical resources.

Our co-operation was intended to resolve this problem, and while Barker will not become a linguist and Galasiński will not be a cultural studies scholar, this book is an attempt to work together and demonstrate what one can offer the other. That is, our book is an attempt to show how CS and DA could benefit from each other.

The day of judgement is upon us . . .

Accordingly, having come to the end of this study we asked ourselves a question: was the effort worthwhile, both for us as academics with certain research interests and for our readers (at least as we see it). Presumably, if we had answered this question negatively, we would not have had the chance to write publicly about it, so readers will not be surprised to learn that the answer to the question is affirmative.

We both feel that we have not only learnt from one another but also ventured into realms of academic research and writing that, although vaguely known to us, we do not systematically read. The amount of literature that is directly relevant to our specialisms is huge enough not to even attempt to keep in touch with some cognate areas. Consequently, the experience of writing this book together allowed us to familiarize ourselves with alternative ways of seeing more systematically than we would normally be able to achieve.

More importantly, we as the authors feel that this book furthers key theoretical arguments with regard to the discursive construction of identity on the level of linguistic data. In other words, for us, the main bonus of the CS and DA co-operation was the ability to translate the theoretical postulates made by scholars dealing with problems of identity into a close micro-linguistic data analysis.

However, in our view the central achievement of this book is not merely to have 'proved' some theoretical points. Rather, we have been able to show how concrete people living everyday lives construct their identities. We have highlighted the kinds of processes that are involved in these constructions including how precisely the anti-essentialist view of identity could be seen in 'real-life' data. In other words, we have not only demonstrated that an anti-essentialist view of identity holds water, we have also shown how it works, in the contexts in which the data were collected. Even though we have focused on data from particular socio-cultural contexts, our analyses, we believe, have more general import – they point to some more common processes of identity formation.

There is another aspect of this book with which we are pleased. That is, we have tried to give (mediated) 'voice' to people who are traditionally under-represented within western academic writing. This is our political project. After some discussion, we not only decided to go out there and speak to 'real' people, rather than use secondary texts from television or magazines, but to collect our data from groups of people who could give voice to under-researched themes. Thus, Poland is 'marginal' to the discursive construction of Europe within the western portion of that continent, and indeed, within the entire English-speaking world. Further, elderly Poles from the village of Korzeniec are placed on the edge of the world both in terms of age and location within Poland. Incidentally, the importance of getting *their* stories heard can be highlighted by the fact that two of the Polish informants died in the year between the interviews and writing up the research. We think there is some urgency in giving voice to those people who have witnessed as adults some of the most horrific events in Europe this century.

Australia is also a long way both literally and metaphorically from the centre of western culture. There are few discourse analytic or cultural studies (as opposed to anthropological or linguistic) within western texts that explicitly base their arguments on data that are not founded on US, or UK English speakers. Our book shows that other data can be easily used to further theoretical and methodological arguments. Indeed, we hope that our readers from the USA and the UK will find the focus of our data refreshing and welcome.

Readers who accept this argument may nevertheless find it difficult to think of men as marginal or without voice. Indeed, cultural studies has 'white male dominance' as one of its central mantras. However, the category of 'men' needs to be treated in a rather less cavalier fashion and given the specificity it requires to forward the lives of all people. Men also need to be considered through lenses that value difference. Thus, three out of the five men we discuss are or have been heroin users, two of whom have spent time in prison. In the context of contemporary culture, marked by the rhetoric of the 'war against drugs', it is not common to find such men given a sympathetic public hearing. Further, two of our subjects are indigenous Australians, who are clearly a marginalized group.

Nevertheless, we consider even this argument to be the easy way out from under the criticism that men do not require public 'voice'. In our view, Maurice, a white middle-class academic, also has anguish and sadness to express. The oppressor and the oppressed are not mutually exclusive binary categories. Though men have many loud public voices it is far less common to hear about the 'private' pain and suffering that a culturally specific discourse of masculinity inflicts on men (as well as women). The idea of gender justice needs to cover men as well as women. Our fathers and our sons were all made for grief.

We hope that for readers of this book there will have been an additional bonus. We have written a book that brings together into one text two traditions of research with the intention of demonstrating the benefits of mutual co-operation. We trust that readers on either side of the CS–DA border, or indeed in other areas of social sciences and humanities, will find this volume a useful guide to the problems of identity as envisaged by *both* traditions. Of course, we hope that our analyses will have convincingly made the necessary analytic points. We also hope that for readers locating themselves within cultural studies the analyses will serve as a sound guide into the discourse analytic approach to data. For readers situated within (critical) discourse analysis we expect that this book will point to some as yet undiscovered theoretical material that will usefully underpin their analytic activities. Finally, for our readers in other areas of social sciences and humanities, perhaps this book will have demonstrated the usefulness of both domains of study, especially when they work in combination.

Appendix

Extract 11

KA, female, aged 82

KA: oni [Ukrainian priests] już to za Niemców wszystko robili. i jak myśmy uciekali z domu bo to ta wojna była strzelali to Niemcy byli tam w rzece za miastem pytali się co my jesteśmy. my mówili że Polak a on mówi a oni mówili tak Polen i Jewrej to pach pach że pozabijają
DG: mchm
KA: ze tylko zostanie Ukrainiec. i oni.

Extract 12

KA, female, aged 82

KA: nikt im tego nie powie oni nie chcą już słyszę żeby im ktoś coś powiedział że Ukrainiec. tu taki jest na górze Ukrainiec tu taki do mnie chodzi do roboty mówi że jak mu powiem jak mu raz powiedział to go bić chciał. nie chce już wiedzieć że: on jest Polak.

Extract 13

KA, female, aged 82

DG: a tylko Polacy byli w szkole?
JZ: Żydzi byli Ukraińcy Polacy:
DG: mchm i jak sie kolegowaliście się wszyscy?
JZ: Żydow nie lubieli Polacy zawsze im dokuczali.
DG: Polacy nie lubili.
JZ: zawsze im dokuczali tak dokuczali.
DG: dokuczali?
JZ: że mieli te pejsy naciagąli ich poza ucho za ucho założył a z tyłu w ławce do siebie tam go pociągnął.

Extract 14

KZ, male, aged 83

KZ: jak by pan przyszedł ja był w Borownicy. Borownica krzyczała żeby tego że tam ich mocno cisną [Ukrainian troops] bo tam wszystkie wsie były ukraińskie dookoła Borownica polska. no to my poszli do Borownicy. byli my w Borownicy. tam pewnego razu proszę pana Ukraińcy zaszli do jednego domu i wyrżli wszystko do tego i wszystko wynieśli do studni.
DG: mchm
KZ: i w studnię powrzucali. przyszli my tylko jedno dziecko tylko dziewczynka uciekła i do Borownicy powiedziała o tym. to jak my przyszli do takiego domu i że papiery wszystko po ziemi krew papiery wszystko porozrzucane w tym domu.
DG: mchm
KZ: o: poszli my szukać zobaczyli my to w studni że to wszystko jest powrzucane do studni. co by pan powiedział?
DG: ja bym nie chciał tego widzieć wie pan. na to nie ma słów.
KZ: no: co by pan powiedział?
DG: nie ma słów.
KZ: to wtenczas Polak jak zobaczył takie coś panie to skórę by z niego ściągał też.

References

Althusser, L. (1971) *Lenin and Philosophy and Other Essays*. London: New Left Books.

Anderson, B. (1983) *Imagined Communities: Reflections on the Origins and Spread of Nationalism*. London: Verso.

Ang, I. (1985) *Watching Dallas: Soap Opera and the Melodramatic Imagination*. London: Methuen.

Austin, J.L. (1962) *How to do Things with Words*. Oxford: Oxford University Press.

Australian Govt Pub. Service (1992) Aboriginal Australia. Canberra: Australian Govt Pub. Service. Produced in co-operation with the Aboriginal and Torres Strait Islander Commission.

Bakhtin, M. (1984) *Rabelais and His World*. Bloomington: University of Indiana Press.

Barker, C. (1997a) 'Television and the reflexive project of the self: soaps, teenage talk and hybrid identities', *British Journal of Sociology*, 44 (4).

Barker, C. (1997b) *Global Television: an Introduction*. London: Blackwell.

Barker, C. (1998) 'Cindy's a slut: moral identities and moral responsibility in the "soap talk" of British Asian girls', *Sociology*, 32 (1).

Barker, C. (1999) *Television, Globalization and Cultural Identities*. Milton Keynes: Open University Press.

Barker, C. (2000) *Cultural Studies: Theory and Practice*. London and Thousand Oaks: Sage.

Barrett, M. and McIntosh, M. (1982) *The Anti-Social Family*. London: Verso.

Barth, F. (1969) *Ethnic Groups and Boundaries*. London: Allen & Unwin.

Barthes, R. (1967) *The Elements of Semiology*. London: Cape.

Barthes, R. (1972) *Mythologies*. London: Cape.

Baudelaire, C. (1964) *The Painter of Modern Life and Other Essays*. Phaidon Press: Oxford.

Beaugrande, R., de (1991) *Linguistic Theory*. London: Longman.

Bennett, T. (1992) 'Putting policy into cultural studies', in L. Grossberg, C. Nelson and P. Treichler (eds), *Cultural Studies*. London and New York: Routledge.

Bennett, T. (1998) *Culture: A Reformer's Science*. St Leonards: Allen & Unwin.

Best, B. (1997) 'Over-the-counter-culture: retheorizing resistance in popular culture', in S. Redhead with D. Wynne and J. O'Connor (eds), *The Club Cultures Reader: Readings in Popular Cultural Studies*. Oxford: Blackwell.

Bhabha, H. (1994) *The Location of Culture*. London and New York: Routledge.

Bhabha, H. (ed.) (1990) *Nation and Narration*. London and New York: Routledge.

Biddulph, S. (1994) *Manhood*. Sydney: Finch.

Billig, M. (1990a) 'Stacking the cards of ideology: the history of the Sun Royal Album', *Discourse and Society*, 1: 17–37.

Billig, M. (1990b) 'Collective memory, ideology and the British Royal Family', in D. Middleton and D. Edwards (eds), *Collective Remembering*. London: Sage.

Billig, M. (1995) *Banal Nationalism*. London: Sage.

Billig, M. (1997) 'From texts to utterances', in M. Ferguson and P. Golding (eds), *Cultural Studies in Question*. London and Newbury Park: Sage.

Billig, M., Condor, S., Edwards, D., Gane, M., Middleton, D. and Radley, A.R. (1988) *Ideological Dilemmas*. London: Sage.

Blommaert, J. (1997) 'Whose background? Comments on a discourse-analytic reconstruction of the Warsaw uprising', *Pragmatics*, 7: 69–81.

Bly, R. (1991) *Iron John: A Book About Men*. London: Element.

Bordo, S. (1993) *Unbearable Weight: Feminism, Western Culture and the Body*. Berkeley, CA: University of California Press.

Bouma, G.D. and Atkinson, G.B.J. (1995) *A Handbook of Social Scientific Research*. Oxford: Oxford University Press.

Bourdieu, P. (1984) *Distinction: A Social Critique of the Judgement of Taste*. London: Routledge.

Bourdieu, P. (1991) *Language and Symbolic Power*. Cambridge: Polity Press.

Bourdieu, P. (2000) 'Making the economic habitus', *Ethnography*, 1 (1): 17–41.

Brah, A. (1996) *Cartographies of Diaspora*. London: Routledge.

Brown, G. and Yule, G. (1983) *Discourse Analysis*. Cambridge: Cambridge University Press.

Brown, P. and Levinson, S. (1987) *Politeness*. Cambridge: Cambridge University Press.

Brown, R. and Gilman, A. (1972) 'The pronouns of power and solidarity', in P.P. Giglioli (ed.), *Language and Social Context*. Harmondsworth: Penguin.

Brunsdon, C. and Morley, D. (1978) *Everyday Television – 'Nationwide'*. London: British Film Institute.

Butler, J. (1990) *Gender Trouble*. New York and London: Routledge.

Butler, J. (1991) 'Imitation and gender subordination', in D. Fuss (ed.), *Inside/Out: Lesbian Theories, Gay Theories*. London: Routledge.

Butler, J. (1993) *Bodies That Matter*. London and New York: Routledge.

Butler, J. (1994) 'Gender as Performance: an interview with Judith Butler', *Radical Philosophy*, 67, Summer: 32–37.

Butler, J. (1997) *The Psychic Life of Power*. Stanford, CA: Stanford University Press.

Caldas-Coulthard, C.R. (1994) 'On reporting: the representation of speech in factual and factional narratives', in M. Coulthard (ed.), *Advances in Written Text Analysis*. London: Routledge. pp. 295–308.

Chodorow, N. (1978) *The Reproduction of Motherhood*. Berkeley: University of California Press.

Chodorow, N. (1989) *Feminism and Psychoanalytic Theory*. Cambridge: Polity Press.

Chouliaraki, L. (1998) 'Regulation in "progressivist" pedagogic discourse: individualized teacher-pupil talk', *Discourse and Society*, 9: 5–32.

Chouliaraki, L. and Fairclough, N. (1999) *Discourse in Late Modernity*. Edinburgh: Edinburgh University Press.

Clifford, J. and Marcus, G. (eds) (1986) *Writing Culture*. Berkeley: University of California Press.

Cohen, S. (1980) 'Symbols of trouble: an introduction to the new edition', in S. Cohen, *Folk Devils and Moral Panics: The Creation of the Mods and Rockers*. London: Martin Robertson.

Connell, I. and Galasiński, D. (1996) 'Cleaning up its act: the CIA on the internet', *Discourse and Society*, 7: 165–86.

Connell, R.W. (1995) *Masculinities*. Cambridge: Polity Press.

Cook, G. (1992) *The Discourse of Advertising*. London: Routledge.

Crook, J. and Fontana, D. (eds) (1990) *Space in Mind*. Shaftesbury: Element Books.

Cunningham, S. (1992a) *Framing Culture*. Sydney: Allen & Unwin.

Cunningham, S. (1992b) 'The cultural policy debate revisited', *Meanjin*, 51 (3).

Cunningham, S. (1993) 'Cultural studies from the viewpoint of cultural policy', in A. Gray and J. McGuigan (eds), *Studying Culture*. London: Arnold.

Dalton, S. and Dunnett, G. (1993) *Living with Personal Construct Psychology*. Chichester: Wiley.

Daniels, C. (ed.) (1998) *Lost Fathers*. London: Macmillan.

Davidson, D. (1980) 'Mental events', in D. Davidson, *Essays on Actions and Events*. Oxford: Clarendon Press.

Davidson, D. (1984) *Inquiries into Truth and Interpretation*. Oxford: Clarendon Press.

Dawkins, R. (1976) *The Selfish Gene*. Oxford: Oxford University Press.

Dawkins, R. (1995) *River Out of Eden: A Darwinian View of Life*. New York: Basic Books.

Derrida, J. (1976) (trans. G. Spivak) *Of Grammatology*. Baltimore: Johns Hopkins University Press.

Dillon, J.T. (1990) *The Practice of Questioning*. London: Routledge.

Du Gay, P., Hall, S., Janes, L., Mackay, H. and Negus, K. (1997) *Doing Cultural Studies*. London: Sage.

Dyer, R., Geraghty, C., Jordan, M., Lovell, T., Paterson, R. and Stewart, J. (1981) *Coronation Street*. London: British Film Institute.

Edwards, D. and Potter, J. (1992) *Discursive Psychology*. London: Sage.

Elias, N. (1978) *The History of Manners: The Civilizing Process. Vol. 1*. Oxford: Blackwell.

Elias, N. (1982) *State Formation and Civilization: The Civilizing Process. Vol. 2*. Oxford: Blackwell.

Fairclough, N. (1989) *Language and Power*. London: Longman.

Fairclough, N. (1992) *Discourse and Social Change*. Oxford: Polity Press.

Fairclough, N. (1995a) *Critical Discourse Analysis*. London: Longman.

Fairclough, N. (1995b) *Media Discourse*. London: Edward Arnold.

Fairclough, N. (2000) *New Labour, New Language?* London: Routledge.

Fairclough, N. and Wodak, R. (1997) 'Critical discourse analysis', in T.A. van Dijk (ed.), *Discourse as Social Interaction*. London: Sage. pp. 258–84.

Faludi, S. (1991) *Backlash: The Undeclared War Against American Women*. London: Vintage.

Faludi, S. (1999) *Stiffed: The Betrayal of the American Man*. London: Chatto and Windus.

Farrell, W. (1993) *The Myth of Male Power*. Sydney: Random House.

Fiske, J. (1987) *Television Culture*. London: Methuen.

Forward, S. (1990) *Toxic Parents: Overcoming Their Hurtful Legacy and Reclaiming Your Life*. New York: Bantam Books.

Foucault, M. (1972) *The Archaeology of Knowledge*. New York: Pantheon.

Foucault, M. (1973) *The Birth of the Clinic*. London: Tavistock.

Foucault, M. (1977) *Discipline and Punishment*. London: Allen Lane.

Foucault, M. (1979) *The History of Sexuality. Vol. 1: The Will to Truth*. London: Penguin Lane.

Foucault, M. (1980) *Power/Knowledge*. New York: Pantheon.

Foucault, M. (1984a) 'Nietzsche, genealogy, history', in P. Rabinow (ed.), *The Foucault Reader*. New York: Pantheon.

Foucault, M. (1984b) 'On the genealogy of ethics: an overview of work in progress', in P. Rabinow (ed.), *The Foucault Reader*. New York: Pantheon.

Foucault, M. (1986) *The Care of the Self: The History of Sexuality. Vol. 3*. London: Penguin.

Foucault, M. (1987) *The Uses of Pleasure*. Harmondsworth: Penguin.

Foucault, M. (1991) 'Governmentality', in G. Burchill, C. Gordon and P. Miller (eds), *The Foucault Effect: Studies in Governmentality*. Hemel Hempstead: Harvester Wheatsheaf.

Fowler, R. (1985) 'Power', in T.A. Van Dijk (ed.), *Handbook of Discourse Analysis. Vol. 4*. London: Academic Press.

Fowler, R. (1991) *Language in the News*. London: Routledge.

Fowler, R. (1996) 'On critical linguistics', in C.R. Caldas-Coulthard and M. Coulthard (eds), *Texts and Practices*. London: Routledge.

Fowler, R., Hodge, B., Kress, G. and Trew, T. (eds) (1979) *Language and Control*. London: Routledge.

Fraser, N. (1995) 'From irony to prophecy to politics: a response to Richard Rorty', in R.S. Goodman (ed.), *Pragmatism*. New York: Routledge.

Gadamer, H-G. (1976) *Philosophical Hermeneutics*. Berkeley: University of California Press.

Galasiński, D. (1997a) 'The making of history. Some remarks on politicians' presentation of historical events', *Pragmatics*, 7: 55–68.

Galasiński, D. (1997b) 'Background and discourse analysis. A response to Jan Blommaert', *Pragmatics*, 7: 83–8.

Galasiński, D. and Marley, C. (1998) 'Agency in foreign news', *Journal of Pragmatics*, 30: 565–87.

Galasiński, D. (2000) *The Language of Deception*. Thousand Oaks: Sage.

Gardner, K. and Shukur, A. (1994) 'I'm Bengali, I'm Asian and I'm living here', in R. Ballard (ed.), *Desh Pradesh: The South Asian Presence in Britain*. London: Hurst & Company.

Garfinkel, H. (1967) *Studies in Ethnomethodology*. Englewood Cliffs, NJ: Prentice Hall.

Geertz, C. (1979) 'From the native's point of view: on the nature of anthropological understanding', in P. Rabinow and W.M. Sullivan (eds), *Interpretative Social Science*. Berkeley, CA: University of California Press.

Gergen, K. (1994) *Realities and Relationships*. Cambridge, MA and London: Harvard University Press.

Giddens, A. (1984) *The Constitution of Society*. Cambridge: Polity Press.

Giddens, A. (1991) *Modernity and Self-Identity*. Cambridge: Polity Press.

Giddens, A. (1992) *The Transformation of Intimacy*. Cambridge: Polity Press.

Gillespie, M. (1995) *Television, Ethnicity and Cultural Change*. London and New York: Routledge.

Gramsci, A. (1971) *Selection from the Prison Notebooks*, edited by Q. Hoare and G. Nowell-Smith. London: Lawrence and Wishart.

Grice, H.P. (1975) 'Logic and conversation', in P. Cole and J. Morgan (eds), *Speech Acts (Syntax and Semantics 3)*. New York: Academic Press. pp. 41–58.

Grossberg, L. (ed.) (1996) 'On postmodernism and articulation: an interview with Stuart Hall', in D. Morley and D.-K. Chen (eds), *Stuart Hall*. London: Routledge.

Hall, S. (1993) 'Minimal selves', in A. Gray and J. McGuigan (eds), *Studying Culture*. London: Arnold.

Hall, S. (1981) 'Encoding/Decoding', in S. Hall, D. Hobson, A. Lowe and P. Willis, *Culture, Media, Language*. London: Hutchinson.

Hall, S. (1990) 'Cultural identity and diaspora', in J. Rutherford (ed.), *Identity: Community, Culture, Difference*. London: Lawrence & Wishart.

Hall, S. (1992a) 'Cultural studies and its theoretical legacies', in L. Grossberg, C. Nelson and P. Treichler (eds), *Cultural Studies*. London and New York: Routledge.

Hall, S. (1992b) 'The question of cultural identity', in S. Hall, D. Held and T. McGrew (eds), *Modernity and its Futures*. Cambridge: Polity Press

Hall, S. (1995) 'Fantasy, identity, politics', in E. Carter, J. Donald and J. Squites (eds), *Cultural Remix: Theories of Politics and the Popular*. London: Lawrence & Wishart.

Hall, S. (1996a) 'Who needs identity?', in S. Hall and P. Du Gay (eds), *Questions of Cultural Identity*. London: Sage.

Hall, S. (1996b) 'For Allon White: metaphors of transformation', in D. Morley and D-K. Chen (eds), *Stuart Hall: Critical Dialogues in Cultural Studies*. London: Routledge.

Hall, S. (1996c) 'Gramsci's relevance for the study of race and ethnicity', in D. Morley and D-K. Chen (eds), *Stuart Hall: Critical Dialogues in Cultural Studies*. London: Routledge.

Hall, S. (1996d) 'The problem of ideology: Marxism without guarantees', in D. Morley and D-K. Chen (eds), *Stuart Hall: Critical Dialogues in Cultural Studies*. London: Routledge.

Hall, S. (ed.) (1997) *Representation: Cultural Representation and Signifying Practices*. London and Thousand Oaks: Sage.

Halliday, M.A.K. (1978) *Language as Social Semiotic*. London: Edward Arnold.

Halliday, M.A.K. and Hasan, R. (1985) *Language, Context, and Text*. Oxford: Oxford University Press.

Halliday, M.A.K. (1994) *An Introduction to Functional Grammar*. 2nd edition. London: Edward Arnold.

Halpern, D. (1992) *Sex Differences in Cognitive Abilities*. London: Lawrence Erlbaum Associates.

Hammersley, M. (1997) 'On the foundations of Critical Discourse Analysis', *Language and Communication*, 17.

Hammersley, M. and Atkinson, P. (1983) *Ethnography: Principles and Practice*. London: Tavistock Books.

Hartley, J. (1982) *Understanding News*. London: Methuen.

Hebdige, D. (1979) *Subculture: the meaning of Style*. London and New York: Routledge.

Henriques, J., Holloway, D., Unwin, C., Venn, C. and Walkerdine, V. (1984) *Changing the Subject*. London: Methuen.

Herman, J. (1992) *Trauma and Recovery*. New York: Basic Books.

Hite, S. (1994) *The Hite Report on the Family*. London: Bloomsbury.

Hobson, D. (1982) *Crossroads: Drama of a Soap Opera*. London: Methuen.

Hodge, R. and Kress, G. (1988) *Social Semiotics*. Oxford: Polity Press.

Hodge, R. and Kress, G. (1993) *Language as Ideology*. London: Routledge.

hooks, b. (1990) *Yearning: Race, Gender and Cultural Politics*. Boston, MA: South End Press.

Hoyenga, K. and Hoyenga, K.T. (1993) *Gender-Related Differences*. New York: Allyn & Bacon.

Illawarra Public Health Unit (1998) *Illawwra Youth Health Survey*. Wollongong: Area Health Authority.

Irigaray, L. (1985a) *Speculum of the Other Women*. Ithaca, NY: Cornell University Press.

Irigaray, L. (1985b) *This Sex which is not One*. Ithaca, NY: Cornell University Press.

Iser, W. (1978) *The Act of Reading: a Theory of Aesthetic Responses*. London and New York: Routledge and Kegan Paul.

Jaworski, A. and Galasiński, D. (1998) 'The last Romantic hero: Lech Walesa's image-building in TV presidential debates', *Text*, 18, 525–544.

Johnson, S. and Meinhof, U. (eds) (1997) *Language and Masculintiy*. Oxford: Blackwell.

Jordan, G. and Weedon, C. (1995) *Cultural Politics: Class, Gender, Race and the Postmodern World*. Oxford: Blackwell.

Kelly, G A. (1955) *The Psychology of Personal Constructs*. New York: Norton.

Kloskowska, A. (1996) *Kultury narodowe u korzeni*. [National cultures at their roots]. Warszawa: Wydawnictwo Naukowe PWN.

Kopp, S. (1978) *An End to Innocence*. London: Macmillan.

Kotlarczyk, J. (1997) *Pomnik za trzy napady na Bircze?* [A monument for three attacks on Bircza?]. Part 1–3. *Wiadomosci Birczanskie*, 2, 3–4, 5.

Kress, G. and van Leeuwen, T. (1996) *Reading Images*. London: Routledge.

Krippendorf, K. (1981) *Content Analysis*. London: Sage

Kristeva, J. (1986a) 'Women's Time', in T. Moi (ed.), *The Kristeva Reader*. Oxford: Blackwell.

Kristeva, J. (1986b) 'Revolution in Poetic Language', in T. Moi (ed.), *The Kristeva Reader*. Oxford: Blackwell.

Kuhn, T.S. (1962) *The Structures of Scientific Revolutions*. Chicago and London: University of Chicago Press.

Lacan, J. (1977) *Ecrits: A Selection*. London: Tavistock.

Laclau, E. (1977) *Politics and Ideology in Marxist Theory*. London: New Left Books.

Laclau, E. and Mouffe, C. (1985) *Hegemony and Socialist Strategy: Toward a Radical Democratic Politics*. London: Verso.

Laing, R.D. (1976) *The Politics of the Family*. Harmondsworth: Penguin Books.

Lakoff, G. and Johnson, N. (1980) *Metaphors We Live By*. Chicago: The University of Chicago Press.

Leach, E. (1974) *Levi-Strauss*. Glasgow: Collins.

Leach, R. (1967) *A Runaway World?* London: British Broadcasting Corporation.

LeDoux, J. (1998) *The Emotional Brain*. London: Phoenix.

Leech, G.N. (1983) *Principles of Pragmatics*. London: Longman.

Luke, A. (1995) 'Text and discourse in education: An introduction to Critical Discourse Analysis', *Review of Research in Education*, 21: 3–48.

Lyotard, J-F. (1984) *The Postmodern Condition*. Minneapolis: University of Minnesota Press.

Massey, D. (1994) *Space, Place and Gender*. Cambridge: Polity Press.

McLanahan, S. and Sandfur, G. (1994) *Growing Up With a Single Parent*. Cambridge, MA: Harvard University Press.

Mclean, C., Carey, M. and White, C. (1996) *Men's Ways of Being*. Boulder: Westview Press.

McNay, L. (1992) *Foucault and Feminism*. Cambridge: Polity Press.

Mead, G.H. (1934) *Mind, Self and Society*. Chicago: University of Chicago Press

Meinhof, U.H. (1997) 'The most important event of my life!': A comparison of male and female written narratives', in S. Johnson and U.H. Meinhof (eds), *Language and Masculinity*. Oxford: Blackwell. pp. 208–28.

Meinhof, U.H. and Galasiński, D. (2000) 'Photography, memory, and the construction of identities on the former East–West German border', *Discourse Studies*, 2 (3): 323–53.

Mellody, P. (1987) *Facing Co-Dependence*. San Francisco: HarperCollins.

Menz, F. (1989) 'Manipulation strategies in newspapers: A program for critical linguistics', in R. Wodak (ed.), *Language, Power and Ideology*. Amsterdam: John Benjamins. pp. 227–49.

Miller, D. (1995) 'The consumption of soap opera: *The Young and the Restless* and mass consumption in Trinidad', in R. Allen (ed.), *To Be Continued . . . Soap Opera Around the World*. London and New York: Routledge.

Mitchell, J. (1974) *Psychoanalysis and Feminism*. London: Allen Lane.

Moi, T. (ed.) (1986) *The Kristeva Reader*. Oxford: Blackwell.

Moir, A. and Moir, B. (1998) *Why Men Don't Iron: The Real Science of Gender Studies*. London: HarperCollins Publishers.

Morley, D. (1980) *The Nationwide Audience*. London: British Film Institute.

Morley, D. (1992) *Television, Audiences and Cultural Studies*. London and New York: Routledge.

Morris, M. (1992) 'A gadfly bites back', *Meanjin*, 51 (3).

Motion, J. and Leitch, S. (1996) 'A discursive perspective from New Zealand: Another World View', *Public Relations Review*, 22: 297–309.

Mühlhäusler, P. and Harré, R. (1990) *Pronouns and People: The Linguistic Construction of Social and Personal Identity*. Oxford: Basil Blackwell.

Mura, S.S. (1983) 'Licensing violations. Legitimate violation of Grice's conversational principle', in R.T. Craig and K. Tracy (eds), *Conversational Coherence: Form, Structure and Strategy*. Beverly Hills: Sage. pp. 101–15.

National Drug Strategy (1995) *Household Survey*. Canberra: Australian Government.

Ng, S.H. and Bradac, J.J. (1993) *Power in Language*. Newbury Park: Sage.

Nicholson, L. (ed.) (1990) *Feminism/Postmodernism*. London and New York: Routledge.

Nixon, S. (1997) 'Exhibiting masculinity', in S. Hall (ed.), *Representation*. London and Thousand Oaks: Sage.

O'Hagen, A. (1999) *Our Fathers*. London: Faber and Faber.

Ossowska, M. (1986) *Ethos rycerski jego odmiany*. [Knight's ethos and it variants]. Warszawa: Panstwowe Wydawnictwo Naukowe.

Panofsky, E. (1955) *Meaning in the Visual Arts*. Garden City, NY: Doubleday Anchor Books.

Pecheux, M. (1982) *Language Semantics and Ideology*. London: Macmillan.

Pfeil, F. (1995) *White Guys*. London: Verso.

Pieterse, J. (1995) 'Globalisation as hybridisation', in M. Featherstone, S. Lash and R. Robertson (eds), *Global Modernities*. Newbury Park and London: Sage.

Pilger, J. (1994) *Distant Voices*. London: Vintage.

Pinker, S. (1994) *The Language Instinct: How the Mind Creates Language*. New York: Morrow.

Popenoe, D. (1996) *Life Without Father*. New York: Free Press.

Potter, J. and Wetherell, M. (1987) *Discourse and Social Psychology: Beyond Attitudes and Behaviour*. London and Thousand Oaks: Sage.

Poynton, P. (1994) *Aboriginal Australia: Land, Law and Culture*. London: Institute of Race Relations.

Real, T. (1998) *I Don't Want to Talk About It: Men and Depression*. Dublin: Newleaf.

Rorty, R. (1980) *Philosophy and the Mirror of Nature*. Cambridge: Cambridge University Press.

Rorty, R. (1989) *Contingency, Irony and Solidarity*. Cambridge: Cambridge University Press.

Rorty, R. (1991a) *Objectivity, Relativism, and Truth: Philosophical Papers Volume 1*. Cambridge: Cambridge University Press.

Rorty, R. (1991b) *Essays on Heidegger and Others: Philosophical Papers Volume 2*. Cambridge: Cambridge University Press.

Rorty, R. (1995) 'Feminism and pragmatism', in R.S. Goodman (ed.), *Pragmatism*. New York: Routledge.

Rorty, R. (1998) *Achieving Our Country*. Cambridge, MA: Harvard University Press.

Rose, J. (1997) *Sexuality in the Field of Vision*. London: Verso.

Rose, N. (1996) 'Identity, genealogy, history', in S. Hall and P. du Gay (eds), *Questions of Cultural Identity*. Newbury Park and London: Sage.

Rowbotham, S. (1981) 'The Trouble with Patriarchy', in R. Samuel (ed.), *People's History and Socialist Theory*. London: Routledge.

Rowe, D. (1988) *Choosing Not Losing*. Chichester: Wiley.

Rowe, D. (1996) *Depression*. London: Routledge.

Salmans, S. (1997) *Depression*. London: HarperCollins.

Saussure, F. de (1960) *Course in General Linguistics*. London: Peter Owen.

Searle, J.R. (1969) *Speech Acts*. Cambridge: Cambridge University Press.

Seidler, V. (1989) *Rediscovering Masculinity: Reason, Language and Sexuality*. London: Routledge.

Seiter, E. (1989) 'Don't treat us like we're stupid', in E. Seiter, H. Borchers, G. Kreutzner and E-M. Warth (eds) (1989), *Remote Control*. London and New York: Routledge.

Seligman, M. (1990) *Learned Optimism*. Sydney: Random House.

Sheedy, G. (1998) *Passages for Men*. Sydney: Simon and Schuster.

Short, M. (1989) 'Speech presentation, the novel and the press', in W. van Peer (ed.), *The Taming of the Text*. London: Routledge.

Shotter, J. (1993) *Conversational Realities*. Newbury Park and London: Sage.

Simpson, P. (1993) *Language, Ideology and Point of View*. London: Routledge.

Smith, A.D. (1990) 'Towards a global culture?', in M. Featherstone (ed.), *Global Culture*. London and Newbury Park: Sage.

Stacey, J. (1996) *In the Name of the Family: Rethinking Family Values in a Postmodern World*. Boston: Beacon Press.

Staten, H. (1984) *Wittgenstein and Derrida*. Lincoln: University of Nebraska Press.

Sterelny, K. and Griffiths, P. (1999) *Sex and Death: An Introduction to Philosophy of Biology*. Chicago and London: The University of Chicago Press.

Stomma, L. (1986) *Antrolopogia wsi polskiej XIX wieku*. [Anthropology of the Polish village of the 19th century]. Warszawa: Instytut Wydawniczy PAX.

Thomas, J. (1995) *Meaning in Interaction*. London: Longman.

Tomlinson, J. (1991) *Cultural Imperialism*. London: Pinter Press.

Van Dijk, T.A. (1993a) 'Principles of critical discourse analysis', *Discourse and Society*, 4.

Van Dijk, T.A. (1993b) *Elite Discourse and Racism*. London: Sage.

Van Dijk, T.A. (ed.) (1997) *Discourse Studies: A Multidisciplinary Introduction. Vol. 1. Discourse as Structure and Process*. London: Sage.

Van Dijk, T.A. (1998) *Ideology*. London: Sage.

Van Leeuwen, T. and Wodak, R. (1999) 'Legitimising immigration: a discourse-historical approach', *Discourse Studies*, 1: 83–118.

Verschueren, J. (1999) 'Whose discipline? Some critical reflections on linguistic pragmatics', *Journal of Pragmatics*, 31: 869–79.

Viney, L. (1996) *Personal Construct Therapy: A Handbook*. Norwood: Ablex.

Volosinov, V.N. (1973) *Marxism and the Philosophy of Language*. London: Seminar Press.

Watts, A. (1968) *Psychotherapy East and West*. New York; Ballatine Books.

Watts, A. (1957) *The Way of Zen*. London: Thames and Hudson.

Weber, R. (1990) *Basic Content Analysis*. London: Sage.

Weedon, C. (1997) *Feminist Practice and Poststructuralist Theory*. Oxford: Blackwell.

West, C. (1993) *Keeping Faith*. London and New York: Routledge.

Widdicombe, S. and Wooffitt, R. (1995) *The Language of Youth Subcultures*. London: Harvester Wheatsheaf.

Williams, R. (1981) *Culture*. London: Fontana.

Williams, R. (1983) *Keywords*. London: Fontana.

Williamson, J. (1978) *Decoding Advertisements*. London: Marion Boyars.

Willis, P. (1980) 'Notes on method', in S. Hall, D. Hobson, A. Lowe and P. Willis (eds), *Culture, Media, Language*. London: Hutchinson.

Willis, P. (1977) *Learning to Labour*. Farnborough: Saxon House.

Willis, P. (1978) *Profane Culture*. London: Routledge and Kegan Paul.

Willis, P. (1990) *Common Culture*. Milton Keynes: Open University Press.

Wilson, J. (1990) *Politically Speaking*. Oxford: Basil Blackwell.

Wittgenstein, L. (1953) *Philosophical Investigations*. Oxford: Basil Blackwell.

Wittgenstein, L. (1969) *On Certainty*. New York: HarperTorch Books.

Wittgenstein, L. (1980) *Culture and Value*. Oxford: Blackwell.

Włodek, L. (1981) *Zarys dziejów Birczy*. [An outline of the history of Bircza] Przemyśl: Polskie Towarzystwo Historyczne.

Wodak, R. (1999) 'Critical discourse analysis at the end of the 20th century', *Research on Language and Social Interaction*, 32: 185–93.

Wodak, R., Cillia, R. de, Reisigl, M. and Liebhart, K. (1999) *The Discursive Construction of National Identity*. Edinburgh: Edinburgh University Press.

Zatwarnicki, W. (1997) *Wgminie Bircza*. [In the community of Bircza] Krosno: PUW Roksana.

Index